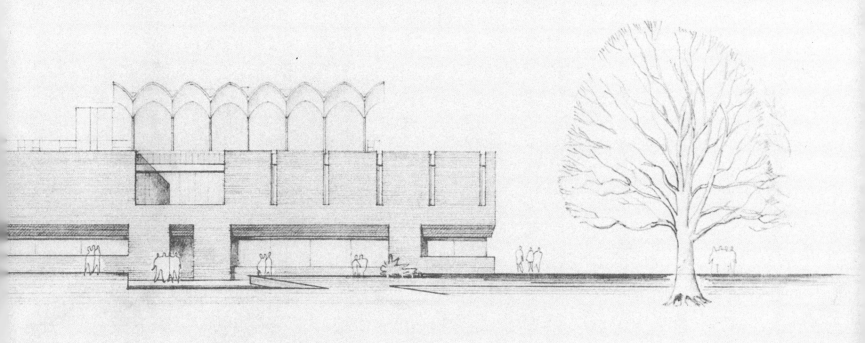

Denys Lasdun & Partners   architects

scale·lin. to 16 ft.   drwg. no. 474/23

FITZWILLIAM

The First 150 Years of a Cambridge College

FITZWILLIAM

The First 150 Years of a Cambridge College

Edited by John Cleaver

with a Foreword
by
David Starkey

THIRD MILLENNIUM
PUBLISHING, LONDON

© 2013 Third Millennium Publishing Limited

First published in 2013 by
Third Millennium Publishing Limited, a subsidiary
of Third Millennium Information Limited

2–5 Benjamin Street
London
United Kingdom
EC1M 5QL
www.tmiltd.com

ISBN: 978 1 906507 78 7

Project Manager: Catharine Walston
Designer: Helen Swansbourne
Production: Bonnie Murray
Repro by Studio Fasoli, Italy
Printed by Gorenjski Tisk, Slovenia

PICTURE ACKNOWLEDGEMENTS

Bruce Photographers (Northampton Street) 159;
Cambridgeshire Collection 27, 64; Ms Alison Carter 107, 183;
Ronald Ching (2010) 178; Dr John Cleaver 2, 4, 18, 22, 33, 43,
44, 52, 54, 55, 56, 64, 80, 84, 86, 89, 90, 92, 93, 94, 96, 97, 98, 99,
100, 101, 102, 103, 104, 105, 106, 107, 116, 118, 119, 125, 126,
127, 138, 142, 143, 145, 149, 150, 152, 153, 154, 156, 157, 160,
167, 168, 169, 172, 177, 180, 181, 184; Commission Air 99;
Alan Davidson (Stills Photography) front cover, 95, 127, 154,
155, 161, 162, 163, 176, 177, 178, 179; Alan Dawber (1965) 89;
Downing College Archives (courtesy of Mrs Alice Fleet) 112;
Mike Evans (1956) 63; Getty Images 38, 67, 136, 137, 150, 151,
152; Andrew Hope (1967) 151; The Imaging Services inside
cover; Dr Ray Kelly 87, 89, 95, 101; Anthony Kersting 34, 58, 65,
72, 73, back cover; Lee Suan Yew (1954) 66; Edward Leigh 116;
Mrs Vera Lethbridge 169; Eaden Lilley 132, 152; Nigel
Luckhurst Photography 67; MRC Laboratory of Molecular
Biology 118; John Müller (2009) 173; National Portrait Gallery
118; Vun Chueng Ng inside cover; Peter Owens (Great
Shelford) 146; Andrew Powell 177; Professor Sally Price 139;
Public Catalogue Foundation 28, 32, 35, 43, 46, 76, 111, 112;
Ramsay and Muspratt 22; Rawood Photography 50; Derek
Reed (1952) 157; John Reynolds 104; RIBA, Lasdun Collection
86, endpapers; Dr Lucy Sheerman 174; Kazuto Shiomitsu
(2009) 108; Stearn and Sons 56, 62, 69, 153; John Thompson
(JET Photographic) 114, 115, 117, 125, 129, 141, 166; Lisa Trei
(1979) 133; Jonathan Webb (Webb Aviation) 164; Nicholas
Whines (1966) 140; Cambridge Union Society Library 135

Images identified by page reference above are either copyright
to or the property of the persons or institutions listed. Whilst
every effort has been made to identify sources, the publishers
will be delighted to acknowledge corrections or any further
information in future editions. All other material, unless
otherwise indicated, is the property of Fitzwilliam College.

CONTENTS

FOREWORD

College histories can be complacent things. This one isn't. Instead, like all the best histories, it reveals an uncomfortable but exciting truth: *Fitzwilliam isn't what you think it is.*

Today, as you wander in from Storey's Way and take in the lovely gardens and pleasing melange of buildings old and new, Fitzwilliam seems a typical Cambridge College, newer than most, nicer than some, but otherwise unremarkable.

Nothing could be further from the truth. For behind its current middle-of-the-road facade – middle class, middle of the results table, though still rather below the average in terms of endowment – lies an odd and remarkably innovative past.

For Fitzwilliam was the first institution in Cambridge to reflect the need for what we now call wider access; to have significant numbers of graduate students; and (as a reflection of Empire) to be international in its composition.

Oddest of all was the fact that for its first century it wasn't a college. Quite deliberately so, since it was the trappings of collegiate life that were seen as making Cambridge accessible only to the rich and privileged.

But, paradoxically, this non-collegiate institution exhibited almost from the beginning a passionate desire for the forbidden fruits of communal – that is, collegiate – life. And it set about acquiring them from the bottom up, with the Fitzwilliam colours of claret and grey, the coat of arms and the very name itself all being invented by the leaders of the student body for the newly-established boat club between 1874 and 1887.

So, whether you like it or not (and I frankly don't), the order of priority is clear: Fitzwilliam was a boat club before it was a college and had its playing fields long before its present buildings or its campus.

This order of priorities – sport first and studies a rather poor second—was shared by Fitzwilliam's academic leadership and carefully nurtured by them up to and indeed beyond the acquisition of collegiate status in 1966.

As embodied in the person of my beloved old tutor Ray Kelly, it had great virtues and aroused deep loyalties. But, as quickly became apparent, it had still greater drawbacks. For it meant that Fitzwilliam was new only in its collegiate status and its buildings; in its ethos it was old-fashioned, even backward-looking, as was shown most conspicuously its initial refusal to countenance the admission of women.

The result was that an unhappy 1970s were followed by decades of struggle: to drive up academic standards; to admit women; to break away from the stranglehold of Denys Lasdun's constricting masterplan for the College buildings; in short, in the words of the College motto (itself of post-1966 coinage), to combine the best of old and new.

However, as both the later chapters of this history and the present condition of the College amply demonstrate, the struggle succeeded. Fitzwilliam changed, and wholly for the better. And it changed without losing the best of its older self.

Of how many British institutions can that be said?

DAVID STARKEY

ACKNOWLEDGEMENTS

The suggestion that a celebration of Fitzwilliam's heritage would be particularly apt at the time of its 150th-Anniversary Appeal originated with the Master, Professor Robert Lethbridge.

A new history is appropriate because of the time that has elapsed since the first Master, Dr Walter Grave, wrote his monumental volume *Fitzwilliam College Cambridge, 1869–1969*. No-one could have been better qualified to write such an account, because of his deep engagement in driving the transition from Fitzwilliam House – a quasi-college operating under the aegis of the Non-Collegiate Students Board of the University – to independence and full collegiate status. Grave's history will never be surpassed as a detailed account for the first hundred years, and I am greatly indebted to it as a primary source for the period.

My election to a Fellowship of the College coincided with Dr Grave's retirement in 1971, and I have seen all the fascinating intervening years: years in which Fitzwilliam has developed immensely both in terms of its physical environment and as an intellectual institution; years too which sadly have been marked by the passing of many of the pioneers who contributed to these developments. Some appear on these pages; perforce others have been omitted, but they remain in the memories of their colleagues and the students whom they have influenced.

A volume like this depends on many contributions, as well as on formal records and on my own recollections. I am indebted in particular to the Development Director and historian Dr Helen Bettinson for her section on *The Great War*; to Professor David Thompson for his sections on *The College Chapel and its Chaplains* and *Leslie Griffiths*; and to Francis Knights for *Music* and *The Chapel Choir*. The Bursar, Andrew Powell, contributed *Building the Endowment*, *What is 'the Endowment'?* and *Finance in a Changing Environment*; Dr Paul Chirico, *Undergraduates – the Perspective of the Senior Tutor*; Dr Bhaskar Vira, *Personal Reflections of a Graduate Tutor*; Nicola Padfield, *Crime, Punishment and Master of Studies Students*; and Robert Lethbridge considered *The Role*

of a 21st-century Master and gave concluding thoughts on *Achievements and Aspirations*.

I would like to thank the individual members of Fitzwilliam who contributed recollections and photographs; all were greatly appreciated, even though space constraints limited the material that could be quoted directly. In particular, John Adams (1958) provided detailed information on the Fitzwilliam Society and the Billygoats. The first Development Director, Dr Iain Reid (1978), provided information on fundraising. During his year in the Development Office, James Harrington (2008) provided essential coordination of the communications with alumni, continued by his successor Benedict Clancy (2009). Quotations such as those from alumni have been abbreviated where necessary, and minor textual amendments have been made to enhance clarity and consistency. Word changes and elucidations to formal and published papers are indicated with square brackets.

A volume like this cannot provide a reference for every statement, but principal textual sources are summarised on p.185. Source information and acknowledgements for images are given on p.4.

For their support during the production of this volume, I would like to thank the publishers, Third Millennium Information Ltd. In particular, I would like to thank the professional editor, Catharine Walston, for her input and advice throughout the project, and for sourcing images. Helen Swansbourne undertook its physical design briskly and effectively. Colleagues have helped with proof-reading and other checking; the remaining errors, omissions and infelicities are mine.

Finally, two personal thanks. Firstly – for the initial step that brought me up the hill from a College closer to the river – to Dr Ken Smith, Life Fellow of the College, who proposed back in 1971 that I should become a Research Fellow at Fitzwilliam. And lastly to my partner, Vun Chueng Ng, who has had to endure my preoccupation with this volume during its production.

JOHN CLEAVER
Cambridge, June 2013

DRAMATIS PERSONAE

Some people appear repeatedly through the volume and are listed here. The list is not exhaustive; omission should not be considered invidious. Throughout, for those who were junior members of Fitzwilliam, names are followed (in brackets) by their matriculation years.

Censors

Ralph Somerset, 1869–81
Francis Howard, 1881–89
Tristram Huddleston, 1890–1907
William Reddaway, 1907–24
William Thatcher (1907), 1924–54
Dr Walter Grave, 1959–66

Masters

Dr Walter Grave, 1966–71
Dr Edward Miller, 1971–81
Professor Sir James Holt, 1981–88
Professor Gordon Cameron, 1988–90
Professor Alan Cuthbert, 1991–99
Professor Brian Johnson, 1999–2005
Professor Robert Lethbridge, 2005–13

Some officers and Fellows

Charles Gaskoin (1895), History; polymath and supporter of amateur dramatics
Frank Thatcher (1909), History; brother of William, Bursar 1917–24
The Rev. Walter Harvey (1907), Divinity; architect, Bursar and Chaplain 1925–40
William Williams (1922), Geography; Bursar 1946–67, Acting Censor 1954–59
Ian Rawlins, Physics; Director of Studies for Natural Sciences 1931–34, Chapel benefactor
Professor Norman Pounds (1931), Geography; Junior Tutor 1944–50
Norman Walters, English; Tutor 1950–66; Senior Tutor 1966–67
Richard Haywood (1936), Engineering; Memorialist
Dr Ray Kelly, Modern Languages; Assistant Tutor 1955–66, Assistant Bursar 1955–60, Domestic Bursar 1960–66, Tutor 1966–81, Domestic Bursar 1966–67 and Bursar 1967–81
Dr Stephen Fleet, Mineralogy; Tutorial Bursar and Junior Bursar, 1964–73, and first Secretary of the Governing Body; later University Registrary, and Master of Downing College
Dr David Kerridge, Biochemistry; first Tutor for Graduate Students

Some members and others

John Alexander (1921), Law; proposed the formation of the Fitzwilliam Society and was its first Secretary, President of the Chartered Institute of Arbitrators
Sir John Stratton (1929), English; major roles in leather industry, leader of the London members of the Negotiating Committee, supporter of rowing
Lee Kuan Yew, known as Harry Lee (1947), Law; first President of Singapore
George Peck, pharmacist and businessman, owner of 31-32 Trumpington Street
Ernest Peck (1893), Chemistry; son of George, pharmacist and Fitzwilliam Society President
Mrs Winifred Armstrong, owner of The Grove

Architects

Sir Denys Lasdun: original master-plan, 1963 and 1966 buildings
David Roberts: squash courts
Sir Richard MacCormac: New Court and the Chapel
Joanna van Heyningen & **Birkin Haward**: Wilson Court
Bob Allies & **Graham Morrison**: Gatehouse Court and the Auditorium
Edward Cullinan: The Olisa Library

TIMELINE

I

ESTABLISHING FITZWILLIAM HALL

1

CAMBRIDGE IN THE NINETEENTH CENTURY

A University ripe for transformation

Fitzwilliam came into being as a college in 1966, not as a new creation but after nearly a century of evolution. Its roots lie in the reforms pressed on a reluctant University of Cambridge in the middle of the nineteenth century. This book is the tale of that evolution, and of its continuation over a further five decades.

In Cambridge, the University was established in 1209 by scholars fleeing Oxford and finding a new home in the small market town amidst the wilds of East Anglia. They had fled because *benefit of clergy* – entitling anyone who could read to trial in an ecclesiastical court, and a lenient sentence – had been infringed. In Oxford, a scholar had killed a townswoman and two or three of his colleagues were hanged in reprisal – with the support of King John, at that time in conflict with Pope Innocent III. Four years later, the King submitted to the Pope and the rights of the University were restored; many of the dispersed scholars returned to Oxford, but a community remained in Cambridge.

Medieval scholars learned their trade much in the same way as craft apprentices, by joining a master and studying under him; a university was similar to a guild of craftsmen. To this day the curious structure of the Cambridge degree reflects craft practice: the *Baccalaureus in Artibus* corresponds to the craft status of *Journeyman* and, after time has elapsed to allow the scholar to gain experience, the award of *Magister in Artibus* makes him a master in his own right, entitled to take pupils.

As the thirteenth century advanced, students in Cambridge established hostels which were regulated by the University; some lasted for several centuries and became quite large, with eighty or more members, and with chapels and libraries. Eventually they provided instruction by lectures and disputations; however, they were without charters or statutes. The college concept that had been originated by Walter de Merton in Oxford was adopted by the Bishop of Ely for a foundation which in 1284 became St Peter's College, with a Master and other college officers and an establishment of Fellows (scholars who already were Bachelors of Arts). Later, colleges began to take junior members, and by the sixteenth century the hostels had largely given way to the developing colleges.

Nineteenth-century engravings show a Cambridge superficially familiar to present-day members of the University. However, the institutions themselves would seem to a modern academic almost as alien as the medieval University. Since the early days, an inversion in power had taken place between the University and the colleges: the University was weak and with very limited resources, whilst the colleges had accumulated wealth and land, and had come largely to determine the teaching. This had a deplorable effect on teaching methods and on the subjects taught. University lectures were given only by the few professors, and were poorly attended. The colleges, often with small numbers of Fellows, did not have the capacity to teach their students to an adequate level and those students who wished to succeed depended on private coaches. With teaching a near-monopoly of coaches and colleges, there was both great reluctance and little ability to introduce the new fields of study that were appropriate for a rapidly-developing country.

The limited role of the University is illustrated dramatically by comparing its income with that of the colleges. In 1851, the University had:

income for general purposes	£7,966
fee income for University Officers (not Professors)	£2,774
sums received by University Professors and others	c. £10,000
other income restricted to specific purposes	£8,711

Its total turnover, under £30,000 a year, equalled less than £17 for each of the 1,760 undergraduates in residence. In addition, the University undertook capital expenditure at a typical annual rate of £2,000. By contrast, the total

Previous page: *Degree Day, 1863* (Robert B. Farren, in the collection of Trinity Hall)

A placid afternoon in 1835 on the river outside the Wren Library, Trinity College (engraved by J. & H.S. Storer)

annual income for all colleges was estimated at more than £185,000 – six times that of the University.

Teaching was only one of many areas where revision was long overdue and so, as mid-century approached, reform of the Universities of Oxford and of Cambridge was being strongly advocated – and strongly opposed. There were still religious tests: Cambridge allowed University membership to non-Anglicans but debarred them from college appointments, from professorships, and from taking their degrees. Even though Masters and Fellows absorbed up to half of the rent and investment revenues of colleges, there were no statutory requirements for Fellows to work even for their own colleges – still less for the University. Fellows were prohibited from marriage, largely precluding long-term careers within the University; on marriage, a Fellow would become a parish priest (often to a living in the gift of his college) or a schoolmaster. And collegiate Cambridge was very expensive.

Elsewhere in England, the monopoly of university education held by Cambridge and Oxford had been broken. University College, London had been founded in 1826 – to be stigmatized by Dr Thomas Arnold, headmaster of

Rugby School, as a 'Godless institution on Gower Street'. It imposed no religious tests, kept fees low, and introduced a wide range of modern subjects to the curriculum. For the urban professional and the non-Anglican, it added a new dimension to intellectual life; for a more traditional education, the University of Durham had been founded in 1832, and King's College, London in 1829. Further afield, German universities had transformed their activities to embrace an ideology that glorified original research and, with very substantial support from the states, had built up their libraries, laboratories and seminars. The world had moved on.

Over a period of two decades, a series of major changes helped to transform the University. Whilst the worst of the eighteenth-century abuses had been removed, progress was slow until in 1847 Cambridge University elected a new Chancellor, the great reformer and enthusiast for technological progress Prince Albert, the husband of Queen Victoria.

One of the less prominent reforms, although still controversial, was the admission of undergraduates without the necessity for them to become members of

H.R.H. FIELD-MARSHAL CHANCELLOR PRINCE ALBERT TAKING THE PONS ASINORUM.

AFTER THE MANNER OF NAPOLEON TAKING THE BRIDGE OF ARCOLA.

Punch imagined the Chancellor overcoming the forces of reaction

colleges, thereby reducing their costs and potentially widening access to the University. This was to culminate in the setting-up, in the summer of 1869, of the Non-Collegiate Students Board; to meet the needs of the non-collegiate students came Fitzwilliam Hall, then Fitzwilliam House – and eventually Fitzwilliam College.

Cambridge emerging from a deep sleep

Cambridge became increasingly factional in the second quarter of the nineteenth century as reforms were advocated and opposed. Self-interest was never far from the surface: colleges feared that the University would gain power at their expense if teaching content was modernized.

In 1834, a group of members of the Senate petitioned Parliament, proposing that religious criteria for degrees should be abolished; a Bill was passed by the Commons but defeated in the Lords. Four years later a Bill for the appointment of a commission of enquiry into the statutes and revenues of the Oxford and Cambridge colleges was introduced. It also failed, but prompted a half-hearted revision of the University Statutes; a committee of Heads of Houses took nearly eleven years to produce a report which merely consolidated the status quo.

With Prince Albert as Chancellor, internal debate was given added impetus and in 1848 a petition was presented to the Prime Minister calling for a *Royal Commission of Enquiry into the best methods of securing the*

improvement of the Universities of Oxford and Cambridge. The signatories included 133 Cambridge graduates (amongst them, Charles Darwin and Charles Babbage) and 62 Oxford graduates; 29 signatories were Fellows of the Royal Society. In the summer of 1850, a Royal Commission was established.

Amidst all the issues of teaching and religion, a small part of the report of the Cambridge Commission addressed concerns about the expenses incurred by students at the Universities, and about the extent to which college membership contributed to the costs. However, as in many other parts of the report, the status quo was supported: 'It has now long been the custom, although there is no express law to that effect, that every student shall be admitted within some College before he can become a matriculated member of the University; and it may be added, that the Elizabethan code of University Statutes is in complete accordance with that usage'. On the admission of students by the University, not attached to any college or hall, they were 'of opinion that it would not be expedient to adopt any change of that nature in the present system of the University ... by which habits of order and moral control are most satisfactorily obtained'.

A subsequent report from the Statutory Commissioners for Cambridge led to a further Act, in 1856. Amongst its many clauses, it made provision for Licensed Masters to set up Private Halls which would

A

BILL

TO

Extend the Benefits of Education in the Universities of Oxford and Cambridge to Students not belonging to any College or Hall.

WHEREAS it is expedient for the Advancement of Learning and Education to make Provision for the Extension of the Benefits of the said Universities :   *Preamble.*

Be it therefore enacted by the Queen's most Excellent Majesty, by and with the Advice and Consent of the Lords Spiritual and Temporal, and Commons, in this present Parliament assembled, and by the Authority of the same, as follows :

1. Notwithstanding anything contained in any Act of Parliament now in force relating to either of the Universities of Oxford and Cambridge, or in the Statutes, Charters, Deeds of Composition, or other Instruments of Foundation, of either of the said Universities, or of any College or Hall within the same, any Person may be matriculated without being entered as a Member of any College or Hall, and may, if he shall think fit, join himself to any College or Hall, with the Consent of the Head thereof, but without being obliged to reside within the same; and every Person so matriculated shall in all respects and for all Intents and Purposes   *Any Person may become a Member of the University without being a Member of any College, and may join any College and be entitled to all Privileges, &c.*

[Bill 71.]

matriculate students, without the need for them to be members of colleges. The first step had been taken to a lower-cost route to University membership.

Controversy over non-collegiate students

The establishment of Private Halls, or hostels, was embodied in Cambridge University Statutes in 1858, to little effect. A hostel for medical students was opened near Addenbrooke's Hospital, but it had closed by 1862 after matriculating only nine students. Few were concerned by its failure. A similar scheme in Oxford failed, but reformers there felt that further action was required and in 1865 set up a committee to consider the extension of the University, particularly for clergy. They proposed that non-collegiate students would live in lodgings, envisaging that such students would neither wish nor be able to afford to create disciplinary problems. Such students would have experiences of a lower standard than colleges could offer – but otherwise they could not come to the University. The committee drafted regulations similar to those ultimately adopted in Cambridge, for an organization with authority over both students and lodging-house keepers, which would appoint Tutors for the students.

At about the same time, revived Parliamentary activity provided additional impetus for the admission of non-collegiate students. *The Oxford and Cambridge Universities Education Bill* – 'A Bill to extend the benefits of Education in the Universities of Oxford and Cambridge to students not belonging to any College or Hall' – was proposed by

William Ewart in 1867. It had two inter-related themes: the provision of more economical direct-entry routes into the Universities of Oxford and of Cambridge, and re-balancing the teaching roles of Universities and colleges.

Regarding economy, Ewart quoted the Commissioners who inquired into University education at Oxford: 'No skill or vigilance in colleges would reduce the cost of living so low as it can be by the ingenuity and interest of a student' so, contrary to claims for economies of scale, 'education would be cheaper under the system proposed. At first sight we might think that Colleges would be cheaper than Universities; they had all the advantages of association, but a certain rivalry among young men at college led to expense. A solitary student was beyond the reach of ridicule and fashion.' Robert Lowe did not consider economy to be unambiguously good; he did not 'believe it was possible to make College living so cheap as to open the Colleges to the poor, whom they wished to comprehend within the University. In these Colleges the sons of the gentry were educated and, though the simplicity of College life should be always kept in view, it would not be right to cut down the habits of these young men to the degree of simplicity which would be fitting in the case of poor men's sons.'

In his Parliamentary speech, Ewart anticipated a problem which eventually would inform the development of Fitzwilliam: 'Another objection ... was the want of society for the ex-college students. But Gibbon consoles us for this, for he says that "society stimulates the intellect, but that solitude is the nurse of genius". But the ex-college students would probably form societies among themselves more free than in the Colleges, where a narrow system of exclusiveness and caste sometimes prevailed, which would be freshened and invigorated by a more open system.'

Concerns were raised about potential problems of discipline, with young men scattered around the town unconstrained by college walls and regulations, but there was surprisingly little mention of the usual religious issues and the need to ensure daily attendance in chapel.

W.E. Gladstone emphasized the need to make more provision for the middle classes and for professional education, and noted that the mercantile classes were essentially 'excommunicated from the higher education of the country'. The Bill was read for a second time, and referred to a Select Committee. It went no further, as the Government changed in the following year.

In Cambridge, the Council of the Senate decided in March 1867 to set up a sub-committee to monitor the progress of the Bill. Thus stimulated, the Council took action towards the admission of non-collegiate students, in November 1867 setting up a Syndicate to 'consider the conditions existing at present in the University for the education of poor students, and whether those provisions may with advantage be extended, and in what manner', with the intention of bringing a Grace to the Senate.

The Syndicate attempted in vain to establish what provisions already existed for poor students, by Scholarships and Exhibitions and by Sizarships (traditionally Sizars worked as servants and as late as 1840 in Trinity they dined off the remains of High Table dinners, but by that time they simply were subsidized students). Early in 1868 the Syndicate prepared a report for the Council; its key statement was that they were 'of the opinion that the benefits of Education in the University might be extended to an increased number of such Students as are contemplated by the Grace, by admitting a greater number of Sizars in Colleges, and by offering facilities for the admission of Students to reside in the University, who may not be Members of any College or Hostel'. The report concluded with draft regulations for non-collegiate students, and recommended their adoption. But the Syndicate was not unanimous; three members refused to sign the report.

The resulting Discussion of the Senate rehearsed arguments that dated back to the 1850 Commission, with claims that the proposal was a godless 'scheme to admit members to this University who would in no way be brought into contact with religion; they would simply be students seeking a degree'. There was no provision for testing students for poverty, and 'the provision made in this report was as much for the rich as for the poor', but a supporter pointed out that 'the Syndicate was told to draw up a scheme of which a poor man might avail himself, not one of which no one else could avail himself'.

Although the Grace was narrowly defeated at the start of the Easter term, the Council was not willing to abandon the scheme, and in Michaelmas 1868 established a second Syndicate which refined it by enhancing the disciplinary and administrative provisions, and by proposing that it should run only for five years in the first instance. The recommendations went to a Grace, and were supported strongly.

A REFORMING MP – WILLIAM EWART

William Ewart was an Oxford-educated lawyer who had been elected MP for Liverpool in 1830, in succession to William Huskisson, the first railway passenger to be run over by a locomotive – by George Stephenson driving the *Rocket*, on the occasion of the opening of the Liverpool and Manchester Railway. He devoted his political life to advanced liberal causes: in 1837 he achieved the abolition of capital punishment for theft from dwelling houses, and in 1834 the abolition of gibbeting of the corpses of executed criminals. Public education was a major interest and, in 1850, he carried a Bill for establishing free libraries supported out of the rates. In 1864 he was instrumental in achieving the legalization of the metric system of weights and measures.

The regulations established a Board to manage the non-collegiate students, controlled migration into and out of colleges, and defined the way in which the officers and staff of the Board could provide all educational and disciplinary measures.

The Privy Council received draft University statutes which made it 'lawful for the University to admit as Students to matriculate and to confer degrees on persons who may not be members of any College or Hall or of any Hostel'. They approved the Statutes promptly, in May 1869, and the Council of the Senate nominated the nine members of the Non-Collegiate Students Board. These included Dr Bateson, Master of St John's College, Mr R.B. Somerset of Trinity College and Professor Humphry (who had been Principal of the ill-fated hostel for medical students).

Before the end of the Easter Term 1869, the basic arrangements were in place to enable planning for the arrival of the first non-collegiate students, at the start of the coming Michaelmas Term. So the precursor of Fitzwilliam began in 1869, with the 150th anniversary to be celebrated in 2019.

2

THE FIRST THREE DECADES

The Non-Collegiate Students Board and its first actions

In the summer of 1869, progress was, by Cambridge standards, extraordinarily rapid. Just a week after the Senate approved the nominations for its members, the Non-Collegiate Students Board held its first meeting: Dr Bateson was appointed Chairman, and served the Board well for its formative first seven years. The following day they met again and agreed to appoint an officer who would be called the Censor (the title had been used by the first Syndicate in its 1868 proposals, and in Oxford). Two days later they agreed that the Censor of Non-Collegiate Students would be one of their number: Mr R.B. Somerset, of Trinity College.

The Board set rules for the admission of students, for monitoring their church membership, and for keeping records of their studies. They resolved for the Censor:

> That his duties embrace all correspondence with applicants for admission; making personal acquaintance with the students on commencing residence; advising them as to their course of study and general superintendence of their conduct; the receipt of the fees prescribed by the Senate as payable to the Board and the keeping of the accounts of all receipts and payments; collecting and laying before the Board once a term the returns to be made by the students of the studies they are pursuing, and of the lectures they are attending or the instruction they are receiving; and preparing and presenting to the Board every term a report of the operation of the Scheme.

For this part-time post, he received a stipend of £100 per annum.

Notices about non-collegiate membership of the University were placed in London and regional newspapers, and over the summer the Censor received 58 written enquiries and some in person. Eight students were admitted in the Michaelmas term of 1869: six new entrants to the University, and two migrants from

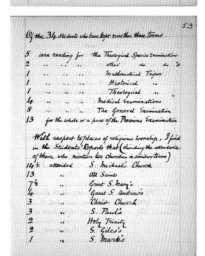

colleges. At least six were mature students: two schoolmasters, a surgeon, and a man who had lectured in Edinburgh and London. The academic performance of the cohort was not encouraging, only three proceeding to degrees. The lecturer achieved First-Class Honours in the Law and History Tripos, but did so after a Whewell Scholarship had enabled him to migrate to Trinity College – he was the first of a long line of students who

Report by Somerset to the Non-Collegiate Students Board in 1875, with details of students' studies and church attendance

R.B. SOMERSET AND F.G. HOWARD

Ralph Benjamin Somerset was born in Derbyshire, and went to Manchester School. In 1852 he came up to Trinity as a relatively impecunious student, initially a Sub-Sizar and then a Sizar; finally, he achieved a Scholarship. He received his BA in 1857, and was 39th Wrangler; a Fellowship followed in 1859. He served as Junior Dean from 1866 until 1869, when he relinquished his Fellowship on marriage. In his parallel Church career, he was ordained Deacon in 1862 and Priest a year later. He acquired his own central-Cambridge parish as Vicar of St Michael's in 1868, and held the position until 1875. His first University function was as Junior Proctor for 1868–69, but he did not become Senior Proctor as he was elected Censor of Non-Collegiate Students. He died in 1891 at his home, 17 Brookside, in Cambridge.

The second Censor, Francis George Howard, was a local man, born in 1843 in Grantchester. After attending St Paul's School in London, he came up to Trinity in 1862 – like Somerset, a Sizar. He graduated in 1866 as 26th Wrangler, but did not obtain a Fellowship. He went directly into the Church, being ordained Deacon in 1866 and Priest in 1867, and returning to Grantchester as a Curate, where he remained for the next eight years. Howard became Chaplain to Non-Collegiate Students in 1873 and Assistant Censor in 1877; he was elected Censor in 1881. He retired due to ill health in 1889 and died at his home in Harvey Road later that year, aged 46.

R.B. Somerset,
Censor
1869–81

F.G. Howard,
Censor 1881–89

Both reliefs by Henry Wiles, a local artist

MANY parents who desire to give their sons the benefit of a University education, at moderate cost, will be glad to know that the University of Cambridge has made very liberal arrangements for the admission of non-collegiate students. Hitherto, students have been received only as members of some college at the University, but henceforth they will be allowed to keep terms by residing in Cambridge with their parents or in lodgings duly licensed, thus escaping the cost of collegiate residence. At the same time all the privileges of the University will be open to them, just as in the case of ordinary students. The terms of admission, and an outline of the general scheme affecting non-collegiate students, will be found in another column; and we have only to add that applications for other particulars may be made to the Rev. R. B. SOMERSET, M.A., Trumpington Road, Cambridge.

From the *Birmingham Daily Post*, 28 June 1869

gained access to Cambridge through the non-collegiate system but achieved distinction after becoming members of colleges.

When the time came for renewal of the non-collegiate scheme, in April 1873, the Board reported on its success, with 90 students admitted, of whom 51 were currently non-collegiate undergraduates; five had proceeded to the degree of BA and 23 had migrated to colleges. Economy had been achieved: 'the Scheme has already enabled some students to live very cheaply while enjoying the advantages of the University. Several have assured the Censor that their whole expenditure in Cambridge was under £50 a-year.' The Grace recommending that the scheme be made permanent was approved at the Congregation of 15 May 1873.

The 1873 report was written when more than half of the students were still in residence; several were still to migrate. Tracking all 90 students through their entire careers:

THE FIRST CLOTHWORKERS' EXHIBITIONERS, EARLY FELLOWS OF THE ROYAL SOCIETY, AND A NOBEL LAUREATE

The first Clothworkers' Exhibitions were awarded in January 1875. The Board divided the £50 between two students; one was an existing student, Edward Taylor, who obtained a Second in the Natural Sciences Tripos.

The other Exhibitioner was Henry Fenton, a new entrant who had studied chemistry at King's College, London. He obtained his First in 1877 – a migrant to Christ's, as a Scholar. Fenton was elected Fellow of the Royal Society (FRS) in 1899, for his work on vigorous oxidation reactions involving hydrogen peroxide and an iron catalyst; these remain valuable for destroying hazardous organic chemicals and for the treatment of highly-contaminated effluents. He received an ScD in 1906.

However, the first person admitted as a non-collegiate student (in 1879, migrating to Gonville and Caius the following year) to be elected FRS (in 1893) was Charles Sherrington. He was President of the Royal Society from 1920 to 1925, and knighted in 1922. The 1932 Nobel Prize in Physiology or Medicine was awarded jointly to him and Edgar Adrian (later Master of Trinity, ennobled as Baron Adrian of Cambridge, and Chancellor of the University), for discoveries regarding the functions of neurons.

Probably the first FRS who completed his studies as non-collegiate was E.W. Reid, who matriculated in 1879 and obtained Firsts in both parts of the Natural Sciences Tripos. At St Mary's Hospital, London, his research was on physical and electrical phenomena in living tissues, including the electrical activity of the excised mammalian heart – amongst the earliest research on electrocardiography. He was elected to the Royal Society in 1898. He spent much of his life as Professor of Physiology in Dundee, and seems to have been frustrated by not obtaining a major English chair. His obituary states: 'His teaching was above the heads of all but a few. He was a devastating critic in his own subject, completely ruthless to shoddy work, looseness of

expression, and playing to the gallery. To one or two exceptionally able students he was guide, philosopher and friend. The mental ability of the majority he treated with contempt.'

Another early non-collegiate FRS was George Michell. Born to Australian parents, he was educated at the Perse School in Cambridge, and matriculated in 1888, but moved to Melbourne a year later. He was an excellent engineering mathematician and contributed to structural theory as well as to the theory of lubrication. He invented the tilting-pad hydrodynamic thrust bearing – always known as the Michell thrust bearing – used, for instance, to constrain propeller shafts in large ships. He became FRS in 1934, and in 1942 the Institution of Mechanical Engineers awarded him the James Watt International Medal.

Above: Charles Sherrington, c. 1890

Right: Brassey's *Naval Annual* for 1919 reported the merits of the Michell thrust bearing

The Michell block. This was the relative position of thrust bearings and journal bearings, when Mr. A. G. M. Michell of Melbourne patented a new type of thrust bearing. As a consequence, higher loads can be carried to-day on thrust bearings than on ordinary journal bearings, so that the position is the reverse of what it was. In some experiments, for example, blocks of the Michell type have been loaded to nearly 5 tons per sq. in., the rubbing speed being 50 ft. per second. In normal marine practice, where great prudence is, of course,

Fixed Collar

Shaft Collar

necessary, the usual load on Michell blocks is from 400 lb. to 500 lb. per sq. in. Hence the whole of the thrust can be carried on a single collar. This results in a considerable saving of material and work, and an appreciable reduction in capital costs. At the same time there is a large decrease in the frictional losses.

45 entered as non-collegiate, and remained non-collegiate, yielding 21 BAs;

30 entered as non-collegiate, and migrated to colleges;

2 entered as non-collegiate, migrated to colleges, but returned, yielding 1 BA;

7 migrated from colleges, and remained non-collegiate, yielding 3 BAs;

2 migrated from colleges, but returned to their original colleges;

4 migrated from colleges, then migrated to other colleges.

So it was a very fluid population, especially as students were not constrained to enter on a specific date; of those who came up as non-collegiate, only about 60%

counted a Michaelmas term as their first term of residence.

In 1875, Somerset produced a report for the Board on the 61 students in residence in the Easter term. Detailed attention was paid to their religious affiliations: 88% were Anglicans, attending 16 different churches, whilst 9% were Non-Conformists and 3% were Roman Catholics. This was to assuage the concerns of those who had considered the admission of non-collegiate students to be an irreligious exercise. Academically:

43 first-year men were preparing for one or more parts of the Previous Examination;

11 second-year men were preparing for the General Examination for the Ordinary BA;

7 third-year men were preparing for a Special Examination for the Ordinary BA;

5 second-year or third-year men were preparing for Tripos Examinations.

The rate of graduation was low: of the 203 students who were admitted in the first seven years, 100 remained non-collegiate throughout their time in Cambridge and of those only 48 graduated. However, of the 103 who migrated to colleges, 95 graduated – nearly twice the yield. The non-collegiate body was being depleted of good-quality students. Further, students might start as non-collegiate to reduce costs, and transfer at a late stage to colleges to gain prestige; this troubled the Censor, concerned for the reputation of the non-collegiate body:

> Those who thus graduate as members of Colleges thenceforth move in the world outside of the University in that character; the scheme under which they have mainly resided loses its natural representatives in the places from which new students should come; and the degree lists contain but few of the names by which a more general attention to the existence of the scheme might be excited.

A particular motivation for migration was that colleges could offer Scholarships or Exhibitions to the academically successful; therefore, if quality was to be built up within the non-collegiate body, financial awards would be needed. In Oxford, approaches had been made to Livery Companies in the City of London, and in Cambridge the Board acted similarly. In 1874, the Clothworkers' Company announced that annually they would provide a three-year Exhibition worth £50 to a non-collegiate student, with preference to be given to a student in Physical Sciences – but that he would lose it if he moved to a college. The Physical Sciences Exhibition ran until 1895, with awards made to 21 students; of those, half were prepared to forfeit the awards when the opportunity arose of migrating.

When the non-collegiate system had been set up, it had been assumed that students would study on their own or take lecture courses organized by colleges. By 1875, disappointed with the performance of the students, Somerset recognized that the teaching provision was not adequate. However, it was only in the time of his successor that it became possible to set up lectures specifically for non-collegiate men.

Trumpington Street

Initially, no space was provided either for the non-collegiate students or for the Censor. Somerset had no vicarage, and worked from his home in Trumpington Road – the address to which potential applicants enquired about admission.

Somerset in 1871 noted of the students that 'The great drawback to their position is still the smallness of their number, which seems to isolate them unduly. They have not hitherto been brought much together and, as they live at considerable distances from one another, they are hardly likely to find themselves associating with each other as members of one body.'

The first step towards providing appropriate space came in November 1873, when the Non-Collegiate Students Board investigated accommodation in a house opposite the Fitzwilliam Museum. The landlord, George Peck, had three rooms available at £55 per annum. This was considered excessive; however, in Lent 1874 this was reduced to £40 and it was agreed to rent three unfurnished rooms on the first floor of 31 Trumpington Street. A further £100 was budgeted for furniture. So now there

Photographs signed by the Censor to define the purchase of property in 1887 by the Non-Collegiate Students Board

Below: The rear view of 31 and 32 Trumpington Street; at left is the rear of 30 Trumpington Street, George Peck's shop

Photographed by Edward Whetton of 5 Downing P.
in May 1887.
9 Nov. 1887.
F. G. Howard
Back of 31 Trumpington St   Back of 32 Trumpington St

Photographed by Edward Wratton of 5 Downing St. Aug. 1887.

3 Nov. 1887 J.G. Howard

Front View of 32 Trumpington St *31 Trumpington St*

Above: The sign over the shop window is that of W. Dodd, cabinet maker and upholsterer; at the extreme left can be seen the canopy of John Burford's perambulator warehouse, at 33 Trumpington Street

were offices for the Censor and his clerk, and a Common Room and Reading Room for the students; in 1880 a fourth room was added to serve as a library.

The once-distinguished house had seen better days since it was constructed in 1727 by John Halstead, a brewer, incorporating an earlier building at the rear. Its site had been occupied by a house known as The Catherine Wheel, in the possession of Corpus Christi College in the sixteenth century. At some stage before the house was sold to Peck in 1873, it had been subdivided and a shop window inserted, and its tenants included a cabinet maker and upholsterer on the ground floor. The 1881 census shows the occupants of 31 Trumpington Street to have been the

cabinet maker and his wife and five children; in 32 were milliner sisters who had lived there since they had been children – their father, a college servant, had been the tenant. There was also an artist's studio.

So the Censor and his clerk joined a variegated population, in a location that did not suit all the members of the Non-Collegiate Students Board (Mr Hill, a member from 1881 to 1884, complained that it was a long way to come from St John's). Soon additional space was needed and in 1883 the Board reported to the Senate on its inadequacy, with small rooms that could not be used together for larger gatherings. If rooms were to be needed for lectures or examinations, 'an

PECK THE CHEMIST

All associated with Fitzwilliam House in Trumpington Street will recall Peck's, the chemist on the corner of Fitzwilliam Street. But the connection with the Peck family is much stronger than mere proximity. In 1851, George Peck took over a pharmacy at 35 Trumpington Street; he was a significant local businessman, a Director of the Cambridge Permanent Benefit Building Society, active in Trumpington Street as a member of the Board of Governors for St Mary the Less and a Select Governor of Addenbrooke's Hospital, and in the City as a Councillor and an Alderman. By 1881, he was living in 30 Trumpington Street and letting out numbers 31 and 32. When he sold them, he retained warehouse space at the back of number 31, adjacent to his shop at 30. By 1901, the family had moved to 25 Fitzwilliam Street.

George's son, Ernest Saville Peck, took the connection further: he matriculated as a non-collegiate student in 1893 and studied for an Ordinary Degree, finishing with the Special Examination in Chemistry and graduating BA in 1896. He inherited the pharmacy business in 1904, and was President of the British Pharmaceutical Conference for fifteen years. During the First World War he was Commandant of the Eastern Anti-Gas School and, for his work in chemical warfare, was awarded the Harrison Memorial Medal of the Pharmaceutical Society (of which he became President in 1935). Like his father, he was active in public service as a Councillor and an Alderman, and became Mayor of Cambridge in 1937. In his capacity as President of the Fitzwilliam Society for 1953–54, he was a signatory of the Memorial presented to the Vice-Chancellor (p. 69).

Eventually, the family no longer lived over the shop and in 1914 Ernest Peck leased those parts of 30 Trumpington Street and the adjacent 25 Fitzwilliam Street that were not needed as business premises. George Peck and Son Ltd. continued for more than twenty years after Ernest Peck's death in 1955, until it was taken over by a pharmacy chain.

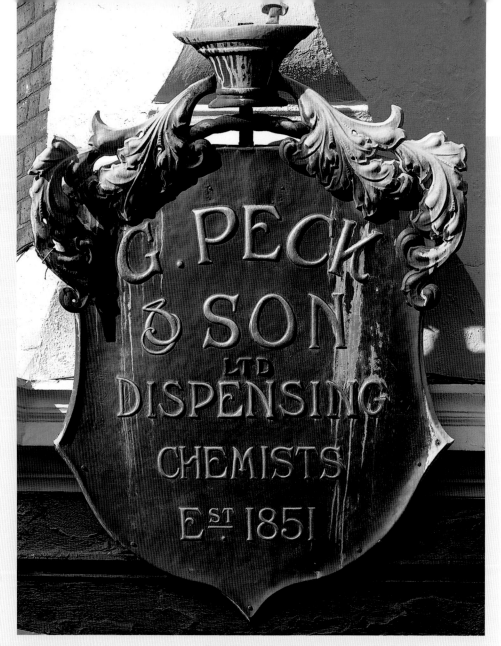

The G. Peck and Son Ltd sign remains over the pharmacy, even though there is no longer a family connection

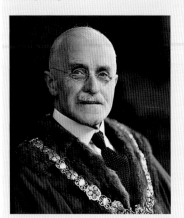

Ernest Saville Peck, Mayor of Cambridge 1937–38

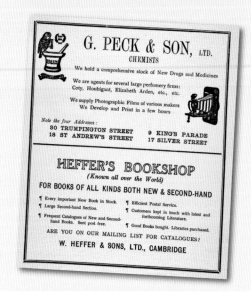

enlarged and more convenient domicile would become imperatively necessary'.

Investigation of potential sites was pre-empted when Peck offered to sell 31 and 32 Trumpington Street to the Board for £3,000. It was recognized that significant work would be needed to adapt the entire building for the use of the Board. This was a long-term objective; initially, only minimal rearrangement was undertaken; tenants remained, and rental income offset the capital cost.

The financial position was favourable, since the Board had been in surplus in most years, in particular having earned £1,500 from fees paid by students at Cavendish College (see below) who generated very few costs; thus a capital sum of £2,000 was available. The Board obtained the balance as a loan of £1,000 at 3½% from the University, which offset it with a loan from the Local Examinations Syndicate. The purchase of 31 and 32 Trumpington Street and the loan arrangements were agreed by the Senate in February 1887.

After just a few years, it was time to take the project to its next stage. Externally, the need was to restore the façade of the building. The interior was to be modified by removing unwanted staircases and providing good rooms for administration and for the men, and accommodation for a porter and his wife.

The Board reported to the Senate in March 1890 on the changes and sought about £950 in grants for the work. The full sum was not forthcoming, but £450 of the debt outstanding on the original purchase was written off. Exhibiting the characteristic spirit that would inform the history of Fitzwilliam, the Board set about raising funds themselves and were able to meet much of their needs by donations: both Somerset and Huddleston were generous and in total there were nearly sixty donors, ranging from the Duke of Devonshire (Chancellor of the University, 1861–91, who had given £6,300 in 1870 to establish the Cavendish Laboratory) and many of the good and great of the University, to two former non-collegiate under-graduates. Fundraising is not exclusively a modern phenomenon.

So it was possible to proceed and, in 1894, the Board reported to the Senate that:

> The ugly shop front and side entrance have been removed, and the original design of the facade has been in part replaced. By the demolition of a huge chimney stack, the large room on the ground floor, previously used as a furniture showroom, and the entrance passage adjoining have been thrown together, and now form a large dining room divisible by a moveable partition. The kitchen and private rooms of the Custodian have been improved, and lavatories added. On the first floor, a large reading room for the use of the Students has been formed by throwing together the two rooms, once used by the Censor and the Clerk, and the passage adjoining, the new room being divided from the adjoining large room (now used as a Lecture Room) by a moveable partition. On the second floor, two rooms have been similarly thrown together, and in course of time may conveniently be used as a Library. By a rearrangement of the roof additional accommodation has been gained in the attics. Until the debt has been extinguished, it has been thought expedient to let off some of the upper rooms, but it will probably not be long before the Board will be able to remove the Library to the second floor, and to assign, if then thought desirable, rooms to each of the three Lecturers. The payments to the Reserve Fund, now temporarily suspended, might then be renewed, so as to form a fund for the purchase in due course of the adjoining premises. A further restoration of the original facade would then complete the unity of the Building.

The building was now in the general form that it would have for the next six decades. By 1904, the Board was clear of debt for both the £3,000 purchase of the building and its £1,639 refurbishment. Largely, funds had come out of revenue, and there had been generosity from the University – but even greater generosity from the individuals whose £973 in donations had done so much to set up Fitzwilliam for the following seven decades.

CAVENDISH COLLEGE

Cavendish College was established by the Rev. Joseph Lloyd Brereton, a serial entrepreneur with two motivations: to open up educational opportunities to those on middle incomes, and to return 5% on capital invested. The College took its name from the family name of the Chancellor of the University. In 1873 the Council of the Senate approved it to admit undergraduates, who were matriculated through the Non-Collegiate Students Board. Nine years later, it became a Public Hostel and matriculated students in its own right.

In the first ten years about 164 students entered Cavendish College, drawn predominantly from professional-class families: clergy and doctors, with some lawyers and merchants.

Like Brereton's other projects, Cavendish College was unsound financially; it closed in 1892. Its buildings on Hills Road form the core of Homerton College.

The life of non-collegiate students

The Board kept few records in the early years – even of student ages. During the first academic year, 23 students matriculated – the nine recorded ages ranged from 14 to 43, with only two aged 20 or 21. Some older men were in employment and studied part-time; there were working residents of Cambridge amongst non-collegiate students at least up to the First World War.

A peculiarity of Cambridge University was the emphasis placed on being in the city and within college walls. Keeping terms received more emphasis than study – hence gate hours, absits and exeats. The scattered non-collegiate students were required to sign in every day that they wished to count for residence – even if they then spent it non-academically. Before there was an office, they could sign in at the college rooms of a member of the Board or at St Paul's Church on Hills Road; later, at St Matthew's Church or the Catholic Church. They could do so also at St Edmund's House from 1900 or Cheshunt College from 1905.

After signing in, the student might (for a modest fee) attend lecture courses organized by colleges or study on his own, but the University Library was not available to him and Departmental facilities did not exist. Later in the day he might have other priorities.

Somerset, who wrote the introduction to the 1874 edition of *The Student's Guide to the University of Cambridge* tells:

But few men study between 2 pm and the ordinary dinner-hour; this time is given by the most industrious to open-air exercise and recreation. The students are English youths, and a large proportion of men have grown up in the great public schools. Athletic sports accordingly are pursued with ardour. In the boat-clubs of the several Colleges the science of rowing is studied by as many men with as much ambition, and perhaps even with as much seriousness, as are shewn in the study of the subjects of the Honour Triposes.

By 1874, the non-collegiate body had increased to nearly one hundred, and more were of normal undergraduate age. Resources were becoming available: one of the rooms in Trumpington Street served as a Common Room, open on weekdays from 11 am to 6 pm and on Sunday afternoons. So a Newspaper and Magazine Club was established, a termly subscription of 1/6 providing sixteen publications ranging from *The Times* and *The Daily Telegraph* to *Punch* and *The Field*. The Debating Society's subscription was only 1/- but, like the other societies and clubs, it was obsessed with formulating rules (of which there were 34) and schedules of fines. Outdoors there was a Boat Club, relatively expensive at 15/- per term (with fines of 1/- for being late at the boathouse and 2/- for absence), and a Cricket Club (with 3/- fine for losing a ball) – whose first match, in May 1874, was played against Trinity. Lawn Tennis and Football Clubs followed.

May Races in 1912

APPLYING AND STUDYING IN THE 1870s

A potential undergraduate would apply to a college or to the Censor of Non-Collegiate Students. Often there were no formal academic prerequisites: non-collegiate and most collegiate students did not take entrance examinations, and the recently-introduced public examinations for school-leavers were not required. Emphasis was placed on the respectability of the candidate: learning and moral character had to be certified by a Cambridge MA.

The first-year course was common, whether students were to be candidates for Honours or whether they had the limited aspirations of a Poll Man, seeking an Ordinary Degree. They sat the first two parts of the Previous Examination, 'Little Go', with questions on: a Gospel in Greek; a Latin Classic; a Greek Classic; Latin and Greek grammar; the Christian apologetics work *View of the Evidences of Christianity* (William Paley, 1794); the works of Euclid; Arithmetic; and Elementary Algebra. Honours candidates had papers in Additional Subjects: Algebra; Trigonometry; and Mechanics. The standard was very low and examinations were tests of stamina rather than intellect; in Arithmetic, a 2½-hour paper would have about two dozen questions of which any number could be answered. Many were appropriate for a ten-year old: 'What is the rent of 10 acres 3 roods 26 poles at £2 8s 10⅔d per acre?'[1]

Second-year Honours candidates started to read for their Tripos papers. Poll Men took a General Examination, continuing the previous melange. Finally, a Poll Man would take a Special Examination, in which choice was possible: Theology; Moral Sciences (moral philosophy and political economy); Law and History; Natural Sciences; and Mechanism and Applied Science.

Honours Examinations usually were taken in the tenth term of residence. To the prestigious Mathematical Tripos and the Classical Tripos, Moral Sciences and Natural Sciences had been added in mid-century, and it was not until 1875 that the Historical Tripos, the Law Tripos, the Theological Tripos and the Triposes in Semitic Languages and Indian Languages held their first examinations.

There was very little University teaching: in 1870–71, only 54 lecture courses, normally three lectures a week for a term, given by Professors. All other teaching took place in colleges or privately. As the range of courses increased, colleges became less self-sufficient and formed groups. Surprisingly, given their traditional rivalry, Trinity and St John's had courses in common. College lectures were not exclusive; non-collegiate students, and men from other colleges, were able to attend for a small fee; the lectures generally were not formal, but more like school classes. It was not until the 1920s that college supervision became established; until then, under-graduates resorted to private tutors – even students taking Ordinary Degrees used them, even if only before examinations, whilst most seeking Honours Degrees found them to be essential throughout their studies.

---

1. Previous Examination, December 1870. Don't even think of using a calculator – the numbers had been chosen carefully to facilitate simplification.

Cricket in 1890: With bat is Prince Kumar Shri Ranjitsinhji, who obtained a Blue and scored over 70 centuries for Sussex, and represented England in Test Matches between 1896 and 1904

Even though it would be many years before the Boat Club demonstrated any prowess, they had clear aspirations: they named themselves *The Herons*, and paid due attention to their plumage: a grey blazer trimmed with ruby, and a white straw hat with grey and ruby striped ribbon. The boat first appeared in the Lent Bumps for 1875; the *Cambridge Independent Press* reported that they showed no sign of going up. Most of its crew took pass degrees and went into the Church, but at seven was Henry Fenton, one of the first Clothworkers' Exhibitioners (p. 19). At six was Charles Williams – only marginally better academically than the incipient clergy, since in 1876 he was to receive the wooden spoon (p. 30) as the last in order of merit for the Mathematics Tripos.

With financially-distinct clubs and a diverse and physically-scattered student body, there was instability, so in January 1884 the clubs joined together as the Non-Collegiate Students Amalgamation Club. At the beginning of the next academic year, the students sought a more inspiring name; there was little progress until March 1886, when a petition went to the Board drawing attention 'to the disadvantages under which we labour, both individually and collectively, from the fact of our bearing no positive and distinctive name', to which they attributed the level of migrations and their effect that was 'seriously to lessen that esprit de corps which it is so desirable to develop'. There was sympathy but no immediate action. However, the Board indicated that a name could well be linked with a location – and at that time they were seeking extended premises.

In Lent 1887, just a few weeks after the Senate had agreed to purchase 31 and 32 Trumpington Street, the students voted on possible names; shortly afterwards, a Board member proposed that the name Fitzwilliam Hall be adopted for the building. So the Club became the Fitzwilliam Hall Amalgamation Club.

The naming was not straightforward: some members of the Board attempted to reverse it (probably concerned that it was reminiscent of Catharine Hall or Trinity Hall). The Censor was instructed to inform the students 'that the name *Fitzwilliam Hall* is simply the designation of the buildings in Trumpington Street in the occupation of the Board; that the title should not be used as an official or collective designation of the Non-Collegiate Students; and that the title *Fitzwilliam* may appropriately be given to any club consisting of Non-Collegiate Students'. So, for instance, Fitzwilliam Cricket Club, not Fitzwilliam Hall Cricket Club – but naturally the more attractive terminology crept back and *Fitzwilliam Hall* came into general usage both for the clubs and for the affiliation of the men themselves.

To go with the name, a flag was needed (particularly for the Boat Club), and with it a Coat of Arms. The Amalgamation Club proposed *the Fitzwilliam Arms, with the University Arms in chief*, and the Board assented, provided that Earl Fitzwilliam gave permission. The use of Arms incurred an annual payment to the Inland Revenue – even though they were heraldically illegitimate, the College of Heralds not having been consulted.

An organization enabling a rational structure, and an inspirational name, did not ensure financial stability for the individual sports: the Boat Club was dormant for a total of five years during the nineteenth century, and the Tennis Club was suspended in 1892. The total income fluctuated, as did the subscription (initially, in 1884, one guinea) as attempts were made to counter the elasticity of demand for membership. It was natural that many students would not be involved with the Amalgamated

Clubs (the later form of name was adopted in 1897). The 1905 Report gives the composition of the student body in residence. Of 90 students, two were advanced students; seven married; 31 with other commitments such as assistants in schools, members of St Edmund's House, lay-reader members of St Matthew's House, and members of the Teachers' Day Training College.

Somerset's account follows the student's day from the sports field to the dinner table. For non-collegiate students, concerned with economy, this commonly would have been in lodgings, although a significant proportion (as late as 1905, about one-fifth) lived with parents or guardians. But the desire for a more sociable and collective system came early, as the Censor reported to the Board in 1882: 'A Hall dinner has been organised by the students at the Bird Bolt Inn, with permission of the Senior Proctor

COSTS FOR COLLEGIATE AND NON-COLLEGIATE STUDENTS

Undergraduates were admitted directly to the University as an economical route into Cambridge. How economical was it?

The Student's Guide to the University of Cambridge, in its 1874 edition, showed that University costs for a non-collegiate student taking an Ordinary Degree totalled about £33. Somerset claimed that a non-collegiate student who spent the minimum time in Cambridge and lived frugally need not expend more than £ 150 over a three-year period:

	£	s	d
University Capitation Tax and payment to the Non-Collegiate Students Board, each year @ £6/2/-	18	6	0
Matriculation, Examination and Degree fees, Professors' lectures	14	13	0
College lectures, 4 courses in 3 terms each year	12	0	0
Academical dress: cap and gown	1	11	0
Expenses in lodgings, board, washing, coals, use of linen, gaslight and service, 23-week years @ £34/10/-	103	10	0

A non-collegiate student who was able to afford a less constrained life estimated annual costs (excluding clothing and travel) as about £85.

An undergraduate in college had additional fees, and was required to purchase furniture for his rooms and re-sell it at a loss; he had to pay for his meals in Hall; when he took meals in his rooms, the servants exploited him. The *Guide* suggested £105 per annum to cover college and University costs, plus up to £90 for grocers' and booksellers' bills and personal expenses. Thus the annual expenditure of an undergraduate in a college, making good use of his opportunities without being extravagant, and seeking an Ordinary Degree, would be around twice that of a non-collegiate student with a quiet social life.

In addition, men who sought high Honours often paid £150 over three years to private tutors, whilst those with more modest aspirations might spend about £50.

The Bird Bolt Hotel; its name refers to a light crossbow bolt used for shooting birds

The very first dinner at Fitzwilliam Hall

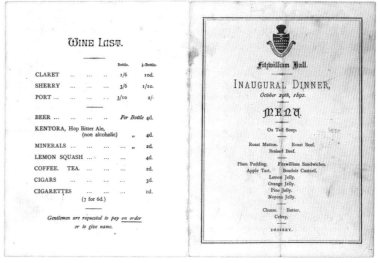

and under regulations drawn up by myself. The hour for dinner during the winter months was 5.30 p.m. and the number of those in attendance was about 25. This term there have been two dinners daily at 1.30 p.m. and 7.00 p.m. and it is proposed to try similar arrangements next term.' The Bird Bolt Hotel, at the intersection of St Andrew's Street with Bird Bolt Lane (now Downing Street) had been a coaching inn. It dated back at least to 1630, when it received an inn licence from the Vice-Chancellor. By that time no licence was needed, as it had become a temperance hotel – not inappropriate for Fitzwilliam men, as at that time aspiring clergy formed a large proportion of their number.

THE FIRST ATTACHED HOUSES

The 1880s were years of great institutional activity in Cambridge. Amongst the foundations was Ayerst Hostel whose objective was '*to enable theological and other students to keep their terms at Cambridge at the same cost as at the younger Universities and at Theological Colleges*'. It had Private Hall status, and started building at a site on Mount Pleasant. But it failed financially and its property was purchased by the Duke of Norfolk for St Edmund's House, set up in 1896 for Roman Catholic ordinands. St Edmund's was not entitled to matriculate students, so any degree examinations were taken under the aegis of the Non-Collegiate Students Board – it became the first Attached House.

Other theological colleges were established in Cambridge at that time, in response to a perceived shortage of priests and ministers. The first Anglican institution, Ridley Hall, was so strongly Puritan that it alienated broad-church members – amongst them Professor Westcott, who set up The Clergy Training School; it became Westcott House in 1902, after his death. Both Ridley and Westcott opened in 1881, and matriculated students through the non-collegiate system.

Westminster College, for training Presbyterian ministers, came from London in 1899; the following year, one of its students matriculated as non-collegiate. Cheshunt College moved to Cambridge in 1906; although not restrictive denominationally, it was associated with Congregationalism. Cheshunt had the greatest number of non-collegiate students: about eight in the first year with eleven in residence in 1910. There was no explicit provision for Methodists until Wesley House was founded in 1921.

3

CONSOLIDATION OF FITZWILLIAM HALL

The Huddleston era

By the last decade of the nineteenth century, the key elements were in place to develop Fitzwilliam Hall and provide for its members. The Trumpington Street building contained a room suitable for lectures, so it was possible to provide regular teaching and address the lack of academic resources that had concerned Somerset from the early non-collegiate days.

The first two teaching appointments had been made in 1885 when Howard was Censor, to give first-year and second-year students the support that colleges provided. Students paid ten shillings for a course with three lectures each week; lecturers received fees of £15 plus a five-shilling capitation payment. Mr C. Geldard (Trinity) was Lecturer in Mathematics, and Mr T.F.C. Huddleston Lecturer in Classics. Huddleston resigned in 1890 when he was appointed Censor, and Geldard in 1893. Looking back, as Censor, Huddleston wondered whether the appointments might have been premature, as fees had to increase, but it was a necessary step.

Huddleston was replaced by Mr E.S. Shuckburgh (Emmanuel) who continued until he died in 1906, to be followed by Mr W.W. Walker (Christ's). Geldard's replacement, Mr W.G. Bell, taught the peculiar first-year combination of Mathematics and Paley's *Evidences of Christianity*.

In 1893 the first Lecturer in History, Mr J.M.B. Masterman (St John's), was appointed – shortly before he completed the Historical Tripos, but subject to his obtaining at least an Upper Second in Part II. An innovation was that rooms were provided for him to live in Fitzwilliam Hall, and he was the first person to be engaged on an annual stipend (initially £25, subsequently doubled), rather than a capitation basis. By 1902, all lecturers received annual stipends. When Masterman left Cambridge, he was replaced by Mr W.F. Reddaway, recruited to teach both History and Essay Writing.

Walter George Bell (1856–1925), Fellow of Trinity Hall; a great supporter of non-collegiate students (and, as a Quaker, a principled supporter of other unpopular causes). He wrote to the 1919 Royal Commission urging the adoption of a collegiate form, and was President of the Amalgamated Clubs for 25 years. By Kenneth Green

The generosity of individuals who underwrote his stipend enabled the appointment in 1901 of Rev. T.W. Crafer (Jesus), to supervise students in Theology. The small amount of Economics teaching needed was provided from 1909 by the appointment of Mr L. Alston (Christ's), without a stipend but in return for rent-free rooms.

So in 1908, when Reddaway issued his first leaflet providing 'Information relating to Non-Collegiate Students in the University of Cambridge', he could include a full complement of teaching officers:

Staff.   LECTURERS. *Classics:* W. W. WALKER, M.A.; *Mathematics:* W. G. BELL, M.A.; *Assistant Lecturer:* R. W. B. GARRETT, B.A.
DIRECTORS OF STUDIES. *Poll Degree:* W. G. BELL, M.A.; *Classics:* W. W. WALKER, M.A.; *Economics:* L. ALSTON, M.A.; *History:* H. W. V. TEMPERLEY, M.A.; *Law:* C. J. B. GASKOIN, M.A.; *Mathematics:* W. G. BELL, M.A.; *Medieval and Modern Languages:* A. J. WYATT, M.A.; *Moral Sciences:* C. FOX, M.A.; *Natural Sciences:* THE PRESIDENT OF QUEENS'; *Music:* E. J. DENT, M.A., Mus.B.; *Theology:* Rev. T. W. CRAFER, M.A., B.D.

T.F.C. HUDDLESTON

Tristram Huddleston, an Eton Scholar, came up to King's in 1867. He took a First in Classics in 1871; he was Powis medallist three times and Browne medallist twice. A Fellowship followed, which he held until 1880. Huddleston was appointed Censor in February 1890 – the first non-clerical Censor.

Hugh Roden (1905) recalled Huddleston at the end of his long period in office as 'an old gentleman, with a grizzled moustache and very thick spectacles. He was fatherly, charming and gentle. On our first Sunday in residence he invited me and another *fresher* ... to dinner at his house in Selwyn Gardens and, together with his wife, courteously entertained us.

'At Fitzwilliam Hall the Censor reigned in a room above the downstairs office, where the good-looking Salmon was sole clerk. The Censor used to get in touch with him by blowing down a tube with a whistle at the base. If one wished to see the Censor, one had to get Salmon to blow up the tube to fix the interview. When one eventually got into the Presence upstairs, dear old *Huddles* opened the door, shook hands with his right hand while placing his left hand, apparently affectionately, on one's right shoulder. I soon learnt from some third-year men, however, that this was his way of ascertaining whether one was wearing a gown or not, his eyesight being too poor for him to see!'

T.F.C. Huddleston, Censor 1890–1907

His failing eyesight led to premature retirement in April 1907, at the age of 59. He lived in Cambridge until shortly before his death in 1936.

A DISTINGUISHED MUSICIAN – SIR HENRY WALFORD DAVIES

One of Fitzwilliam's most distinguished musicians was Sir Henry Walford Davies, who matriculated in 1889 and received the MusB in 1892 and the MusD in 1898. He went on to important church-music and academic posts, and in 1918 became the first Director of Music for the newly created Royal Air Force; he wrote the *RAF March Past*, still the official march for the service. He succeeded Elgar in 1934 as Master of the King's Musick, and held the post until his death in 1941. Walford Davies was knighted in 1922. Many of his hymn and carol arrangements continue in use, including *God Be in My Head* and *The Holly and the Ivy*.

Cigarette card, from the
Radio Celebrities series, 1934

There was little progress in other areas, and at the turn of the century non-collegiate students could be regarded as socially inferior to college members. They experienced difficulties when attempting to enlist in the Cambridge University Rifle Volunteers (precursor to the OTC); Huddleston engaged in futile correspondence and meetings for two years with the Adjutant. In the Boer War, however, death showed no such discrimination: Hugh Fife, a reverse migrant (from Clare, he became non-collegiate and stayed for just two months in 1891 – long enough to row for the Hall and to fail Little Go – before leaving to join the Army), was killed at Johannesburg in 1900.

The Reddaway era

On Huddleston's retirement in 1907, the Non-Collegiate Students Board had a good field of candidates for his successor. They made an excellent choice: W.F. Reddaway who, as lecturer since 1896, had strong connections to the Hall. He was to transform its resources and its self-perception – not only by inspiration, but substantially at his own expense, generously providing working capital as donations and loss-making loans.

AN EARLY GRADUATE STUDENT – T.H. LABY, FRS

For most of the last century, on the desks of engineers and physicists have been copies of *Kaye and Laby* – the eponymous designation for *Tables of Physical and Chemical Constants, and some Mathematical Functions*, which was first published in 1911 and ran through 16 editions until 1995; its contents are available online from the National Physical Laboratory. Kaye and Laby met when they were both undertaking research in physics in Cambridge, in the glory days of the Cavendish Laboratory when it was the centre of the world of experimental physics.

T.H. Laby came from a small town in the Australian bush, and was largely self-taught in physics, chemistry and mathematics; he did not have sufficient academic subjects for a conventional university education. He obtained a junior position in the chemical laboratory of the New South Wales Department of Agriculture, where he did excellent practical work and made rapid progress as an independent and original scientific worker – so that in 1904 he received an award from the Royal Commission for the Exhibition of 1851 to enable him to

come to England. He joined the Cavendish Laboratory, and in 1905–06 he was a non-collegiate student. But inevitably he migrated, to Emmanuel.

After four years in Cambridge he was appointed to the Chair of Physics in Wellington, New Zealand; in his reference for that post, Professor Sir J.J. Thomson wrote that he had 'been greatly impressed by Mr Laby's skill as an experimenter, in fact I do not remember any one who has excelled him in this respect'. Laby played a major role in physics, in university reform, and in public life in both New Zealand and Australia; he was elected a Fellow of the Royal Society in 1931.

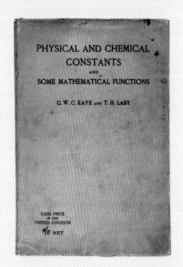

PHYSICAL AND CHEMICAL CONSTANTS
AND
SOME MATHEMATICAL FUNCTIONS

G. W. C. KAYE and T. H. LABY

CASH PRICE
IN THE
UNITED KINGDOM
4/6 NET

Left: The first edition of *Kaye and Laby*

Above: In the sixteenth edition, eight decades later

98 ACOUSTICS
Properties of sound in liquids (contd)

Liquid	t /°C	c /m s⁻¹	dc/dt /m s⁻¹ K⁻¹	10^{-15} neper m⁻¹ Hz⁻² (α/f^2)
Carbon tetrachloride				
Chloroform				
Chlorobenzene				
Cyclohexane	25	921		
Cyclohexanol	25	984		
Ethyl alcohol	20	1270	−3.0	
Ethylene glycol (ethane-1,2-diol)	25	1280	−3.5	
Freon (C51–12)	25	1465	−3.9	535
Glycerol	25	1145	−5.4	370
*Helium (⁴He)		1660	−3.7	140 (<200)
n-Hexanol	25		−3.3	~180
Hydrogen	25	524	−2.1	−500 (<45)
Indium	−269	1920		51
Lead	25	180	−3.4	120
Mercury	−255	1303	−1.9	

ROBERT PASK AND HIS WOODEN SPOON

In the nineteenth century the class list for the Mathematical Tripos gave the full order of the results, from the Senior Wrangler down to the lowest of the Junior Optimes, whose peers would present him with a huge and elaborately-decorated wooden spoon. Back in 1876, Charles Williams (p. 25) was the last man in the list, but no trace survives of his wooden spoon. Robert Pask was the recipient of this 'honour' in 1908, almost at the final opportunity; the following year was the last in which candidates were listed in sequence, so the custom ended.

R. Pask. 1908.

The proud possessor, and with good reason – Pask was the first man from Fitzwilliam Hall even to appear in the Mathematical Tripos class lists for half a decade

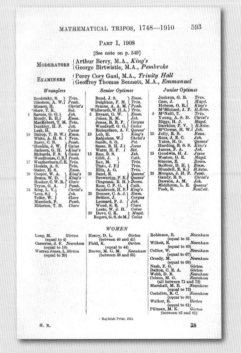

The 1908 class list, with candidates in order. Women are listed separately; they were allowed to take examinations, but could not receive degrees

H. W. MALDEN.   C. W. JANVRIN.   L. J. LOCK.   A. BROOKES.   W. F. REDDAWAY.   L. WHITEWAY.
(HON. SEC.)   (CAPT.)

MATCHES WON: 12.   LOST: 0.

The achievements during Reddaway's period as Censor included the establishment of the Fitzwilliam Hall Trust, which purchased property in Fitzwilliam Street; a substantial reduction in migration to colleges; and the provision of both a Chapel and the Oxford Road sports ground. But he failed to change the formal non-collegiate status, and resigned at the early age of 51, in 1924.

The non-collegiate students played games on hired fields. With his sporting inclinations, Reddaway sought better provision, and in 1908 the opportunity arose. He learned that a field behind the houses in Oxford Road was on the market (perhaps from L.J. Lock (1905), who was both a theological student and a medical practitioner, and lived nearby in Huntingdon Road; he was Captain of the 1909 tennis team, above), but no funds were available. Reddaway's characteristically generous action was to acquire the field at his own expense: the cost in April 1908 was £650, which provided about 6½ acres linked to Oxford Road by two entrance strips (one he sold soon afterwards).

What he had purchased was not a sports ground. It was a rough field – worse than a rough field, as it had been used for dumping earth when the nearby roads were being constructed. This provided one more challenge for Reddaway, who by November could write: 'steady progress has been made with the task of turning a meadow, originally self-sown and for twenty-five years uncared for, into a ground of the class which Cambridge now expects. ... the hedges, fences and ditches were set in order, a new

approach from Oxford Road constructed, plans and estimates procured, our small pavilion removed from the old football field, and, above all, the cleansing of the turf begun. This last seems to have succeeded beyond all expectation. In April every kind of weed luxuriated, and we took 250 plantains from seven square yards of soil. Before the end of September the field showed as pure a surface as some which have received many years of treatment.'

The final statement is highly characteristic of his combative enthusiasm for all things Fitzwilliam. And the previous one is significant, too. Although labourers were brought in for some of the heavy work, W.S. Thatcher recalled: 'Mr Reddaway organised us into working gangs, and, in the course of several years, we levelled it ourselves. He had a way of luring us on and in. My first introduction to the ground was on a damp, dank day in the Lent term. A simple invitation to view having arrived, I found Mr Reddaway and two others spudding up plantains. ... The scene called for little enthusiasm and one answered with politeness. Yet, after a very short time, one found oneself with a spudder in one's hand and a bent back.'

By February 1909, the *Magazine* could report: 'At the southern end a dead level, amply large enough for five grass courts, has been excavated, built up, turfed and kept under careful supervision during many weeks. It promises to be firm and true enough to satisfy all requirements in the coming term ... . If summer – as a cynic once said – sets in with its usual severity, enthusiasts may have recourse to the ash-courts close at hand.'

W.F. REDDAWAY

W.F. Reddaway, Censor 1907–24, by Philip de László

William Fiddian Reddaway was, in the opinion of many of its members, the true begetter of Fitzwilliam. That opinion is not fair to his predecessors, but it does embody substantial truths – that Reddaway was able to draw the non-collegiate students into a corporate structure, albeit one that placed very heavy emphasis on the clubs and their activities, and that he fought unrelentingly on its behalf.

Reddaway was born in Lancashire in 1872, the son of a Methodist minister, and was educated in Cambridge at the Leys School before entering King's in 1891; he was a Scholar from 1893, and obtained a First in the History Tripos in 1894.

Reddaway first became involved with non-collegiate students when he was appointed Lecturer in 1896. He had been a Fellow of King's since 1895, a position that he retained throughout his life; he was a modern-European historian who sacrificed his personal work when he became Censor (at a stipend of £300 plus a capitation allowance of 7/- per student); in 1924 he resumed his studies, holding a University Lectureship from 1927 until 1937, and publishing until his death in 1949.

Blessed with an exceptional memory – he never forgot a name and rarely an initial – Reddaway regarded office organization as unnecessary. Even the telephone was merely tolerated, and was on the ground floor, downstairs from his rooms. Normally he did not employ a clerk, but made use of the students: partly to provide some financial support for them; partly as an economy; but above all because of his contempt for office work for 'what did a clerk do but make lines in a book?'. Even when it was pointed out that the lines had to be in the right places he remained unconvinced. Fortunately for the Hall, from 1909 one of the students who worked part-time was Frank Thatcher (elder brother of the future Censor) who was a trained accountant, and who returned to the Hall as Bursar from 1917 to 1924.

W.S. Thatcher recalled that 'Reddaway disliked being organised even to the slight extent that was customary at that time, for instance showing quiet opposition to the requests and regulations of the office of the University Registrary; one morning, having settled himself at a table he remarked "Let me see, what can we do today to annoy the Registrary?"' And when Thatcher became Censor, he was handicapped because Reddaway's memory provided the only records – one of his first actions was to purchase filing cabinets.

Thatcher came up as a freshman in the same year that Reddaway became Censor. 'Reddaway at that time must have been a young man in his middle thirties but, to the undergraduate, tutors are ageless though never young. ... There was always a tone and manner in those interviews and conversations. One's remarks were listened to gravely while the rather hesitant manner of reply gave one the impression that the speaker was considering seriously what one had said. ... It implied that he was talking to an equal though one might be younger: that what one thought and said was worthy of consideration. Immediately, one found oneself vested with a new dignity and one's self-confidence was increased.'

Although many students inclined to some sort of corporate life, Reddaway directed it and gave it purpose. He went to all their matches, he ran with the Boat, he attended debates; he was always there. So in his time originated the Chapel, the Fitzwilliam Hall Trust, the Playing Field and Red Cottage, and the Fitzwilliam Society. Reddaway had great capacity for leadership, and instilled into those around him something of his own enthusiastic belief. Thatcher considered him an 'outstanding personality, and that this made even his weaknesses lovable. He was essentially Victorian in that he was a democrat and yet an aristocrat – he left no doubt that he was Censor, and yet he worked always through the men. He was familiar with them in their clubs. He developed the practice of dining, sitting with the men and talking freely, but always as a leader, maintaining reserve but warmed by his living affection for Fitzwilliam and its men.' His influence developed so that they 'picked up some of his indomitable will and enthusiasm. There gathered round him a group of men whom he called his 'Old Guard'. It was like him to choose such a title, but we felt it to be an honour to be so included. ... To migrate became the equivalent to desertion. It was not done. It is astonishing how quickly it ceased as a flow, though now and then it still happened. There will always be climbers.'

He was an enthusiastic fighter, litigious even over trivialities: Thatcher recalled meeting him 'on Castle Hill and discovered that he was rushing to his greengrocer to dispute his bill. The sum to be disputed was exactly one penny. He also went to court shortly after he had bought the playing field, over a short ditch which he claimed as his. The Judge was very tart with him, but he had enjoyed himself.'

But a full assessment of Reddaway cannot be made without considering his personal generosity. Not only did he purchase the Oxford Road ground and several Fitzwilliam Street houses; when eventually he sold them to the Fitzwilliam Hall Trust, he contributed to the appeal for funds – repaying himself with his own contribution!

And his advocacy of Fitzwilliam never faltered, as Thatcher wrote: 'I frankly do not know who edited the earlier *Magazines*, but ... I catch the lordly tone of Mr Reddaway who had a genius for magnificent phrasing and for an optimism about things which used to make us think he had missed his real vocation, Thus ... "Few colleges in Cambridge, we venture to think, have more to offer in the way of collegiate life than is known to that large group of non-collegiate students who have made a practice of dining at the Hall and turning up to our very full programme of debates and concerts" ... Such noble exaggerations, but they display a great truth which was manifest in Mr Reddaway and his work that, important as are bricks and mortar and all those advantages which flow from spacious and well-appointed buildings, it is the human spirit which counts. The material surroundings are but an outward manifestation of that spirit.'

Above: Red Cottage

Below: War-memorial tablet on Red Cottage

The last development that Reddaway undertook at Oxford Road was the construction of Red Cottage as a house for the groundsman, again at his own expense. Characteristically, the venture depended on the talent of an undergraduate of the Hall: Red Cottage was designed by Reginald Tollit (1909), a practising architect as well as a Theology student.

O THE FORTY THREE FROM
ITZWILLIAM HALL WHO
ELL IN THE GREAT WAR THIS
LAYING FIELD IS DEDICATED
Y THEIR SUCCESSORS 1923

ALSO THIS HOUSE BY
THEIR PARENTS FRIENDS
AND SUCCESSORS 1925

In November 1909, with the ground largely in use, Reddaway leased it to the Amalgamated Clubs at the modest rate of 3½% per annum of the costs he had incurred in its purchase and preparation, about £1,000, with a further £7 p.a. to cover the construction of the ash tennis courts; £42 p.a. in total. At the end of his Censorship, he sold the ground to the Fitzwilliam Hall Trust at purchase cost, making no allowance for land-price inflation (perhaps twofold) and sacrificing the potential capital gain on land that he had owned for fifteen years.

Spiritual provision at the Hall also became a possibility. The non-collegiate body contained substantial numbers of clergy and of those destined for the cloth; students were not obliged to attend a service every day, but the majority were regular church-goers. Initially there was no possibility of all the students worshiping at a single location. However, a major step was taken in 1905 when the Rev. T.W. Crafer (p. 28) initiated regular services in a side-chapel in King's and communion services in All Saints' Church in Jesus Lane. As life in Fitzwilliam Hall became more corporate, the possibility arose of having a Chapel and a Chaplain.

In 1911 the Board resolved to appoint a resident Chaplain. Crafer initially acted as honorary Chaplain, until Mr A.O.N. Lee (who had graduated in Theology in 1909) was available in 1914 to take up the position. For the post (combined with that of Steward), he received £140 per annum – of which £40 was contributed by Reddaway. The arrangement was a success, as Reddaway reported to the Board for 1915–16: 'It is difficult to express adequately my sense of [the Chaplain's] work under the difficult conditions of the war. All who have known him regard the idea of Fitzwilliam Hall without a resident Chaplain as now almost inconceivable. It may be convenient to mention here ... that a fund for the permanent endowment of the Resident Chaplaincy has been set on foot.' The Chaplaincy Endowment Fund raised £500 in the period 1916 to 1923, when the proceeds were used to purchase 10 Fitzwilliam Street, to generate rent income.

Whilst a Sports Ground and a Chapel would have seemed to Reddaway's students to have been the greatest advances under his Censorship, and to him the greatest fight was over nomenclature and the status of the non-collegiate students, his most important long-term contribution to Fitzwilliam was in purchasing houses in Fitzwilliam Street and establishing the Fitzwilliam Hall Trust.

THE CHAPEL IN FITZWILLIAM HALL

The Chapel in 1913; note the stained glass above altar

The establishment of a Chapel in Fitzwilliam Hall was motivated by its junior members, and made possible by the generosity of both young and old. Students in the Theological Society petitioned in December 1910 for services within the building; the Board responded positively, and the first services took place in the Library on the first floor. After joint use for only six months, a further petition sought exclusive use of the room. More than 100 undergraduates, including many Nonconformists and non-Christians, signed, claiming a 'general need of corporate worship; the fact that there are now resident some forty professed Ordinands: that this lack is the one thing which robs us of full collegiate life'. Many generous gifts of money and furniture enabled the Chapel to be fitted out, and it was dedicated by the Bishop of Ely (formerly a Chairman of the Board) in April 1913.

The Chapel c. 1950

The Chapel was elaborately equipped, with oak altar, riddel-posts, cross and candlesticks, credence-table, prayer-desk, and altar book-stand by the local furniture designer and cabinetmaker George Philo. The style was strongly influenced by the Gothic Revival, with the woodwork described as 'eleventh-century' and with both the silk and linen tapestry altar frontal and the wool-tapestry riddels hand-woven by the firm of Morris and Co. The heraldic stained glass, with the shields of Fitzwilliam Hall, the University, the Diocese of Ely, and the Clothworkers' Company, were by F.R. Leach and Sons, also a local firm; the glass is now in the Crypt of the present Chapel.

By 1930, refurbishment was necessary, to deal with damp and with problems of lighting and noise. Plans were prepared by the Chaplain, the Rev. Walter Harvey, and expenditure approved by the Bursar, the Rev. Walter Harvey – plural office-holding was common for much of the history of Fitzwilliam. Two plain-glass windows replaced a stained-glass window above the altar, probably a Burne-Jones design of *Our Lord in Glory* made by Morris and Co. Here, Harvey's enthusiasm was unwise, as Thatcher recalled: 'This window … was particularly abhorrent to the Bursar. He could not abide it, so go it did. … Only when the deed was done and when Reddaway had come into the Chapel did we learn what we had done. Reddaway missed it at once and enquired what had become of it and when informed quietly replied "Indeed, but it was a gift from the Master of Selwyn …", It was then too late to do anything, so when some time later the Master of Selwyn came to visit us we had to lay plans to keep him out of the Chapel.' The Master of Selwyn was the son-in-law of the first Censor, in whose memory the stained-glass window had been given.

Reddaway became Censor 15 years after the Trumpington Street building had been refurbished. There was need for additional space, and an almost complete lack of nearby accommodation for the students; meeting these needs became a major objective – to be tackled by Reddaway with his characteristic combination of buccaneering and generosity.

The first step was to add space connecting directly with the main building; this was accomplished in 1914 by leasing all the upper-floor space in 30 Trumpington Street and the contiguous 25 Fitzwilliam Street from Peck (p. 22).

This provided space for a library (to replace that given to the Chapel) and for accommodation – always known as The Hostel. Reddaway leased the premises at his own expense, then sub-let to the Board. This arrangement continued until Reddaway's retirement; then, until 1963, they were leased by Peck to the University. By Michaelmas 1919, further properties had been acquired, all by Reddaway in person: in Fitzwilliam Street, six houses purchased and one rented; two houses in Trumpington Street rented. Three houses were acquired subsequently. Reddaway intended that students would be tenants of the

GASKOIN AND DRAMA

One of the most colourful members of Fitzwilliam was Charles Jacinth Bellairs Gaskoin – with such a name, how could he not be? Gaskoin was born in 1873 and educated at home, too delicate for school life. At 19, apprenticed to a bookseller in Oxford, he studied Law as a non-collegiate student. His family moved to Cambridge and he joined Fitzwilliam Hall in 1895, reading History and obtaining Firsts at every opportunity, culminating in the top First in the History Tripos; he migrated to Jesus with a Scholarship and obtained the top First in Part I of the Law Tripos in 1899.

A highly able man without a Fellowship, Gaskoin coached students in History and in Law, lectured to Pass and Tripos men, and directed studies in History at Fitzwilliam for nearly thirty years. In the First World War he showed a flair for cracking codes and was put in charge of a Postal Censorship Code Department in London; he returned to this in the Second World War. In 1934, he was appointed to a lectureship in Indian History.

C.J.B. Gaskoin, by H.S. Buss

Thatcher recalled: 'Gaskoin belonged to a world which has passed away. Though Director in History, he was paid no salary, which was not uncommon in those days. ... But he had no duties, these he created as he went along. He entertained a great deal and was fond of that now-forgotten meal, the social breakfast, when history, amateur dramatics, eggs and bacon, got all mixed up together.'

And amateur dramatics was central to this very full life. Harold Burton (1920), who recounted his early life from Fulham to Fitzwilliam in *There Was a Young Man*, wrote: 'Gasky had really little interest in the drama, but was completely obsessed by the fun and games of acting. He must have realized that his distinctive voice and figure restricted his own range of parts, but he did not need to be playing an important part; he enjoyed just being there while others were planning, discussing, rehearsing, and talking theatre.'

The Fitzwilliam House Amateur Dramatic Society (FHADS) was his main vehicle, although his enthusiasm involved him in many other productions. The first recorded is a mock trial in 1913, which bears witness to the Edwardian obsession for dressing up. Gaskoin was the Judge and from his account in the *Fitzwilliam Hall Magazine* it is clear that he delighted in donning the black cap. Another mock trial ten years later brought FHADS members and law students together, but with a real Judge, several law dons, and senior police officers.

Characteristically for the period, FHADS performed drawing-room comedies, and the programme for 1928 at the ADC is typical: a double bill with Clemence Dane's *A Traveller Returns* as the curtain-raiser, followed by Noël Coward's *Hay Fever*. A review stated that *Hay Fever* 'provided a delightful evening's entertainment. Due praise must be given to the FHADS ... for the vitality that they brought to the piece and for the lively spirit in which they attacked it.' And, 'If this was the first FHADS production of Mr Coward's play, it does them tremendous credit, and H.M. Burton, who produced, should be very pleased with himself and the company. His acting ... was the best male performance.'

Above: The mock trial in 1913

Right: FHADS casts in 1928, for *A Traveller Returns* and *Hay Fever*

AN EDWARDIAN UNDERGRADUATE

Edgar Semple never forgot that his life was transformed by Fitzwilliam and the support he received from Reddaway. He obtained Thirds in both parts of the History Tripos, and was the first president of the Athletics Club. Fifty years later, he reminisced: 'My father's business having collapsed just at the time that I was hoping to begin my training for Holy Orders, I realised that I should have to pay my own way. ... I read that with strict economy it was possible to take the course for the BA degree as a non-collegiate student for £55 a year. I decided that I could just manage that, so I wrote to Fitzwilliam Hall and was accepted for entry in October 1909.

'I soon discovered that the social life was regarded as of vital importance. Inspired by the great Censor, Mr W.F. Reddaway, a fine third year led and encouraged the exuberant freshmen; ... while ... W. Harvey and W.S. Thatcher were among the giants of those days. I found that apparently nobody ever worked in the afternoon. Everybody played in some sport, though recognised variations were a punt or canoe on the Cam or the Upper River during the Easter Term.

'The most popular social meal was tea, greatly appreciated after a strenuous game and a bath, and current prices permitted a grand spread for a very small expenditure. Tea was 1/- a lb, so was coffee, so was butter. A full size chocolate Swiss roll was 6d.; a large Madeira cake was 6d.; cream éclairs were 2d. each. After tea a good smoke, with Waverley Mixture at 5d. an ounce, John Cotton at 9d.; and cigarettes were always at hand, for 'Virgins' were 2/- per 100, while 'Turks' or 'Gyppies' were 5/- per 100. Great swells known as 'Knuts' might offer a 6d. Havana or some 'Gold Block' tobacco at the fabulous price of 1/- an ounce! Coffee parties after hall were very popular, strictly only until swotting time at about 9 p.m.'

Many students were members of the Officers' Training Corps. 'The Fitzwilliam section was in 'F' Company, with Clare and King's. Some of us were on duty in Windsor Castle for King Edward VII's funeral, and outside Buckingham Palace for King George V's coronation. The F.H. tent had a grand time at the annual camp at Farnborough.

'Sunday was a big day in those Church-going times. Great St Mary's and Holy Trinity were crammed to the doors for the special sermons. ... [But] the chief spiritual event for Ordinands was the Corporate Communion at All Saints' Church, followed by breakfast with the Reverend T.W. Crafer, our Theological Director. But we all were determined to have a Fitzwilliam Hall Chapel, and it was my privilege to see that dream realised before I went down.'

As a cleric who had been involved in the OTC, Semple naturally became a Chaplain to the Forces in the Great War; his enthusiasm for his role is evident in his *E.G. Semple C.F.* on the photograph from Alexandria. His correspondence with Reddaway repeats thanks and good wishes – and more practical matters: writing from Khartoum, he included a cheque for £3 as a donation for needy members of Fitzwilliam Hall, to replace one sent earlier but lost when a ship was torpedoed.

Above: Semple in Alexandria

Below: Semple in OTC camp (with Wilfrid Hirst and Frank Thatcher – both with caps, respectively standing and seated)

Hall, as in The Hostel. However, house prices had been exorbitant and furniture needed to be replaced; costs could be recovered only slowly from rent income, despite augmentation by donations. By 1922, all but one of the houses on the Addenbrooke's side of the street had been sold off. Those on the other side were extensively refurnished, and some were let to landladies.

In 1913, the first proposal had been made for setting up trustees to hold property and administer funds for the benefit of Fitzwilliam Hall, but the war intervened and it was not until June 1921 that the Fitzwilliam Hall Trust was incorporated. It took over responsibility for the field and the properties (excluding The Hostel) from Reddaway, incurring indebtedness to him and repaying him from rental income. The peak sum owed to Reddaway by the Trust was nearly £8,000, but by June 1924 this had been reduced to about £4,500. It took until October 1933 for Reddaway to be repaid – nominally in full but, since the repayments always ignored potential capital gains, in effect he made substantial donations to the Trust.

Initially the scope of the Trust was defined very widely; it overlapped primary functions of the Board including the provision of instruction, books, rooms, and research support (including Fellowships and travel funds). Following the report by a Syndicate that in 1924 examined the Board's operation, those were stripped and the Trust was restricted to providing accommodation, sports facilities, facilities for religious worship, and to supporting students by Scholarships and Exhibitions and in cases of hardship.

The Council of the Senate had set up the Syndicate because the Board was in severe financial difficulties. Recurrent income was down: the high post-war student numbers had not been maintained – in 1920 they had reached 314, but were halved three years later – whilst fees had not been increased since 1896. And student debts had reached about £1,600, half irrecoverable.

The Syndicate recognized that the majority of non-collegiate students benefited from the existence of Fitzwilliam and therefore that it needed to be sustained, on a stable footing. They recommended that the University should (out of its Government grant) pay £1,000 annually to the Board; of this, £200 would be earmarked as a Censor's Gift Fund to assist poor students. So, with annual costs of £2,000, income of £1,200 would be needed: fees would be increased so over three years a student would pay a total of £33.6s.0d. (reduced to £22.1s.0d. for those, such

as Attached-House students, who made no call on Fitzwilliam resources). The University also wrote off bad debts, and recommended a termly prepayment scheme to limit the accumulation of new debt.

In addition to these practical salvage measures, the Syndicate recommended, and the Senate approved, that the institution should change its name to Fitzwilliam House 'to avoid any confusion with older foundations'. Although this change was linked to the use for the first time of the Fitzwilliam name in the Statutes and Ordinances of the University, and so a step towards further recognition, it was resented by many who had come to take great pride in the title of Fitzwilliam Hall, the more so as it was not accompanied by any change of designation in the degree-class lists: still *Non-Coll*.

The University's financial provisions had an indirect benefit: Red Cottage became a war memorial, owned by the Fitzwilliam Hall Trust. By the time of the Syndicate, Reddaway had partially disentangled his finances from those of the Hall, but still needed to dispose of Red Cottage. Six years earlier, as the end of the war approached, an appeal had been launched 'to found a worthy memorial of our heroes fallen in the war'. The initial subscribers were relatives and friends of the fallen, with Reddaway himself the largest single donor. The announcement in the *Fitzwilliam Hall Magazine* went on to give the objectives of the fund: 'An abiding monument in our Chapel, Exhibitions for their successors who need them – these their own kinsfolk have sanctioned as the perfect tribute ...'. By 1924 there was a substantial balance on the account; also, provision for needy students had changed significantly, as the University support of the Censor's gift fund was an order of magnitude greater than could have been generated by investment of the war-memorial account.

So Reddaway found an alternative use for the war-memorial funds. This was simple as he was the sole trustee, and by December 1924 he had obtained permission from the subscribers to change the use from the provision of Exhibitions to the purchase of Red Cottage: on 27 June 1925 he passed the £535.13s.10d. balance of the fund to the Fitzwilliam House Trustees, on the condition that they would purchase Red Cottage from him and hold it on behalf of the Amalgamated Clubs. In this way, several of Reddaway's objectives had come together: a tangible War Memorial existed, and the Sports Ground and Red Cottage were on a common financial

SUBHAS CHANDRA BOSE AND JOSEPH BAPTISTA – LEADERS OF INDIAN INDEPENDENCE

Probably the most controversial figure ever to pass through Fitzwilliam was Subhas Chandra Bose, who matriculated in 1919. Bose was from southern Bengal and was high-caste, born to a father with a law degree, and destined for life in government service; in his youth, he was more fluent in English than in Bengali. He entered Calcutta University in 1913 to read Philosophy, but was rusticated after a professor was assaulted; he was re-admitted in 1917 and went on to take First-Class Honours in Philosophy. He expected to continue for a Masters degree but his father proposed that he should go into the Indian Civil Service; for this he needed to take the ICS examinations in England.

At very short notice, he came to London. There, the Adviser to Indian Students indicated that he had no hope of entering Cambridge; however, some students from his home town encouraged him and 'One of them who belonged to Fitzwilliam Hall took me to Mr Reddaway, the Censor, and introduced me to him. Mr Reddaway was exceedingly kind and sympathetic, gave me a patient hearing, and at the end wound up by saying that he would admit me straightaway. The problem of admission settled, the next question was about the current term which had begun two weeks ago. If I lost that term then I probably would have to spend nearly a year more in order to qualify for a degree. On this point also, Mr Reddaway was accommodating beyond my expectation. He [persuaded] the University authorities to stretch a point in my favour ... the result was that I did not lose that term. Without Mr Reddaway, I do not know what I would have done in England.'

All smiles – but substantial underlying differences. Gandhi and Bose at the March 1938 meeting of the Indian National Congress

Bose found Cambridge rather conservative: 'One could detect in the average Britisher a feeling of superiority beneath a veneer of bonhomie'. However, he greatly admired the Union Society debates, where 'there was perfect freedom to talk what you liked or attack whomsoever you wished'. More generally, 'What greatly impressed an outsider like myself was the measure of freedom allowed to the students, and the general esteem in which

basis, owned by the Trust – not simply an investment, but on behalf of the Clubs.

Non-Collegiate status and Reddaway's resignation

'It is interesting to note that all the Censors have ultimately become rebels, a phenomenon which is well worth investigation, for on the whole they have been a sober body of men.' So wrote Thatcher in his final *Letter* in the *Fitzwilliam House Magazine* for 1954, shortly before he retired. Valid for him, but even more valid for his predecessor.

As his Censorship went by and successive elements of corporate life were attained, Reddaway became ever more concerned with the status and the designation of the Non-Collegiate Students – a title that he detested. Earlier Censors had deplored it, and the men had replaced it for sporting purposes with Fitzwilliam Hall, but it remained *Non-Coll.* on the class lists, defining the graduates for the rest of their lives.

The question of the proper title for the students was raised by Reddaway in his very first term as Censor, at the Board meeting in December 1907. The following spring the they were held by all and sundry. What a change, I thought, from a police-ridden city like Calcutta where every student was looked upon as a potential revolutionary and suspect.'

He had become strongly aware of the position of Indians under the Empire, and felt he should work for independence; this was reinforced by the Amritsar massacre which had taken place shortly before he left India – so he had great reservations about working for the British. Bose was placed fourth in order of merit in the ICS examinations but was unwilling to proceed; many people, from his father to the Permanent Under-Secretary of State for India, encouraged him to stay but in April 1921 he formally resigned from the ICS. Next day he wrote 'I had a talk with the Censor of Fitzwilliam Hall, Mr Reddaway, about my resignation. Contrary to my expectations, he heartily approved of my ideas. He said he was surprised, almost shocked, to hear that I had changed my mind, since no Indian within his knowledge had ever done that before.' In 1921 he gained a Third in Part I of the Moral Sciences Tripos and returned to India.

He visited Gandhi immediately and threw himself into Congress Party politics. He spent years in prisons under very poor conditions, contributing to his ill-health; medical treatment led him to Vienna and elsewhere in Europe, giving him first-hand experience of the developments of the 1930s. He became an international figure and enhanced the stature of the Congress Party. In 1938, whilst visiting Britain and having extensive discussions with political and intellectual figures, he was elected president of the Indian National Congress and returned to India to chair its 51st session. Bose was a modernizer with socialist tendencies who recognized the importance of urban and technological development, and wished to advance Indians irrespective of caste or religion. Consequently he had a difficult relationship with the older Gandhi whose vision was of a 'traditional' India with self-sufficiency at a basic village level. The Congress Party was divided, and in 1939 Bose was banned from holding any elective office in the party.

At the onset of war, Bose was determined not to be deflected from his objective of independence. After a spell in prison, he made his escape from India and his way to Berlin. He was without sympathy for Nazi ideology; nevertheless, for the sake of Indian independence he broadcast to India from Berlin and took part in recruiting prisoners of war to form an Indian Legion – but fewer than a quarter joined. He realized that he would produce more effect further east, and eventually was transported by submarine to Tokyo. He became the leader of the Indian National Army, formed by the Japanese from Indians captured at Singapore, and engaged in propaganda and in planning for a free India. The INA attacked the British in Burma, but had to retreat into Thailand. On 18 August 1945, Bose was injured fatally in an air crash in Formosa, en route to Tokyo.

Subhas Chandra Bose is widely respected in India as a hero of the independence movement, and was nicknamed Netaji (meaning Revered Leader); Calcutta's international airport is named after him.

Bose was not the first Indian graduate to attain prominence in the independence movement. In 1895, Joseph Baptista came to Fitzwilliam Hall to study Law. He had studied Civil Engineering at the University of Bombay and had joined the Provincial Government there; he was radicalized in service, and seems to have come to Cambridge to prepare for a wider role in public life. After obtaining Thirds in both parts of the Law Tripos, he received both his BA and his LLB in 1899. He was called to the Bar as a member of Gray's Inn.

In Cambridge, Baptista was politically active, moving at the Cambridge Union a motion against recent prosecutions for sedition in India; this gained him attention as a public speaker, and he addressed political meetings and took part in by-elections, including campaigning in Cambridge for the Liberal candidate. When campaigning at York, he shared a platform with Lloyd George. Back at the Cambridge Union, he demonstrated his wider liberal credentials by advocating the admission of women to University degrees – not to be achieved for another half century – and it is said that he 'became the favourite of Girton and Newnham and the local ladies, with no end of tea parties'.

Baptista joined the Bombay Municipal Corporation, practised at the bar, and wrote on the commercial law of India and the Empire. He was prominent in Indian Home Rule and prepared a draft constitution for India, based on the Canadian model with a federal structure and Dominion status within the Empire. He was elected President of the Home Rule League, and went back to England in 1917 in a delegation to meet Labour Party leaders. As a Roman Catholic, he wished to maintain a clear separation of Religion and State. He was also active as a labour leader, and was one of the founders of the All India Trade Union Congress in 1921, becoming President in the following year. Towards the end of his life, for the year 1925–26, he was Mayor of Bombay; he is commemorated there by the Joseph Baptista Gardens.

Board set up a Committee on Migration and Disabilities to 'make enquiry into the alleged disabilities of non-collegiate students in competing for educational appointments, and to recommend action to remove the possibility of students, who have been in reality non-collegiate during the whole of their residence, graduating as members of a College'. The Board resolved that migration should not be allowed in the later stages of a student's career, except to take up a Scholarship or an Exhibition.

A major complication for Reddaway was that his attempts to enhance status were taking place at the same time as a Royal Commission was reviewing the Universities of Oxford and Cambridge. They had major concerns about costs for students and proper accounting – particularly for the costs of catering, which took extraordinary prominence in their Report in 1922. Its legacy was the 1923 Oxford and Cambridge Universities Act, which resulted in substantial changes to both University and College Statutes, including the Statutory Accounts structure used for more than 80 years. It also ended the practice of awarding college Fellowships for life simply for achievement when young.

As part of their consideration of costs, the Royal Commission commented very favourably on the arrangements for non-collegiate students, wishing to see an increase in their number and emphasizing that their status should not be less than that of collegiate students. They recognized that 'the Non-Collegiate bodies are capable of taking a leading part in the life of both Universities to a far greater extent than in the past, and of securing for an increasing number of students the benefits of a first-rate education in conditions which ... are the normal conditions at Universities in all parts of the world.'

They emphasized the importance of advanced students, who symbiotically would enhance the intellectual level of the non-collegiate body that supported them. Thus: 'We have referred ... to the position of graduate students from other Universities at Oxford and Cambridge, and have expressed the view that it is unnecessary and undesirable to create for them a special position as students attached to the University and not to the Non-Collegiate organisation. ... It is desirable that the Non-Collegiate students should have among their number men of intellectual distinction from other Universities who come up as Research Students or for short courses. The Non-Collegiate bodies should set themselves to attract such students, and foreign and special students generally, by studying their needs and providing all possible facilities for them.'

For leavening of the undergraduate body was needed: 'In addition, we think it is important that they should take steps to raise the general intellectual standard of the Non-Collegiate students, by adopting, for ordinary candidates intending to read for the BA degree, an entrance standard as high as that of Colleges, and by aiming at an increase in the number of students reading for Honours courses.'

The Commissioners noted that resources were inadequate, and considered that support should come from the general Government grant that they recommended for the University.

Whilst the general tenor of these comments was positive, strongly commending Fitzwilliam Hall for increasing the attractiveness of non-collegiate life, many of them went directly against Reddaway's policies – in particular, the emphasis on research students and foreign students, whom he regarded as diluting his core of corporately-minded clubbable sportsmen. The sting was in the conclusion: 'we do not recommend, in spite of some arguments which we have heard, either the taking of further steps to alter the character of the Non-Collegiate bodies or the adoption of a Collegiate title in lieu of the title 'Non-Collegiate'. The probable result of such a change would be a demand for the re-establishment of a Non-Collegiate body on fresh lines afterwards, in order once more to secure the full advantages of Non-Collegiate residence.'

The obstacles to Reddaway's ambitions had been reinforced. Not long afterwards, he put in for leave of absence; W.S. Thatcher, who had been appointed Assistant Censor early in 1923, became acting Censor. So it was Thatcher who had to deal with the Syndicate that reviewed the operation of the Non-Collegiate Students Board in the spring of 1924, resulting in the curtailment of the scope of the Fitzwilliam Hall Trust that was so central to Reddaway's ambitions for Fitzwilliam. Reddaway never returned as Censor; he resigned in June 1924.

4

WAR, PEACE AND DEPRESSION

The Great War

On Sunday 2 August 1914, as Reddaway was celebrating his 42nd birthday at his seaside home (which he had named Fitzwilliam Cottage) in Hunstanton, news came through that Germany had declared war on Russia. Two months later Reddaway returned to find Cambridge 'a hive inhabited by successive swarms of soldiers'. The town appeared full of Belgian refugees, but they were soon 'submerged by the khaki torrent'. Some students unable to get commissions began to join the ranks – 'a proceeding that could be privately admired though not officially encouraged' and almost every eligible undergraduate joined the Officers' Training Corps. A squad of dons drilled on the playing field, discovering that 'a certain maturity in study gives no immunity against the recruit's notorious inability to distinguish his right hand from his left'.

Early in Lent, commissions came through for men who had joined the OTC during Michaelmas, and numbers fell across the University. Oswald Elliott, joining the 10th Gordon Highlanders, wrote to Reddaway, 'I often think of you all at Cambridge and wonder how the old place carries on. My stay there seems quite a dream of the past, as this time last year it was one of the future. I hope we may all return some day, though I do not think it will be in less than twelve months.' A dwindling roll was serious, not only for the social and sporting life of the Hall; fees were its life-blood. The Censor was keen to reassure Fitzwilliam men that, whilst their absence would 'accentuate our sense of deprivation', it would strengthen 'our resolve that, come what may, the Hall that you have built up shall not decline'.

Reddaway believed it his duty to furnish men serving abroad with news of Cambridge and of one another; the *Fitzwilliam Hall Magazine*, sent to France, Belgium, Gallipoli, Mesopotamia, India, and Africa, was his vehicle. In January 1916, as a historian writing self-consciously for an unseen readership, he wished 'to dedicate to our remote successors some attempt, feeble it may be, but frank, to describe what we see and feel in one of the greatest hours in human history'.

It is clear from the correspondence that flowed in to Cambridge, often in pencil on flimsy paper, that servicemen treasured this link with their former lives. 'It was a great delight to receive the "Billy" mag last week and I read with great interest the doings of the old crowd ... In this life one thinks most tenderly of Blighty and all connected with it ... The Cambridge experience looms large. What would I give to boot the ball with Brookes and Co of 1907–12?' asked John Stephens. In Dar-es-Salaam, Wilfrid Copplestone received his copy whilst recuperating 'from a complaint brought on by the heat and general unhealthiness of German East Africa ... It is ripping, out in this benighted country, to hear how one's friends are going.'

Name	Address of Registration	Age
C.A. Neeve.	The Old Vicarage. Grantchester.	22
		Year of Birth
		1893

Occupation	College
Theological student.	Fitzwilliam Hall.

| If Married | — | General Remarks | Date Nov 25. 1915 |
| If Single | Single | Conscientious objector. | |

Not everyone succumbed to enthusiasm for the war

W. P. B. HOLLIS (Corp. R.E., Prisoner-of-War).   H. E. MARTIN (Lieut., 8th Res., Middlesex, T.).   C. G. JOSEPH (2nd Lieut. C.U.O.T.C.).
J. W. HURRELL (Lieut. 2nd Beds.).   (Rev.) E. G. SEMPLE.   J. LONGSTAFF (2nd Lieut. 12th Durham L.I.).
W. H. STOKES (Schoolmaster).   L. V. MILLER (Sergt. Instructor Signals).   C. A. HARGREAVES (2nd Lieut. 6th Manchester, T.).   ✝ W. B. HIRST (2nd Lieut. 4th Lincs.T.)

Frequently, however, the going was not good. It was through the *Magazine* that many learned of the Hall's first casualty, the hugely popular Wilfrid 'Jerry' Hirst, killed by a sniper in April 1915. Briefly stationed in Dranoutre, a few months later, Fred Scott was able to write that he had found 'Jerry Hirst's grave and had the privilege of paying respect to a great man by placing a bunch of flowers on his grave. It was the best I could do – I had not time nor opportunity to obtain a wreath.' The losses did not dampen Scott's enthusiasm: 'Big things are afoot. I would not be out of it for anything now. My only regret is that my brother cannot share our coming glory. He made the supreme sacrifice a fortnight ago near Ypres – and I wish for myself no better end.'

The place of Fitzwilliam in serving men's hearts is demonstrated not only by their frequent letters to the Censor, but also by their visits during periods of leave. The dining hall and combination room were not so different from the officers' messes they left behind, and the humour and empathy there may have been easier to bear than the loving concern of parents and sisters. Alec Boucher, the first from Fitzwilliam to be awarded the Military Cross, spent a term in the Hostel as a convalescent. 'He brought home most vividly to all of us both the realities of the war and his own magnificent character,' Reddaway wrote in the December 1916 edition of the *Magazine* shortly after his death.

The experiences of Fitzwilliam men varied enormously. Some, such as Frank Cook, were classed 'medically unfit'. Not all the able-bodied approved of fighting: C.A. Neeve registered as a Conscientious Objector. Others were deprived of action, by being stationed at home or being taken prisoner. W.P.B. Hollis had the unusual distinction of having arrived on 12 August 1914 in France; he served as a dispatch rider for a week before being captured, and remained a prisoner throughout the war.

Not all served on the Western Front. William Haslam tired of waiting for his commission and joined the Sherwood Foresters as a private. He was shipped to Dublin in April 1916 to suppress the Easter Uprising, gleefully reporting to Reddaway: 'I am pleased to say I rather enjoyed the whole business in spite of the hardships of Active Service conditions, and the pavement bed with one blanket.' Haslam did not achieve his desire of serving in France until the end of 1917 – and did not survive the spring of 1918.

One of the most intriguing wartime journeys was that of George Scott, who had been working as a teacher and journalist in Petrograd in 1914. He found his way back to England via Finland, Sweden and Norway and was appointed Assistant Military Attaché in Tbilisi. Following the Russian Revolution, Scott and his colleagues endured a chaotic year before escaping from the advancing Germans in April 1918. 'I was successful in eluding the

THE ROLL OF HONOUR TRIPTYCH

Commemoration in the Chapel of the 44 members of the Hall who died in the Great War is by a memorial Triptych, which was placed above the altar in 1928. The natural-oak Triptych has vellum panels by Albert Cousins, from the Fitzwilliam Museum, who specialized in calligraphy and illumination; the outer panels list the names in burnished gold.

The Triptych was created independently of Reddaway's appeal for a memorial (p. 37); it was arranged by the Bursar, Walter Harvey, with Chapel funds. He considered that it 'will worthily emulate the finest work of the Medieval craftsmen' and he looked forward to a 'future time [when] we have to move to some new Fitzwilliam House of a splendour and dignity as yet by few of our members imagined, it can and will go with us to our new home'. It did: it now contributes to the beauty of the modern Chapel.

The Roll of Honour Triptych

Bolshevik spies for a period of no less than three months ... I was then captured, made to march from Vladikavkaz to Moscow, via the Astrakhan Steppe and Saratov, and finally ended up in Moscow convict gaol, where I languished in solitary confinement from January till May 1919. Subsequently, two days prior to the carrying out of my death sentence, I was exchanged for an important Bolshevik "Admiral" by the name of Raskolnikov, and arrived in England, June 1919. I spent two months in a mad house.'

Geoffrey Fyson (1892–1948), poet of the war and the inter-war years

Given the composition of the Fitzwilliam community, it is not surprising that many became army chaplains. Rev. John Stephens, serving with the 2nd London Regiment, notified Reddaway about several of them: Gamble at a Casualty Clearing Station, Crookall with an infantry brigade, McArthur at a YMCA post, R.E. Thomas acting as a quartermaster before becoming a chaplain. Stephens described the difficulties associated with conducting services near the front line: 'I am now an expert at the graceful duck, and cling to mother earth most lovingly. I have no dignity but flop down when I hear the well-known screech in my vicinity. However there is no absolute protection from such arguments and only last Sunday I was nearly caught.' Frederick Bywaters held services in a cinema pavilion, and boasted that he 'packed over 1,000 inside on Sunday morning'.

Religious life continued at the Hall despite the much-lamented loss of the Chaplain, who had departed for Burma. There was a debate as to whether Chapel should become compulsory; it remained voluntary, and Reddaway considered the turn-out to be excellent, the daily service averaging a quarter of all students and the mid-week communions more.

By this time numbers had fallen to a dangerous low. Reddaway published a list of matriculated residents to give absentees a flavour of the Hall's make-up in wartime: 'Cheshunt College 2, St. Edmund's House 2, Westminster College, Ridley Hall and Clergy Training School 0, West African Students 2, Egyptians 2, Indians 11, Cinghalese 2,

THE HIRST-PLAYER FUND

Wilfrid Hirst and Eric Player matriculated in 1911, both destined for Holy Orders. It was fitting that Hirst should be the first from the Hall to die; his strength of body and mind had made him a natural leader in every kind of game. When he was sent to France, he rejoiced: it was 'supremely gratifying; of all the most horrible things I can think of, a trip to Egypt, or India, with one's Regiment at such a time would be the worst. Fitzwilliam Hall for the firing line, just as it should be.'

The family and friends of Captain Eric Player (also killed by a sniper) had been among the first to respond to the Censor's call for a memorial bursary, and by 1921 it had achieved the impressive sum of over £300, £65 donated by the Reddaways. The bursary was later amalgamated with that of Hirst, and Hirst-Player Studentships continue to provide financial support to students of the College reading Theology.

Altar cruets in memory of Hirst and of Player

Japanese 1, Russians 1, OTC Cadets 1; of other British Undergraduates – engaged on work of national importance 2, Ministers of Religion 3, Anglican Ordinands 2, medically rejected 6, awaiting call to the colours 2, South African 1, Anglo-Indian 1.' A year later, in December 1917, he admitted that 'we have now reached the end of our financial tether, and the only wonder is that this has not happened long before. Last year showed a deficit on the year's run of some £250, which, in spite of a windfall in the shape of returned income tax, practically extinguished our Reserve Fund. This year we must expect the receipts from our slenderer numbers to fall still further short of the irreducible expenses.' The playing field at Oxford Road not only brought an income from letting for sheep-grazing, but proved valuable for growing potatoes – an obsession of the remaining students.

The letters from across the globe still provide a direct link, as they did for Reddaway, with the experiences and thoughts of this cohort of Fitzwilliam men. Generally their tone is cheery. Fred Scott's frequent reports from the Western Front provide a fascinating glimpse of life in 'Mudland' with the Leicesters: 'We made a lovely raid on 'em one night, and next morning they were quite cross about it until our guns showed them it was wiser to control their tempers.' Occasionally even his light tone is leavened with harsher description: 'On the knoll a labyrinth. And over everywhere, in the dominated radius, not a blade of grass. Of trees, a few here and there, bereft of branches, and with splintered trunks. Rubble heaps mark the places where cottages once stood and, round about, the limp-

looking skeletons of former busy pit-heads peer shakily over black and ugly heaps of mine-spoil. Crater-gashed and pock-marked, the precious crest is still German, while on the forward slope we maintain a precarious footing. We took over the sector, and the frost departed. With it went what bit of cover from view our mudlanes gave us, with the result that enemy eyes aligned along telescopic sights watched our every movement.' Wounded on three separate occasions, Scott was awarded the Military Cross. He was later captured at Reims and shot dead.

Injury and sickness were occupational hazards for serving men, who tended to downplay the seriousness of their wounds. Kenneth Keay wrote, 'You probably read of the hot time the Scottish Division had at Longueval. I got through that all right but was hit on the way down after we had been relieved probably by a stray bullet, which entered almost at the middle of my back and lodged in my side. It proved however after the bullet had been taken out to be only a flesh wound and is practically healed up already.'

Like his correspondents, Reddaway tended to disseminate news – other than death notices – in a breezy manner. The following is typical: 'Captain Adam was twice wounded near Loos in a great but rather hopeless charge. The first bullet, in the arm, knocked him down without inflicting great pain, producing, in fact, a feeling of amusement. He continued to charge but fell again, shot through the thigh. He was saved by the precaution of having taken with him the inner tube of a motorbicycle tire, which apparently forms the perfect tourniquet, and he is now well on the way to complete recovery.'

It is not difficult to imagine Reddaway's anguish when he was informed of a Fitzwilliam death. The July 1916 *Magazine* editorial contains the news that, despite having been shot in the chest, Horace Martin was considered out of danger. Two pages later there appears the following postscript: 'And having written thus far with joy and thankfulness, I am handed a telegram and the whole sky is changed. "Captain Martin died in the presence of his parents, Treport, nineteenth." Horace Martin, whom for four years everyone knew and everyone esteemed... To him it is indeed hard to say farewell.'

The College archives contain many examples of the Censor's correspondence with bereaved families who were clearly touched by his sincere condolences and often felt the need to explain the circumstances of their loved one's death. In October 1916 Reddaway received a letter from Oswald Elliott's younger brother, Duncan, then a schoolboy: 'I thought you would just like to know how he died like a soldier and a gentleman in defence of his king and country's rights.'

A letter from the Cambridge-based mother of Philip Rolfe was addressed to Mrs Reddaway, thanking her for the friendship that she and her husband had shown Philip during his time at Fitzwilliam. The Reddaways had two small sons of their own, well known to undergraduates. She closed her letter, 'It is sad indeed to think of all the young lives sacrificed, of so many who would have served their Country by living well. May the young manhood of your dear boys reap the good harvesting of this bitter sowing.'

Post-war recovery

The end of the war was greeted with a collective sigh of relief. Reddaway painted the scene in the *Magazine* for December 1918: 'It was at a quarter to twelve on Monday that the bells rang out. I closed my lecture on the instant, and five minutes later found that the windows of a local publication regarded as pacifist had been broken on King's Parade. We returned to the Hall, found that the residents had given up work for the day and soon our flag was flying once again... I should say that it took us several days to realise that we had really won the war, and perhaps as long again to begin to grumble at the slowness of the demobilisation.'

Numbers grew quickly. Having fallen to around 40 in 1918, there were almost a hundred students by the following March, with many new and returning men coming up in Michaelmas 1919. Behind this lay the University's decision to make generous concessions to ex-servicemen, allowing them to count war-service as residence up to a maximum of four terms. This applied equally to new entrants and to those who had matriculated and gone away on war service. There was also an influx of American ex-servicemen keen to study at a British university for a short period before returning home; 41 were registered as members of the Hall in March 1919.

A new chapter was about to begin, and all were aware that times had changed. 'Naturally everyone asks how the new Cambridge differs from the old. Greater courtesy, says one, with eagerness to get as far from the war as possible and live to the full the traditional University life.' H.M. Burton wrote: 'immediately after the war more than half the undergraduates were mature; they had matured in the harsh and testing atmosphere of war. They did not, as a class, lack the brilliance of the younger men, but there were depths below the superficial sparkle, while their earnestness, although no less sincere, was at least tinged with disillusionment.'

Senior members in 1934. Seated, from L: Reddaway, Thatcher, F.I.G. Rawlins, Gaskoin; standing: R.S. Ball, F. Thatcher, G.W. Butterfield, W. Harvey

W.S. THATCHER

W.S. Thatcher, Censor 1924–54, by Edward Halliday

Generations of Fitzwilliam men have expressed their lifelong debt to W.S. Thatcher, not least because it seemed to them that it was through his personal intercession that they had the opportunity to come to Cambridge. An implausible majority recall their interviews on Cambridge Railway Station, when Thatcher's intuition about their potential was transformed into the offer of a place.

And the personal contact continued. When New Court was dedicated to the memory of W.S. Thatcher (p. 93), Sir Daniel Pettit recalled his 'dedication and intellectual stature triumphed over much adversity'. Leslie Wayper and Norman Pounds wrote 'It was, of course, Thatcher's relationship with students that endeared him to us all. ... We all came to know him well; all were entertained for tea once or twice in the year, and in Hall he sat amongst us and chatted wisely and wittily on any matter that came up. He attended club dinners, which he did his utmost to encourage, and was, whenever other matters permitted, present on touchline and towpath.'

William Sutherland Thatcher came up to Fitzwilliam Hall in 1907 and retired as Censor of Fitzwilliam House in 1954 – a half-century which saw much of the development of Fitzwilliam, and great transformation of the University. In his many writings in the *Magazine* and the *Journal,* Thatcher demonstrates great nostalgia for the world of his youth and a reluctance to reconcile himself with the Cambridge of his later years, a period which now seems as remote as the Edwardian era did from the 1950s.

Thatcher was a characteristic product of the early-Reddaway era: one of Reddaway's *Old Guard,* helping to clear weeds from the Oxford Road ground; playing football on it, in a successful team in 1910–11; and helping out in the office. In 1911, he took his degree, and went out to India as Professor of Economics at the University of Allahabad. He joined the Indian Army Reserve of Officers in 1914 and was commissioned in the 129th Baluchis; later, he was to write their regimental history for the Great War. He served in Flanders and in East Africa; he was awarded the Military Cross for gallantry in leading an attack at Kibata in 1916, where he received a severe head wound which left him disfigured for life. Reddaway wrote: 'The bullet passed so precisely down the ear-hole that it was difficult to make out what had happened, and the wounded man had to be carried in a hammock for 70 miles down the coast before receiving any treatment. His Baluchis denied themselves water all day that he might receive a dose every ten minutes, and to this his preservation was doubtless due.'

When he was discharged from hospital in 1918, Thatcher returned to Cambridge to rebuild his life. He considered studying for the recently-introduced degree of PhD, but the Professor of Political Economy considered it unnecessary, expostulating 'For God's sake don't do that, it's only for foreigners'. Thatcher became Director in Economics for Non-Collegiate Students in May 1919.

The Times wrote of Thatcher's influence: that he 'gave the young Lee [Kuan Yew] an unbending Victorian sense of moral correctness and an extraordinary example of fortitude in leading an ordinary life despite the debilitating effects of ... [wounds] suffered in the first World War'.

The academic developments in Cambridge were not altogether to his liking. Thatcher had a traditional concept of liberal education, and considered that there was a dichotomy – which in retrospect does not seem inherent, and was not consistent with his own study of the applicable field of economics – between the development of expertise and the attainment of liberal values. This led him to defend the Ordinary Degree which, except as compensation for failure in a Tripos, had almost faded away by the time he retired. 'I still think a general Pass Degree would be a very good thing ... if it were taken seriously .... The present attitude is based upon snobbery and a misconception of the functions of a University. There ought to be room in a University for the non-academically-minded man ....'

A false dichotomy, but a romantic notion: 'For in a university there has to be time to stand and stare. Time to talk and ruminate. That's why the old habit of country walking was so good. One could ruminate.'

Left: Football team in 1910–11, Thatcher in middle row, second from right

Right: Thatcher's permit to ride a bicycle in academical dress; it shows him living at Red Cottage

11 October 1910

St John's College. Cambridge.

Mr W.S.Thatcher has permission to ride a bicycle in academical dress after dark & on Sundays so long as he is resident at Red Cottage, Oxford Road

H.F. Stewart
Senior Proctor

The recovery was short-lived. Fitzwilliam Hall benefited from some economies of scale when numbers in residence rose rapidly to a peak of 314 in Michaelmas 1920. But they fell back by a third in the subsequent two years. Inflation in the early 1920s compounded the problem; thus the Hall made a peak profit of £919 in the year 1919–20 but declined to a loss of £601 in 1921–22, leaving a capital balance of only £632.

Collegiality and non-collegiality: a corporate Fitzwilliam?

Fitzwilliam was created by rebellion against the University policy of 1869. So, to what extent was the conversion of the non-collegiate body to a quasi-collegiate body appropriate? For many years this would be ambiguous, and the advantages became overwhelming only when generous undergraduate grants followed the Butler Education Act of 1944. The issue has echoes even now, for instance with the refusal of UK Research Councils to pay college fees for their research students. In retrospect, it is natural to treat the sequence from the start of the Non-Collegiate Students Board to the present as progress – monotonic, unmitigated and inevitable. But was it? And how severely were the original expectations for non-collegiate students compromised?

Migration to colleges was deplored because it weakened the non-collegiate body; however, it was natural since college Scholarships provided both support and recognition for students. The non-collegiate route enabled people with moderate finances to enter Cambridge; then they took steps to advance further – opening opportunities for the able and fortunate. W.E. Gladstone was in no doubt that they formed 'a standing reserve established in favour of the Colleges' and benefited 'the country at large by drawing in more and more largely fresh infusions of vigorous blood'. Early non-collegiate students did not ostracize their migrant peers; migrants attended dinners, and at a meeting of the Amalgamation Club in 1890 the outgoing Secretary was congratulated on his Scholarship to St Catharine's (whether St Catharine's was satisfied is not obvious, as the ultimate class for this Scholar was a Third in the Special Examination in Theology!).

The diverse population of students who interacted with the University through Fitzwilliam included the members of the Attached-House Theological Colleges, whose lives centred on their own institutions. Attached Houses utilized in turn the Board, the House and the College to give their members access to the University by matriculation and to receive degrees. There were tensions, perhaps because the existence of Fitzwilliam impeded their own ambitions. Their students fitted more readily the original non-collegiate concept rather than a quasi-collegiate model, as the Tutor of Cheshunt College indicated at a Discussion in the Senate House in 1923 when he objected to the Board's recommendation to increase the total fee over three years from 18 to 24 guineas: this was an undue imposition on students at the Attached Houses, 'institutions which, if the Senate wished it, would be capable of ruling themselves under the direct control of the Senate'.

The first concerns about the consequences of quasi-collegiality appeared early. In 1876, long before there was any dining provision at Trumpington Street, Somerset reported that 15 or 16 of the younger students were dining together daily; 'With this experiment I have not interfered; I have only watched it, as I had the opportunity, so as to suggest precautions against increasing expenses'. A key motive for non-collegiality was avoidance of the competitive expenditure that arises naturally within any social grouping – it was recognized as a particular problem in colleges, but could arise also amongst non-collegiate students.

Much of the drive to promote corporate identity was associated with the Amalgamated Clubs, and with Censors; often, their concepts coincided. Reddaway wrote in the *Fitzwilliam Hall Magazine* in 1910: 'Of the Clubs, which contribute so much to our prestige and to our daily enjoyment, it may suffice to say that they now constitute Fitzwilliam Hall in its widest sense'. His approach, regarding club captains as the natural leaders for the institution, persisted for at least a further half-century; it arose in an interview in *Varsity* given by the Assistant Bursar in 1958. When Ray Kelly was asked about the development plans for Fitzwilliam, he was reported as hoping for 40 or 50 sets of rooms, and indicated that they would be allotted to the clubs' officers – still positioning the clubs centrally within the College.

When Thatcher became Censor, as befitted a member of the 'Old Guard' he inherited Reddaway's objectives and pursued them in a very literal manner. For him, the composition of the student body was a major concern: he was reluctant to see the corporately-motivated diluted by others who might have different priorities.

So, in the Censor's Report for 1933–34, at a time when numbers were declining: 'Students in residence may be divided into: (1) the normal three-year undergraduates attached directly to Fitzwilliam House, (2) undergraduates attached through membership of the attached Houses, (3) miscellaneous students including research students, one-year students, students professionally employed during the daytime, (4) Oriental students. The serious fall has taken place in (1), who form the solid core round which the others group themselves. These men supply the real drive in the active life of Fitzwilliam House. The rest are largely passive.'

This wish for a corporate identity had an invidious side – a wish to exclude those considered insufficiently collegiate. Throughout the inter-war years, advanced students were viewed with suspicion, as were overseas students (very often, the categories overlapped). Thus Thatcher sought to limit Oriental students – at that time primarily Indian – to 10% of the population of the House, and was very concerned about his obligation to take all the research students admitted by Departments who did not receive places at colleges.

To put his concerns into context, in 1925 the composition of the non-collegiate student body was:

Fitzwilliam Hall students from:	
UK	70
Dominions, Continental Europe, USA	22
India	21
Other Asia	10
Africa	2
Total of direct Fitzwilliam Hall students	125
Students indirectly via Theological Colleges	35
TOTAL	160

Thatcher was unsympathetic to the needs of the University. In 1927 he wrote to the Secretary of the Board of Research Studies; explicitly by its arguments and implicitly by its language, the letter showed his attitudes and assumptions. He claimed that a high proportion of Oriental students was undesirable because: '(1) It is not good for the Oriental students themselves as they herd together and are thus deprived of the benefit they ought to obtain from mixing with English students; (2) It reacts adversely upon Fitzwilliam House, as, owing to the public prejudice both in the University and outside, public opinion condemns any institution with too many Orientals; (3) It results in the lowering of the vitality of the institution taking too many such students.'

Reddaway missed no opportunity to project the corporate characteristics of the Hall: information from 1908

INFORMATION RELATING TO NON-COLLEGIATE STUDENTS

IN THE

UNIVERSITY OF CAMBRIDGE.

NON-COLLEGIATE Students are members of the University without being members of any College or Hostel. They are governed by the Chancellor and other Officers of the University, and by a Board of nine members appointed by the Senate. They are supervised by a Censor. They keep Terms by residing in Cambridge in lodgings duly licensed, or with their parents, or, in special cases sanctioned by the University authorities, under the care of other persons, or in their own or in hired houses. They are matriculated, examined, and admitted to Degrees in the same manner and possess the same status and privileges as Collegiate Students. Thus they may use the University Library, Museums and Laboratories, attend the Professors' and all Intercollegiate Lectures, and compete for Scholarships and Prizes open to the whole University, under the same conditions as other Students.

Fitzwilliam Hall.   The centre of their corporate life is Fitzwilliam Hall, a house built in 1727 and situate opposite the Fitzwilliam Museum in Trumpington Street. It contains Reading and Writing Rooms, a Library, a Dining Room, Censor's and Lecturers' Rooms, Clerk's Office, etc. At present the Director of Students in Economics, L. ALSTON, M.A., the Censor's Secretary, J. E. STALEY, B.A., and the Clerk to the Board, F. W. SALMON, reside in the building.

Above: 'The Cosmopolitans' in 1900

He reiterated his policy of raising 'the status of Fitzwilliam House both in the University and in the outside world'; it should not serve as 'a Cave of Adullam for those deemed undesirable by the colleges'. He claimed that colleges were refusing to accept Oriental students 'on the grounds that they are turning away English students whereas we are not doing so, I would reply that the paucity of English applicants to Fitzwilliam House is due largely to the high percentage of Orientals who by their presence prejudice us in the eyes of would-be applicants'.

This attitude was as contrary to progress as had been the nineteenth-century complacency which had required so much effort to reform – reforms which included starting the non-collegiate system.

Building up the research students was vital for the transformation of the University from its nineteenth-century condition, in which a small minority of highly significant scholars formed the intellectual core of an organization whose junior members predominantly were either the affluent seeking a congenial finishing school or candidates for the Anglican priesthood, to the modern world-leading research institution whose Senior Members, by dint of extreme hard work, are still able to make time to undertake the education of undergraduates of the highest intellectual quality, drawn from the entire world.

Right: Thatcher implied that only British students contributed to the corporate–social core of the House, but students from the Empire are well represented in sports teams: tennis in 1931

Starting the Fitzwilliam Society

Looking back at the end of the 1920s, Thatcher expressed surprise that the Fitzwilliam Society was not founded earlier. 'Perhaps it might have been but for the War, which retarded most social developments by at least ten years. Certainly everything was ready for such a Society in 1914.'

It was not until June 1924 that the possibility of an alumni society was mooted, at a meeting of the Amalgamated Clubs. The proponent, J.R.W. Alexander, a final-year undergraduate, received unanimous support and instructions to canvass alumni and set up a meeting in London. By November, letters were sent to 1,350 alumni, inviting them to the Holborn Restaurant, Kingsway; 188 replies were received, all but 11 supportive, and about 35 Fitzwilliam men assembled on 9 December 1924.

The meeting endorsed four objectives for the Society:

(a) To promote closer relationship among old Fitzwilliam Hall men and between them and the Hall;

(c) To ensure the permanence and success of the Society's Dinner held annually at the Holborn Restaurant ... on the day of the Inter-University Rugby Union Football Match;

(d) To collect material for a Fitzwilliam Hall register;

(e) To further the interests of Fitzwilliam Hall.

Objective (b) was rejected, on grounds of cost: to circulate an annual report and a *Fitzwilliam Hall Magazine* free to every member of the Society.

Reddaway was elected President, with Thatcher and Gaskoin as Vice-Presidents; Alexander became Honorary Secretary and Treasurer. So, with the life subscription set at one guinea, it was time to discuss other issues before moving to dinner.

The main topic was implicit in the obsolescent terminology of the objectives: to deplore the recommendations of the 1924 Syndicate, and to mourn the loss of the Fitzwilliam Hall title. They had the notion that, with sufficient support from Fitzwilliam men, the old name would not have been lost and the Syndicate would not have emphasized the non-collegiate function – so the Society was created as a pressure group. Members ignored the recognition by the Syndicate of the corporate existence of Fitzwilliam, and that its title – albeit as Fitzwilliam House – would appear in the Statutes and Ordinances of the University.

London Dinner at the Criterion restaurant, in 1936

But the Society had troubles of its own, with membership and income. By September 1924 fewer than one in five of the 242 indications of support had resulted in a subscription, and three years would pass before the 100th payment was received.

The basic pattern of committee meetings, London Dinners, journals, and attempts to increase membership ran on, augmented from 1928 by Cambridge Reunions. Alexander succumbed to pressure of work in 1927 and gave up the Secretaryship – although he remained in contact throughout his life. The Society commemorated his name in book awards for Law students reading for the LLM.

In succession to Alexander, the Society elected G. Milner Walton, who had been General Secretary of the Amalgamated Clubs when Alexander made his proposal. Milner Walton was one of the people who gave prodigious service to Fitzwilliam over very many years; he was Secretary and Treasurer from 1927 to 1966 (except for the year in which he was President), and was Editor of the *Journal* for that entire period. He produced its first freestanding issue; this was Volume 1 No. 2; the first issue was a supplement to the June 1926 *Fitzwilliam House Magazine* (produced termly since 1908). He is commemorated by the Fitzwilliam Society Milner Walton Awards.

Much of the attention of the Society was directed towards survival, as amongst the older cohorts those few who would take up membership had largely done so, and new graduates were less than enthusiastic. By 1929 there were only 156 members. The number of paid-up members doubled in a year once final-year students could be charged on their Easter-term accounts. From 1955, undergraduates were billed termly over three years, and nearly all took up life membership.

The core members of the Society aspired to help Fitzwilliam in its development, despite the small membership and weak financial position. In 1935 the Society took the long-awaited replacement of *Non-Coll.* by *Fitzw.* in class lists as a cue for launching a building fund for the House. The proposal was referred to the Council of the Senate by the Non-Collegiate Students Board, noting that there was neither building scheme nor cost estimate.

The Council was even more cautious: it was not until late 1936 that the appeal was approved, but with the condition that *Building* was not to appear in the title of the fund. Emasculated and delayed, the appeal failed to exploit the raised emotions of 1935, and by the start of the war had collected only £290; it closed in 1956, having generated about £1,500.

Thus in the pre-war era the Society made little practical progress beyond bringing a relatively small membership together, but it was to provide the nucleus of the body that took part in the campaign for full collegiate status in the 1950s.

THE FIRST CAMBRIDGE REUNION AND THE PAVILION

benefited the field from his undergraduate days to the present hour'. Harvey had trained as an architect before coming up in 1907 and, whilst an undergraduate, had supervised the levelling of the field. He designed the pavilion; its cost, about £830, was met by a combination of donations, an increase in the Amalgamated Club fees, and half the rent from Red Cottage.

London Dinners in December were not convenient for everyone, particularly not for schoolmasters, so a reunion was arranged in Cambridge in July 1928. Its form has been followed each year for three-quarters of a century, with a General Meeting, sports matches, and a reception and dinner.

At Oxford Road, members could see 'the New Pavilion, where the arms presented by the Bursar, the Rev. W. Harvey, give the finishing touch to the long and self-sacrificing labours, manual and mental, by which he has

Above: The New Pavilion: sketch by Walter Harvey

Right: Pavilion Fund donations from the *Magazine* of June 1928 – students made donations, as did Reddaway and the Censor

II

FITZWILLIAM HOUSE TO FITZWILLIAM COLLEGE

5

ANOTHER WAR, ANOTHER RECOVERY

The Second World War

The Second World War had a severe and immediate effect on Fitzwilliam – much greater than that of the First. Because Cambridge was considered safer than London, it provided a home for many evacuated institutions; however, the first displacement was when Addenbrooke's Hospital took the students' common room and reading room for offices. The students used the Parlour and the senior members withdrew to the Censor's office – one of the very few rooms retained by Fitzwilliam throughout the war.

Subsequently the House was taken over almost completely by Bedford College for Women, evacuated from Regent's Park; this first exposure to the opposite sex had severe consequences, as Thatcher wrote: 'Women can be seen – and heard – in the dining hall. ... We have stood up to it as to other war strains and shocks; the heavens have not fallen, though the ceiling paper is somewhat loosened'. Bedford College did not return to London until the summer of 1944. Even then, normality was not restored, as other organizations such as the Polish Club and the British Council occupied Fitzwilliam rooms.

Life was austere: 'High Table kept its continuity in the form of coffee and spam sandwiches eaten by a few of the faithful in the Censor's room once a week. It was a horrible meal but eaten with grim determination that if *London could take it* so could we. They were particularly bad sandwiches and the coffee was always cold.'

The loss of space was accompanied by loss of senior members and assistant staff, so eventually only Thatcher and the Clerk, Barrett, were left. Student numbers fell, reaching a minimum of about 19 in 1944, of whom nine were research students. That autumn, there were initially only seven Freshmen: two from the United Kingdom, and three Poles, one German refugee, and one Czech.

But adversity bred resilience, and there was a humane and even an optimistic spirit when dining resumed in Michaelmas 1944. Thatcher recalled 'about sixteen dining, of whom two were natives of the British Isles – one an invalided soldier and the other a lamb, though rather a

In memory of those who gave their lives in the Second World War 1939–1945

G.C.BOND · A.B.BRYAN
J.L.COHEN · S.B.DEARING
D.DONAHUE · N.S.EMBIRICOS
I.P.L.FLEMING · C.R.FRENKIEL
F.W.M.GREAVES · R.C.HORTON
E.T.HUMPHREYS · D.G.IMAGE
E.V.KNOWLES · G.T.LOWRY
J.N.MAAS · G.F.MEASURES
H.T.MEASURES · C.W.OLIVER
J.E.OLIVER · M.H.PARRY
D.L.PETRIE · L.E.PILL
A.L.SADD · J.J.E.SCHMITZ
G.L.STEWART · P.C.WHEELER

May they rest in peace and may perpetual light shine upon them.

GIVEN IN MEMORY OF
THE REVD JOHN BELL
(1946)
WHO SERVED
AND RETURNED.

Previous page: Silver presented to Fitzwilliam to mark the attainment of collegiate status

The Warwick vase, which bears an inscription from Virgil, *The Aeneid*: *Quique sui memores aliquos fecere merendo*

large one, not yet old enough for the slaughter. The others came from the whole earth. It was a most pleasant and happy table and a shining example of what things might be if only we humans could forget our nationality, colour, and race, and remember only we are men.'

Away from the House, Fitzwilliam men were occupied across the spectrum of wartime activities. Some had good wars. John Stratton (1930), who already had reached the level of General Manager at John Lewis, became Director of Service Footwear and Leather Equipment, expanding into the top position of Controller of Leather and Footwear and eventually leading the Stratton Mission into occupied Germany to investigate their leather and ersatz-leather industry; he received his CBE in 1948. Dick Haywood (1936), later the first Engineering Fellow of Fitzwilliam, was chief steam-turbine test engineer for the English Electric Company, in charge of experimental work at power stations. Both Stratton and Haywood were to be heavily involved in the post-war campaign over the future for Fitzwilliam House. On the electrical side, Dr Percy Dunsheath (1910) was very active in a research and advisory role: on sweeping magnetic mines, and for PLUTO (the Pipe Line Under The Ocean that supplied

petrol to France in 1944). He was President of the Institution of Electrical Engineers for 1945.

Most got through the war with the mixture of boredom, frustration, deprivation and fear that – rather than excitement and bravery – largely occupies men in wartime. But others did not survive. Their names are engraved on silver and carved on a cross in the Chapel. The recorded deaths occurred under a much greater variety of circumstances than in the First World War.

Of the 26 on the Roll of Honour, two civilians were killed in air-raids on London, whilst a Dutch civilian drowned while attempting to escape to England in a home-made boat. Only a minority were in the Army, including one who died in training. Active-service deaths in the Army ranged from Benghazi to Italy and to the Netherlands; six are known, including one Army Chaplain.

There was a strong representation of Fitzwilliam men in the air, including P.C. Wheeler who was the first to die, in December 1939. Four others died in the RAF, M.H. Parry in a raid on Peenemunde. Two died in the Fleet Air Arm, including G.F. Measures; tragically, his brother also died, with the Army in Abyssinia. Two Naval members were killed.

ALFRED SADD

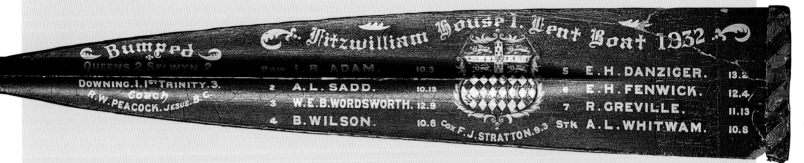

The Rev. Alfred Sadd was a missionary, who was executed by Japanese troops in the Gilbert Islands.

Sadd came from Maldon, on the Essex coast, where the family business was timber importing. From his earliest years he was at home on the sea, so that it was natural for him to work amongst the islands and atolls of the Pacific Ocean.

He was not a scholar, but extra tuition at The Leys School enabled him to enter the University, and in 1928 he started to train for the Congregationalist ministry. He went to Cheshunt College, becoming an Attached-House student of Fitzwilliam House. A simple and fervent personality, he threw himself into life – from preaching, to hazardous cycling, to rowing. After his BA, in 1931, he remained at Cheshunt and continued to row for Fitzwilliam, twice in boats that got their oars.

Sadd joined the London Missionary Society in 1933. His reputation preceded him to the Gilbert Islands: 'his writing is illegible, his spelling original, and his punctuation erratic, but he is of the salt of the earth'. He became ever more committed to the islands and in 1942, with Japanese forces approaching and missionaries with families evacuated, remained alone in Beru. When Japanese forces landed in April, he did not make concessions. Twice they tried to humiliate him, laying a Union Flag in his path; he avoided walking on it and the second time picked it up and folded it respectfully. Obviously he was going to be difficult, and he was sent to the Tarawa atoll some 450 km away, where he and other Europeans were put to forced labour.

Six months later, an Australian warship sank several Japanese ships off Tarawa. In response, the Japanese ordered all 22 prisoners (mostly New Zealanders) to be executed. Sadd attempted to comfort them and – to set an example – took the first place to be beheaded.

Participants in the 1932 Lents, with very different fates: Alfred Sadd at 2, and John Stratton as Cox

Altar cross and candlesticks in memory of Alfred Sadd

Given the variety of origins of Fitzwilliam men, it is not surprising that the dead included a Polish Jew and a Greek – and on both sides of the conflict: J.J.E. Schmitz was killed in action at Stalingrad. Members who survived the war served in the Polish, the Swiss, and the Turkish armies.

In the Eastern theatres, A.L. Sadd was executed by Japanese forces and E.T. Humphreys, captured in Burma, died whilst a prisoner of war. Two others, however, survived: M.F. Smith, captured when Singapore fell; and

S.E. Davies, a missionary captured by the Japanese in Northern China. But G.T. Lowry, in the Colonial Service and a member of the Hong Kong Volunteer Defence Force, was killed when Hong Kong was over-run in 1941.

After the war, the Amalgamated Clubs took the lead in the commemoration of the dead, and an appeal for a war-memorial fund was launched in 1947. The objects of the appeal included commemorative silver: a replica of the Warwick Vase bears the names of the 26 members of the

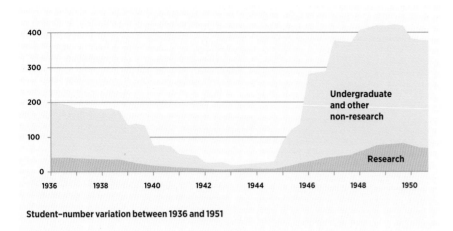

Student–number variation between 1936 and 1951

House who lost their lives. For the permanent Chapel, matching the 1914–18 Triptych (p. 43), a memorial was carved, the bequest of Rev. John Bell, a veteran who came up in 1946.

Immediate post-war life

Student numbers started to increase even before the war had ended. By Christmas 1945 there were 86 students, and 51 more joined during the academic year. As 27 years previously, there was a sudden surge as men demobilized from the services sought places in Cambridge, and there were 1,200 applicants in the period to summer 1946. Students whose studies had been interrupted returned; some had been at other colleges, some at Fitzwilliam. The Non-Collegiate Students Board had agreed in 1944 to take up to 300 students in the immediate post-war period, provided that an additional officer was appointed to support the Bursar and the Junior Tutor. Harvey and Gaskoin had retired, and two key posts were taken by Fitzwilliam men: Norman Pounds became Junior Tutor in Michaelmas 1944 and W.W. Williams, recently out of the Army, became Bursar and Assistant Censor in 1946. In the office, Miss Barrett returned as Censor's Secretary.

Even before numbers had built up there were enormous difficulties in obtaining supplies and staff, and with labour relations: twice the kitchen staff left with an hour's notice, and only the Housekeeper's determination made it possible for dinners to be served. As always, self-help came into play – with a shortage of waiters, the students took turns to wait on each other.

Food presented very severe problems for the House and for its members, as rationing continued; with the dire economic situation, the position became worse. Potatoes and bread were rationed, as they never had been during the war, and Thatcher noted the difficulty of feeding ex-warriors on 1d worth of meat per man. Alan Shakespeare (1945) remembered 'strict food rationing, which made dinner in Hall quite interesting: my favourite meal was jugged hare (not rationed!). Whale meat was on the menu two or three times a week. Horrid, even when disguised in a curry.'

The return to normality was slow, but Geoffrey Cole (1946) recalled that the House 'started to make available a satisfying lunch ... otherwise, at lunchtime you had to find a lunch in town somewhere, as landladies were not noted for their generosity with a mid-day meal'. In all the recollections of the period, one source of sustenance recurs: 'Thankfully, all over the country for a few years, Wartime Government had developed British Restaurants to provide a simple nourishing meal – in 1946, for one shilling. Meat, potatoes, a vegetable and often spotted-dick sponge and custard or rice, and you could have a cup of tea for an extra 3d!'

The British Restaurant in Jesus Lane occupied the Pitt Club, a development that had been commemorated by Sir Arthur Quiller-Couch, Professor of English Literature and Fellow of Jesus College:

> Though our Club has had notice to quit,
> Yet as Britons we still claim admittance;
> So our last one-and-eightpence we'll split,
> And we'll feast at the Pitt for a pittance.

Not feasting, not even a balanced diet. Clyde Cartwright (1946) received advice: veterans reading medicine 'seemed to be generous, and usually helpful, with their comments. For example, schoolboys (including myself) tended to suffer from boils, especially on the neck, and received the advice that these were due to Vitamin C deficiency. I could not remember when my family last had fruit. It became an aim, therefore, to contrive access to non-private fruit in the countryside, particularly blackberries.'

The winter of 1946–47 was very severe and extended far into the spring, compounding the consequences of fuel shortages and rationing. In Cole's experience: 'January arrived and with it Eastern Britain suffered snow and the tightening grip of prolonged frost. Coal was scarce; transport of coal to the gasworks and the power stations was at full stretch. Students in lecture theatre wore their overcoats, ex-sailors their duffle coats.'

Fitzwilliam House in 1950

They met the challenge of these adverse conditions. 'For sport and exercise, I was determined to sample rowing with practices two or three times a week, or when the river Cam didn't freeze. As the Lent races neared, to toughen us up, our three eights would row down the Cam and through the lock into the Fens and on to Ely – 15 miles, returning several days later to row back. Sweets were rationed to three-quarters of a pound per ration book. I used to buy Mars Bars with mine to boost me up in those gruelling trips.'

Who were the undergraduates who were subject to these Spartan conditions? The Ministry of Labour and National Service required 90% of the places to be reserved for former servicemen, so that only 10% were available for those coming up directly from school. This emphasized the differences between two very distinct categories of student. Cartwright, a Yorkshire grammar school boy with a State Scholarship for 1946, was unable to take up his place at Wadham because their schoolboy quota was already allocated. Eventually he found one at Fitzwilliam, and recalled: 'one was quite likely to share a [Supervisor] with a warrior. The age of the latter might help, or it might not. I remember the experience of finding out what one's colleague had been doing – for instance: aged 26, a Wing Commander in the RAF, flying Pathfinder raids over Germany. He would never broach the subject, yet one wondered what he thought of 18 year olds whose main interests might be girls, and/or football, or eventual travel to France or Italy. ... The warriors tended to be more focused, more serious, of course.'

Lee Kuan Yew (1947) recalled: 'I had studied with that unusual generation of returned warriors in their 20s, some even in their 30s, married and with children. They were serious men who had seen death and destruction. Some had been through hell. One student in Fitzwilliam, who had been badly burnt when his plane crashed, was painful to look at despite repeated plastic surgery. But he overcame his disabilities. He knew his disfigured face frightened and upset people meeting him for the first few times, so he set out to act normally, to be reassuring and without self-pity. Unbowed, he made the best of his life.'

Thatcher wrote in the *Fitzwilliam Journal* about the organizational problems. Teaching loads doubled, supervision group sizes increased, and colleges were rationed for student numbers in laboratory-based subjects. The admissions process was complicated by unpredictable demobilization arrangements. But his final words in the *Journal* piece were highly positive: 'in spite of everything it is an exhilarating sight to see the place alive again. Better to die of overwork than fade out with anaemia.'

Restoring Fitzwilliam

Post-war reconstruction was not just a matter of practical provision for a large and fluctuating student population. Fitzwilliam, with its members scattered across Cambridge, needed to be restored as a coherent institution: that task engaged Thatcher, W.W. Williams, Norman Pounds and, later, Norman Walters.

Pounds took the leading role with the societies: he was the first post-war President of the Historical Society, which in 1946–47 made a good start with distinguished speakers from across the University. He was President also of the similarly-ambitious Music Society, which provided Hindemith and Stravinsky as well as the staples of chamber and vocal music (p. 141). Much use was made of gramophone recitals – essential in a world in which broadcast music was typified by *Music While You Work* on the BBC *Light Programme*. The Amateur Dramatic Society was enterprising with its first production in Lent 1949: Ibsen's *The Master Builder*. By 1953 the pre-war pattern of comedies was back, with Hart and Kaufman's *You Can't Take It With You* and, the following year, James Thurber's *The Male Animal*.

Senior members in 1950. Top left: Wayper; front row: Williams, Thatcher, Pounds

PROFESSOR NORMAN POUNDS

Norman Pounds, a highly prolific geographical writer and an outstanding lecturer, came up in 1931. His was an archetypal Fitzwilliam background; a scholarship boy at his grammar school who came to Fitzwilliam because he could not afford a college, he was supported on a national scheme that obliged him to be a schoolmaster after graduation. Reading History, he was disappointed by the prevailing academic standards, and was inspired to change to Geography by the great historical geographer H.C. Darby, then a young Fellow of King's.

Supported strongly by Thatcher, who brought him back to Cambridge in 1944 as Tutor and Director of Studies in Geography, in turn he supported Thatcher in his increasing antagonism with Williams (who had been a colonial surveyor, and for whom Pounds had little respect). Pounds was disappointed at not being integrated into the Department of Geography and went to the University of Wisconsin-Madison, then in 1950 to the University of Indiana as Professor of Geography. On retirement, he returned to England and lived near the College.

Norman was a workaholic who wrote more than 30 books. Peter Searby, in his Memorial Address, quotes him as exclaiming at a health crisis in 2000 'I can't die yet: I've got another book to write'; he wrote three more before his death in 2006 at the age of 94 – only two years after decreasing mobility ended his lecturing to large and appreciative audiences at the University of the Third Age.

He was addicted to rugby union, and in 1946–47 not only refereed all the Fitzwilliam home matches but even turned out to play – he played into his 50s, and paid the penalty in knee problems later in life.

Pounds was generous to the College. In 1989, he established a fund in memory of his wife for the support of music in College; he donated *The First Undergraduate* statue in 1995; and made a very substantial bequest at his death. He is commemorated by the *Norman Pounds Special Collections Room* in the Library.

Norman Pounds in 2002, by Benedict Rubbra

In addition to local successes, Fitzwilliam men were making an impact on wider University life. In 1950, Norman St John Stevas was President of the Cambridge Union, and there were three Blues and two Half-Blues, as well as many uncapped but regular players.

When Pounds left Cambridge, his place as Tutor was taken by Norman Walters. Walters, a Jesuan, was Director of Studies in English. As Grave wrote: 'to Mr Walters the College was primarily a body of undergraduates. He brought them here by his management of College admissions; he looked after many of them during their ... years of residence ...; he presented them for their degrees and, as Praelector, he also welcomed them back when they proceeded MA.' He was deeply committed to Fitzwilliam in every way so 'as treasurer of the Amalgamated Clubs for some years he set himself to do everything possible to help the men in their different clubs and societies'.

Christopher Bradnock (1961) wrote: 'Norman was known to his friends as "Fatty Walters" – he was a very big man! He was also a wonderfully supportive and delightful person who worked tirelessly for the College and its members. He brought to the College a wonderful body of carefully-selected undergraduates who were proud to be a part of Fitzwilliam and contributed in so many ways to College and University life.' Roger Wilkins (1967) recalled that this was the period when Fitzwilliam excelled in many sporting fields; Walters 'had clearly determined that sporting success was a way of raising the status and recognition of what was still a very new College. It was a great success. I was part of the rugby union team that won Cuppers that season. I went on to row for the College and to box for the University, gaining my Blue in 1970.' The College was well known in the late 1960s for achievements in team sports, and strongly represented in individual sports.

A.G. Hunt (Fellow, 1963–83, subsequently Life Fellow) recalled Walters' remarkable memory, retentive of faces and names and of factual details; he could repeat a complicated set of admission statistics after apparently a single glance; 'he excelled in recounting exactly a particular player's contribution to one of the many games he made time to attend as supporter of a College team, and he was superb in relating the *ipsissima verba* of a conversation with more than a hint of the speaker's tone and gestures.' With his essential kindliness, he was tolerant of almost all faults except pomposity and humbug.

LANDLADIES IN THE POST-WAR ERA

Finding accommodation for the post-war glut of students became the primary task for Norman Pounds. This required sharp practice. Many landladies who had taken students before the war were accommodating exiled London University students at its end, and Pounds by dubious means got their addresses and charmed them into taking Fitzwilliam students, rather than reverting to their previous colleges. Only once was he accused of poaching! When his lists ran out, he cold-called in likely parts of the town; he visited more than 4,000 houses and secured 200 sets of rooms.

The situation was complicated by the gate-hour regulations: all students had to be locked in by 10 pm, unless they had written permission from their Tutors. All lodgings had to be licensed by the Lodging-House Syndicate, and Pounds recalled an occasion when the Secretary to the Syndicate refused to license a house because it had only an outside toilet – inaccessible overnight to the student. There were no other rooms at the time; the infuriated Pounds threatened the Secretary with writing to *The Times* to expose the denial of a warrior's opportunity to take up his place – and the Secretary backed down.

Pounds had to go into the villages to find lodgings, and this could cause problems. Karol Krotki (1945) wrote to the Bursar 'As my intended lodgings are more than 3 miles away from the Mill Lane Lecture Rooms and the Marshall Library, assuming only two rides to Cambridge per day, i.e. 13–14 miles of cycling per day with a consequent loss of time … . After six weeks of living in Trumpington I might be ready for a bicycle championship, but I doubt whether this could help me in my exams.' Landladies could be churlish, unwilling to provide meals or charging excessively for them. Even worse, they could steal their lodgers' ration coupons. But Krotki had a good test to characterize landladies: 'those who charge for the place where the bicycle is kept, and those who do not'.

The traditional Cambridge landlady died out long ago; her successors service the more lucrative and malleable language-school market. There is much more accommodation in colleges; otherwise, students live in shared houses. But until New Court was constructed, giving all undergraduates a minimum of two years in College, dealing with lodgings and landladies was an integral part of the Fitzwilliam experience.

Richard Aldrich (1955) spent his first winter in 'a cold spot and a cold house, and even after the purchase of a small oil stove I spent most of the first two terms huddled in the obligatory duffle coat … . I later discovered that Fitzwilliam students had a poor reputation amongst landladies. This was because they had fewer facilities in college and chances to dine there, and so were always asking to have something cooked.'

Digs could be primitive. Roger Wilkins (1967) recalled a downstairs sitting-room and an upstairs bedroom in Oxford Road, backing onto the rugby field: 'Although she and her husband had just installed the latest gas water heater in the bathroom, she didn't like to use it (citing a combination of a fear of the gas exploding and the cost), so I was awakened every morning to face a large jug of hot water that I could use in the sink to wash and shave. A weekly bath (no shower available) cost a shilling a time and had to be pre-booked. The delays and moaning were enough to ensure that I never took advantage of this option.' Showers at sports fields or at Fenners were preferable.

But sometimes landladies' attitudes moved beyond the tiresome to the totally unacceptable. Lorenz Pereira (1961) wrote of racial prejudice; he had just moved into new digs when a graduate friend from Ceylon, of darker complexion, came over to see him – and was barred from entering. Pereira pointed out that both were from the same country, but she responded 'with a great deal of conviction and a touch of satisfaction, that I was different, that I was semi-coloured.' He had no option but to move out.

Sometimes, situations could approach the darkly comical, as Alex Fisher (1963) recounts: 'My digs were in Halifax Road, where the landlady's very ill husband died in the second year. She bore the loss stoically but, when shortly afterwards her black cat disappeared, the poor lady flipped and she herself disappeared.' She was found later suffering from paranoia. Her lodgers benefited, being allocated emergency accommodation in the new Huntingdon Road buildings.

EARLY YEARS OF THE RESEARCH CLUB

Research students were admitted throughout the twentieth century – and at times perceived as secondary to the undergraduate body. After the Second World War, it was to the great credit of Fitzwilliam that action was taken to integrate research students into the House, taking note that their interests and needs differed from those of the undergraduates. In Michaelmas 1950, with 82 research students in residence, a Research Club was founded; initially it held coffee-meetings at which each member gave a brief account of his work, and later it brought in senior-member and external speakers.

By 1952, the founding Secretary, Alfred Leonard, could report in the *Fitzwilliam Magazine* on the example that Fitzwilliam was setting Cambridge: 'the Club will take over two rooms on the first floor of 19 Fitzwilliam Street. The House will therefore be first in providing research students with a common-room and a writing-room for permanent use. We would like to take this opportunity to express our appreciation of the efforts made by the Censor and his colleagues to give us this accommodation at a very difficult time for the House. The success or failure of this bold venture will now depend entirely on us.'

Ray Kelly with the Research Club Committee, in 1959

A year later they were well established: 'The new Club rooms ... include a writing room, a comfortably furnished sitting room and a kitchen. Newspapers, periodicals, playing cards, a chess-set and a modern eleven-waveband radio set are provided in the sitting room, while coffee, tea and beer can be obtained from the kitchen. The Club premises are open, and all the above amenities are maintained throughout the year.'

Special dining arrangements were made for the research students, with exclusive provision for dining in Hall each week in term; dining was arranged also in the vacations (undergraduates went away promptly at end of term and student facilities shut down).

For several years the Club flourished, attracting distinguished external speakers. In Michaelmas 1952, 'activities included a talk by Professor N.B.L. Pevsner, MA, PhD on Sir Christopher Wren and one by Professor F.G. Young FRS, DSc, on Hormones and Animal Growth.'

On the sporting side, much squash and tennis took place, and there was a motoring section which engaged in rallying and excursions. There were excursions too on the river, and more competitive endeavours initiated by Peter Brittain: in 1955, a research students' eight took part in the Mays, and believed they were the first in any college – they had the satisfaction of bumping the Fourth Boat.

Norman Walters died at the very early age of 44. Grave recalled the last time he saw Walters; it was the last night of the 1967 May Bumps, when Walters told him that the First Boat had caught Jesus, very late on the course. That night he was taken ill, and died a week later. The re-arrangements made clear how much Walters had done for the College, in the first year of its new status. Jack Revell temporarily became Senior Tutor, Alan Watson became Tutor, Rev. Nott Praelector, and Admissions was handled jointly by Grave and Hunt. Dominic Baker-Smith, then a Research Fellow at Queens', became Director of Studies in English, and later joined the Fellowship.

POPPY DAYS

Until the 1960s, with their anti-establishment and anti-military tenor, the Rag Day in Cambridge was specifically a Poppy Day event, on the Saturday nearest to Armistice Day, 11 November. All proceeds went to the Earl Haig Fund for ex-servicemen.

Poppy Day was supported enthusiastically across Cambridge; the inter-college rivalry was nowhere stronger than in Fitzwilliam – with its natural competitive spirit, seeking to outdo the 'real' colleges. And perhaps the prospect of a firkin of ale from a local brewery for the highest-collecting college and a kilderkin for the highest per-capita collection might have had something to do with it.

Whilst many of the elements of rag days are timeless – the over-sized babies in prams never seem to grow up, and the penchant for cross-dressing seems irresistible – there were contemporary allusions on Poppy Day floats. The 1958 float alludes to the conflict between mainland China and Formosa across the intervening strait; shelling took place between the mainland and Quemoy. That year, the House collected £1,213, one-eighth of the University total, and won the kilderkin by taking more than twice the per-capita sum for the next-ranking college.

This was but part of a much longer run of successes throughout the 1950s, as collections built up from a Fitzwilliam total of £72 in 1948 to £272 in 1951; that was the first of three successive years in which the House received firkins, with 1956 a fourth time. On any day, there were many events in the centre of Cambridge as well as the parade of floats: in 1953, a team of 'Mrs Mopps' gave attention to a zebra crossing and earned their share of the firkin as a reward for getting soaked on a bitterly cold day.

But that era, in which there was great empathy between the collectors and the citizens of Cambridge, had less than a decade to run before the special nature of Poppy Day was subsumed into a commonplace rag day and it was moved to the Lent term. The citizens, naturally, lost interest – and nowadays its only impact is that it brings the highly-stressed traffic system of Cambridge ever closer to its ultimate gridlock.

Above: The 1958 float outside Fitzwilliam House; in the autumn of 1958, the two sides of the Chinese conflict bombarded each other on alternate days with shells containing propaganda leaflets

Left: Punt jousting on the Mill Pond, with the Silver Street Bridge under construction

THE LITTLE ROSE

The glory has departed from Trumpington Street. Not only has Fitzwilliam gone, but also its local, The Little Rose, has been converted into a sea-food restaurant.

Just as for centuries Peterhouse had Little St Mary's as its chapel, so Fitzwilliam had The Little Rose as its de facto bar, separated from the House by the few little buildings of Tunwell Court. With little space inside the House, it was the natural place to retire after dinner for a half of bitter and a quiet chat. Or for more.

The 1948 *Fitzwilliam Magazine* included a panegyric by One of the Old Brigade, who wrote:

'The Little Rose is our pub. Not that Harry disputes the claim, although, at first, perhaps, he didn't quite know what to make of the Old Brigade when they began to invade his 'public' in 1946. Mind you, nobody could have blamed Harry had he come the old acid, for, what with blokes like P** L** and T** S** ... aren't they enough sometimes to make any man say things his better nature would never utter?'

The genial environment, reminiscent of mess bars across the world, attracted the returning warriors. 'Celebrations, carousals and capers occur almost nightly, and the modest half-pint is made to do things not even brewers and glass manufacturers could think possible. ... To come back to Cambridge will always mean returning to the Rose.'

Harry Bond retained the affection of generations of Fitzwilliam men, even though he did come the old acid for many years – acquiring a duly certificated reputation (right).

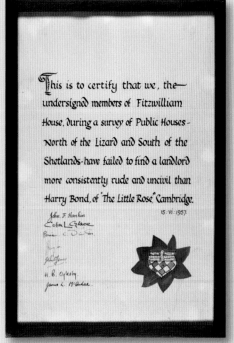

A Little Rose is still displayed above the Loch Fyne Restaurant

The identification of corporate spirit with sporting activity had been inherited from Reddaway's great emphasis on the Clubs, but was becoming anachronistic. Its spirit lived on with Williams, who had read Geography at Fitzwilliam Hall from 1922 to 1925, and who was Bursar from 1946 to 1967 and Acting Censor from 1955 to 1958. This was recognized by a student who came up in 1947: 'Mr Williams, Director of Studies, always reminding ex-service students that they worked too hard and played too little. The truth was that most of us had lost four years in the race to get a footing on the career ladder and our objective was to obtain a good degree and a rapid entry into a settled lifestyle.'

THE POLISH MEMBERS

During the Second World War, much of the Air Force was based in East Anglia. It contained many airmen from Poland, exiles after the German invasion. Post-war communism was no more attractive, and many remained in the region. Once hostilities ceased, many applied to Cambridge and numbers built up rapidly. Fitzwilliam matriculated 14 Polish students in Michaelmas 1945, increasing over that year to 23 out of a total of 112 students. In the second post-war academic year there were fewer, about 7 out of 175. Subsequently numbers fell to about two per year, and after 1955 there were only one or two in residence at any time.

Polish Officers received a warm welcome in the House, with Thatcher very supportive; an association for Polish students, formed in 1946, was based in Fitzwilliam. Shortly after his retirement, the Polish Government-in-Exile awarded him the Order of the Polonia Restituta, in recognition of his services to exiled Poles. Thatcher was very proud of his reputation of being the only man in Cambridge able to understand a Pole when he got excited.

The Polish connection was not confined to junior members; assistant staff were recruited, notably for the kitchens and the Hall, and some served for many years, as Paul Humberstone (1964) wrote in the *Magazine*. In the 1960s, the Head Waiter was Mr E.W. Walizeck; reliable, conscientious, and self-effacing, 'Wally' obtained a job in Fitzwilliam in 1949. He learned English through conversation and by reading newspapers, and took his work very seriously, seeking to maintain good relations between the waiting staff and the students. Herbert Stosiek joined the House after working in the kitchens at Downing. Once he had mastered English, he took evening courses at the Technical College, winning a Silver Medal and a First Prize in a catering competition. He became Head Chef in 1960. Even though most of his craftsmanship was directed to the senior members, he had the attitude that 'it doesn't matter if you are doing a meal for 2s. 6d. or for 10s. 6d., you take just as much interest – for your own satisfaction, you see'.

THE TRAGEDY OF PARK NO-SU

In popular perception, Cambridge is associated with espionage and treason. Fitzwilliam had its own incident – with tragic consequences.

In the heyday of the Cold War, Park No-Su was accused of espionage and inappropriate contacts with North Korea. Park was a South Korean graduate law student at Fitzwilliam from 1961 to 1968. In February 1969, he and his wife returned home to Seoul; that spring, they were accused of involvement with a North Korean spy-ring with, allegedly, a Cambridge base. Park was charged with contravening the National Security Law and the Anti-Communist Act: visiting North Korea and East Berlin, receiving North Korean money, travelling on a North Korean passport, and joining the North Korean Communist Party. He was sentenced to death. In the Supreme Court, subsidiary charges were dropped but the charge that his visit to North Korea in 1968 was for a purpose prejudicial to South Korea was sustained and the sentence was confirmed. His wife received a suspended sentence.

David Pearl, then a young Law Fellow of the College, wrote about the response in Cambridge. 'Pak No-Su had many friends here. From the start it had seemed impossible to believe that the man known to these friends was the master-mind of an international espionage ring.

'A petition to the President of the Republic of South Korea to commute the death sentence was signed by over 4,300 people, including many senior members of the University and a number of Members of Parliament. Towards the end of August 1970, a delegation of three, led by Lord Caradon, sometime the UK Delegate to the United Nations, visited Seoul to make a personal appeal on humanitarian grounds.

'As Lord Caradon said, "It is the belief of those who knew him best that, whatever misjudgements or mistakes he might have made, he would not be guilty of such serious crimes as those of which he was first suspected. In his long hours of trial his friends of many years have sought to stand by him and help him." '

There was to be no satisfactory outcome. Park No-Su was hanged. His extensive collection of books on international law, bequeathed to the College, forms The Park Collection in the Library.

LEE KUAN YEW

The most significant statesman to be a member of Fitzwilliam is Lee Kuan Yew, who was Prime Minister of Singapore for the first three decades of its independence.

Lee was born in 1923 into an English-speaking family of Hakka origin that had come to Singapore in the 1860s from southern China. He was educated at Raffles Institution, where in 1940 he came first in the school (and amongst all pupils in Singapore and Malaya) and won a scholarship to Raffles College. His university education ended in 1941 when the Japanese invaded, putting him at considerable personal risk, as many young Chinese men were massacred.

Lee Kuan Yew, by Bernard Hailstone, given by Donovan Hailstone (1953)

1950 Hockey team with Dennis Lee as Captain

After the war, Lee determined to go to England and read Law. At the London School of Economics, he was overwhelmed by living in London and sought a more congenial environment in Cambridge. One of his fellow Raffles College students introduced him to Thatcher, who admitted him for the 1947 Lent term, telling him 'Lee, when you come up to Cambridge, you are joining something special, like joining the Life Guards and not just joining the army. You have to stand that extra inch taller'.

As well as his studies, Harry Lee (as he was known within his family and during his Cambridge years) joined the Boat Club, undergoing several sessions of bank-tubbing and progressing to an eight. However, 'On the afternoon of my second scheduled outing, a snowstorm broke and I assumed the practice was cancelled. I was severely reproached. Seven others and the cox had turned up but could not take the rowing eight out because I was missing. I decided the English were mad and left the Boat Club.'

Lee and Kwa, with Thatcher outside the Senate House

Professor and Mrs Lethbridge with Lee Suan Yew in 2011

His fiancée, Kwa Geok Choo (the only person who had beaten him in English and in Economics at Raffles College), also wished to read Law in Cambridge. She got a place at Girton, but Lee was disconcerted to find how far Girton was from his south-Cambridge lodgings. He appealed to Thatcher, who wrote 'You plead that it is a long way to go to see your fiancée .... Not really so far as you make out, especially if love provides the motive power. I don't know whether you read the great myths, but you will remember the gentleman who swam the Bosphorus every night to see his lady love. Going to Girton is a slight thing compared to that. Unhappily, the gentleman got drowned ... but I doubt whether you need die of exhaustion on the road.' Lee married Kwa secretly during the Christmas vacation of her first year.

Despite all the disruption to his education, his ability and determination ensured that he graduated First Class in both parts of the Tripos; in Part II Law in 1949, he obtained the only Distinction in his year.

Politics was central to his life, but although he met nationalist groups in England he did not integrate with them. In 1950, while reading for the Bar at the Middle Temple, he took part in the election campaign for a friend who was a Labour Party candidate. Back in Singapore, as a barrister he represented many cases of actual or alleged rebellious behaviour against the colonial government. The Malayan Communist Party was fomenting trouble, but Lee established the non-Communist People's Action Party in 1954 and became the first Prime Minister in 1959, when Britain ceded all internal responsibilities to Singapore.

At that time, Lee favoured a merger between Singapore and Malaya, and in 1963 the fully-independent Federation of Malaysia was formed, incorporating Singapore, peninsular Malaya, and Sabah and Sarawak in Borneo. This gave Fitzwilliam an intriguing memento of the vicissitudes of state formation. Amongst the silver marking collegiate status (pp. 48 and 79) are four pieces inscribed that they were donated in 1965 by a group of alumni living in Malaysia, Lee amongst them. True – but only for a short time: most of the donors were based in Singapore, and only a few months later Singapore left the Federation and became independent. Long-standing racial discrimination by the Malay-dominated Federation Government against the Chinese and the Indian populations had made union unworkable.

After independence and during Singapore's transformation to a flourishing first-world nation, Lee held the office of Prime Minister. He retired in 1990, but for several years exerted influence under the title of Minister Mentor.

Lee Kuan Yew was elected to an Honorary Fellowship of Fitzwilliam in 1969, and so the most senior of the College's Honorary Fellows.

He was not the only member of his family to come to Fitzwilliam. His younger brother Lee Kim Yew (Dennis) followed him a year later, also to read Law, and in 1954 his youngest brother, Lee Suan Yew, came up to read Medicine. A significant cohort of Singaporeans came to Fitzwilliam, and went on to become leaders in their rapidly-developing community.

S.D. SHARMA AND M.S. SWAMINATHAN – TWO INDIAN RESEARCH STUDENTS

Shankar Dayal Sharma with Professor Bottoms and Professor Cuthbert

In Michaelmas 1945, even though Fitzwilliam was filling up beyond capacity with demobilized British students, a few overseas research students were admitted. Amongst them was Shankar Dayal Sharma, who had been top student in his year at Lucknow University, studying for a PhD in Law. His topic, *The interpretation of legislative powers under the Government of India Act 1935*, might seem improbable in consequence of Indian independence, but much of this legislation carried over to the constitutions of India and Pakistan. It contributed to many problems such as the anomalous survival of the Princely States, including Bhopal, Sharma's home state.

Whilst in England, Sharma was called to the Bar at Lincoln's Inn. He also taught classes for Part II of the Law Tripos, on both Hindu and Muslim Law. He was not approved for his degree until 1952; he had better reasons for delay than most research students.

As a student in Allahabad, where he had obtained his BA in 1937, Sharma had come under the influence of Nehru and the Congress Party. His ambitions were academic, and he had gone on to the University of Lucknow. Leaving Cambridge in October 1948, he returned to Lucknow, to a Readership in Law. For activists in Bhopal, he drafted a letter demanding its merger with the adjacent democratic state of Madhya Pradesh. In December 1948 he was arrested by the forces of the Nawab of Bhopal after they suppressed a demonstration with extreme violence and loss of life. But the trend towards integration and democracy was inexorable; Sharma was released, and two years later was persuaded to return from Lucknow and was elected unanimously as President of the District Congress Committee. In 1952, he became Chief Minister of the State of Bhopal and drove forward its modernisation from poor and feudal beginnings.

In 1956, Bhopal merged with Madhya Pradesh and Sharma became Minister of Education. He held several State Governorships and the Presidency of the All-India Congress Committee, before becoming the eighth Vice-President of India (1987–92) and the ninth President of India (1992–97). He died two years after the end of his term as President.

In later years, Sharma came twice to Fitzwilliam: as Vice-President in 1989; and as President in 1993, when he received an Honorary LLD and the College made him an Honorary Fellow.

While Sharma was politically active in Bhopal, another Indian research student joined Fitzwilliam. Maankombu Sambasivan Swaminathan, who matriculated in 1950, was very significant in an utterly different way. He was a highly-driven agricultural scientist, who got into conflict with his landlady who insisted that he came home in time for an evening meal at 6 pm – incompatible with experimental studies. In 1953, he obtained his PhD for research into potato genetics at the Plant Breeding Institute, then a part of the School of Agriculture.

Swaminathan had considerable experience before coming to Cambridge: two bachelor's degrees, in Zoology and in Agricultural Science, followed by research at the Indian Agricultural Research Institute (IARI) and in the Netherlands. He returned to IARI in 1954 and worked mostly on wheat and rice; subsequently, he engaged increasingly with government and international programmes to enhance crops and agricultural practices in India – playing a very major role in the Green Revolution which greatly increased crop yields. The Nobel Peace Prize Laureate Dr Norman Borlaug (who created Mexican dwarf wheat) said 'The green revolution has been a team effort … . However, to you, Dr Swaminathan, a great deal of the credit must go for first recognising the potential value of the Mexican dwarfs. Had this not occurred, it is quite possible that there would not have been a green revolution in Asia.'

Swaminathan has been acclaimed both in India and internationally, and in the second half of his professional life has worked extensively in policy development – not only in agriculture but in areas as diverse as population policy and global security. His work, and the Green Revolution, have not been free of controversy, but certainly have resulted in great increases in crops and in improvement of nutrition across Asia.

Dr M S Swaminathan, Chairman of the M S Swaminathan Research Foundation, at his Institute in Tamil Nadu

6

SURVIVAL IN THE POST-WAR WORLD

A role for Fitzwilliam?

Even after the immediate post-war student peak had passed, the inadequacies of provision in Fitzwilliam were manifest. Consideration of new buildings for the House (p. 82) had made little progress. So in January 1953, the Censor presented to the Non-Collegiate Students Board a memorandum on student numbers and buildings, and proposed an additional Tutor and consideration of the Officers' stipends.

He also raised the perennial issue of status: 'We would venture, at this point, to remind the Board but particularly the University Authorities, that Fitzwilliam House though by regulation a department of the University is, by its very nature *sui generis*. While not a college *de jure*, it is so *de facto*. The whole history of its development, from its very inception, is that of a body of men who in spite of the old title *Non Collegiate* and the old attitudes, have passionately desired a corporate life and standing. ... Fitzwilliam House has a very real life and pride, though these are constantly frustrated by the inadequacy of its buildings and the unhelpful attitude of the University Authorities. This last statement is made with reluctance, but one is compelled to make it. Too little is known of Fitzwilliam House and its problems by those in Authority and too often decisions are made by those who have never put foot inside the building and who know nothing of its working, its life and its hopes.'

This touched a chord with the Board, who developed it into a report that was sent to the Council of the Senate in March 1953, and thence to the Financial Board. A special committee was set up, which delayed the appointment of a new Censor; Thatcher, due to retire in September 1954, would continue in an acting capacity with the title of Senior Tutor. The target number of students would be 300 (excluding Attached House members).

But the special committee's second report queried the raison d'être for Fitzwilliam House. They recognized

that students admitted to the University by the Board of Research Studies should enter Fitzwilliam if no college took them, and also graduate students on taught courses. But they saw no need to provide for undergraduates. 'The University is essentially collegiate in character, and special reasons are necessary to justify it in continuing to maintain a non-collegiate student body similar in composition to those of the Colleges.' Under the Butler Education Act, awards of sufficient value to maintain their holders at colleges were

THE COURT.

11. Subject always to these Articles, the Foundation shall be governed and its affairs administered by a Court consisting of the following persons, who shall be known as Governors (and who shall be treated as " the Directors " wherever the same shall be applicable for all the purposes of the Act) :—

A. ~~The Master, Vice-Master, the Senior Bursar and the Senior Tutor of Fitzwilliam Hall.~~

B. ~~Five persons to be elected by the Council from among their own number.~~

B. C. The Chairman of the Council of Governors of ~~the~~ Fitzwilliam Hall Trust and the President of the Fitzwilliam Society.

C. D. Seven persons to be elected by the Foundation in General Meeting from among those members of the Foundation not in residence in the University.

D. E. ~~Four~~ *Five* persons to be elected by the Court from among Heads of Houses, holders of administrative posts of professorial and higher rank in the University, and holders of University teaching posts. ⟦A member of the Court elected under this paragraph shall not vote on any resolution for election proposed under this paragraph.⟧

E. F. A member of the Council of the Senate of the University to be elected by the said Council.

A. Nine members of the Council of whom the Master, Vice-Master, the Senior Bursar and the Senior Tutor of Fitzwilliam Hall shall be members virtute officii and the remaining members shall be elected by the Council from among their own number.

The draft Memorandum of Association with a heavily-annotated governance page

The Negotiating Committee, 1955; John Stratton seated centrally next to Thatcher

available, and the committee speculated that it was 'possible that a poor man who is state-aided will fare better financially at certain of the Colleges than he would at Fitzwilliam House'.

Two of the three Board members on the committee refused to sign the report and appended forthright comments. At the Council of the Senate, discussion of the report was adjourned twice; eventually, the provisions for

THE BUTLER EDUCATION ACT AND THE 1962 ACT

Long before the Second World War had been won, the politicians gathered to spend the peace dividend. Many aspects of that brave new world have been discredited. But one stands out for providing clear benefits: the Education Act of 1944, always linked with the name of R.A. Butler MP, President of the Board of Education (later Lord Butler, and Master of Trinity College 1965–78).

Whilst the Act was primarily concerned with school-level education, there was one small clause relevant to universities, well down in the Miscellaneous Provisions section. It empowered Local Authorities 'to grant scholarships, exhibitions, bursaries, and other allowances in respect of pupils over compulsory school age' but it did not require them to do so. Under the Education Act 1962, it became obligatory for every Local Education Authority to make awards for full-time first-degree courses at universities.

The 1944 Act initiated an era of Local Authority Grants much wider than the pre-war system of State Scholarships. University and college fees were paid in full; the living allowance was means-tested based on family income, but even a partial award could contribute usefully towards expenses. So the financial obstacle to students of limited means coming to Cambridge had been removed.

undergraduates were rejected unanimously – assuring the survival of the House.

The fate of Fitzwilliam had become a topic for rumours and a live issue in the University, so in the *Cambridge Review*: 'It is unlikely that even the Council could be so foolish or so out of touch with University opinion as to put forward any proposals for liquidating an institution which for many years has played such a useful part in the University'.

The question of collegiate status was developed in the following weeks. A meeting early in April was attended by Officers and Directors of Studies, Fitzwilliam graduates in University posts, and Heads of Attached Houses. Members of the Fitzwilliam Society were unable to attend. It was agreed to send a Memorial to the Council of the Senate on the future of Fitzwilliam House, and to set up an Acting Committee of six Directors of Studies under the chairmanship of R.W. Haywood (University Lecturer in Engineering, and President of the Fitzwilliam Society for 1954–55). The signatories of the document, which was submitted at the end of April 1954, became known as the 'Memorialists'.

Submission of the Memorial led quickly to a discussion between representatives of the Council, senior members of the House and representatives of the Fitzwilliam Society, at which the claims for fully-independent status were reiterated. The Council response was positive, the Vice-Chancellor writing that it would be reasonable to seek the opinion of the University on the abolition of non-collegiate status and the establishment of Fitzwilliam House as a Recognised Institution.

Thus far, so good – and in remarkably quick time. But the next steps introduced complications that would cause the scheme to unravel. These arose from Fitzwilliam Society members based in London; led by John Stratton, they had provided advice and support for Thatcher, and were now to play a more overt role when they joined the Acting Committee to form a larger Negotiating Committee.

The Negotiating Committee successfully advanced the argument that Fitzwilliam should gain independence as an Approved Foundation rather than merely as a Recognised Institution. A Report of the Council of the Senate made the key recommendation that 'approval be given to the general proposition that steps shall be taken to terminate the present Non-Collegiate system, provided that Fitzwilliam House can be recognised as an Approved

Foundation bound to limitation of the number of its undergraduate members and to the performance of certain functions now performed by it as an institution for Non-Collegiate Students'. This Grace was approved, without a vote, by the Regent House on 27 November 1954. It was time to build on that victory.

So the Negotiating Committee moved to the next stages: looking for a location and funds for a new building; and framing a constitution for Fitzwilliam as an Approved Foundation (to be registered under the 1948 Companies Act) – a prerequisite for the Council of the Senate to support an appeal for funds.

One point suggestive of underlying attitudes was the name proposed for the company: Fitzwilliam Hall. So, just as had the founders of the Fitzwilliam Society (p. 50), the London members looked backwards to their youth rather than accepting the developments of the previous three decades.

How would the Memorandum and Articles of Association of the Company be constructed? The objectives were uncontroversial: to 'found and carry on a self-governing Approved Foundation ... for the higher education of men, and to promote its development into and to carry it on as a college of the University' and to 'advance education, learning and research in the University'.

Governance was quite another matter. A Council of teaching and administrative officers of the Hall would be responsible for academic policy and day-to-day administration. But over-riding powers would be vested in a Governing Body or Court; despite bearing the same title as the Governing Body of a college, it would have had a very different composition – containing and chaired by non-resident members. This was inconsistent with the constitution of a college – self-government is inherent – and so not a rational step towards full collegiate status.

The structure was reviewed by a sub-committee of the Negotiating Committee, and they made it worse by proposing an increase in the number of non-resident members. The representatives of the Council of the Senate recommended reversal of the increase; this was unacceptable to the London members who resigned forthwith, seeing their future influence weakened. In his resignation letter, Stratton stated his opinion that 'in this day and age potential benefactors might wish not only to be informed about the objects of an institution they were being asked to support, but also for an opportunity of continuing their interest in the conduct of its affairs'.

It was fortunate that the issue arose fairly quickly, and the inappropriate governance structure was eliminated. The dispute became unpleasant; it was even implied that the Fitzwilliam officers had been self-seeking in trying to maintain a conventional Cambridge-based structure rather than one led from London.

In Michaelmas 1956 the Negotiating Committee, reconstituted without the London members, prepared a scheme of governance incorporating advice from the Registrary: there would still be a two-tier structure, but the Governing Body would have a balanced composition with both Fitzwilliam officers and members, members from the Board, and other experienced people from Cambridge.

The Approved Foundation scheme faded. It could not be implemented without funds and, since a future scheme might take a different form, the Council of the Senate did not approve the submission of the Memorandum of Association to the Board of Trade to establish the company.

The preceding years had not been wasted, however. Although the Memorialists' scheme had come to nothing, and there was no immediate prospect of Fitzwilliam becoming an Approved Foundation, the question of the development of Fitzwilliam House had received an extensive airing. The notion of conversion to an institution for graduate students, with Attached House members as the only undergraduates, had been tested and rejected. So there had been a step forward and progress had been locked in; subsequent developments would be able to build on the agreement 'that steps shall be taken to terminate the present Non-Collegiate system'.

House to College

The transformation of Fitzwilliam House from a University Department to an independent body had foundered on its need to be financially self-sufficient. This was linked to the need for new buildings, since it was recognized that the Trumpington Street building and its Fitzwilliam Street neighbours were completely inadequate for a body with 300 junior members. In the later 1950s, these issues were transformed from separate difficulties compounding each other to linked aspects of a common solution.

The person who put the aspects together was S.C. (later Sir Sydney) Roberts, Chairman of the Non-Collegiate Students Board and a member of the Council of the Senate. As early as Michaelmas 1955, before the

Sir Sydney Roberts, by Peter Greenham. Reproduced by kind permission of the Master and Fellows of Pembroke College

was to fund Universities, not independent colleges or similar bodies. Representatives of the Council of the Senate and of the Negotiating Committee met in late March 1956 and it was agreed that an approach should be made to the UGC since, although the grant would be made to the University, it should not be assumed that the University would not be permitted to use it for a building for Fitzwilliam House – even though, by the time the building was complete, the House might have become autonomous. This seems ever so slightly Jesuitical, but it should be remembered that it was taking place in a very expansive era, in which a long-overdue increase to the woefully inadequate university capacity in England led to a group of new universities such as Sussex and Warwick.

At the end of May, the Registrary reported that the soundings had been successful. The long-running investigation of potential locations for new buildings had settled on the Huntingdon Road site of The Grove. Thus the complementary elements of the scheme were in place and a submission to the UGC could proceed. In March 1957, the Statement of Needs for 1957–62 had as its second-placed capital-project request an administrative building for Fitzwilliam House, to cost about £200,000 and suit an institution with between 350 and 400 students (who would not be accommodated in the building).

Memorialists' initiative had collapsed in acrimony, Roberts and the Board began to consider whether provision for an administrative building for Fitzwilliam House might be incorporated with high priority into the University's Statement of Needs for the quinquennium 1957–62. There was an immediate issue: funds would come from the University Grants Committee, but its remit

THE SECRETARY OF THE AMALGAMATED CLUBS AND THE VICE-CHANCELLOR

In the spring of 1958, the General Secretary of the Fitzwilliam House Amalgamated Clubs was Geoff Harrison. The appointment of Grave as Censor had recently been announced, occasioning not only surprise that the Acting Censor had not received the post but also dismay since it had not been accompanied by news on progress towards collegiate status. So Harrison obtained permission from Williams to write to the Vice-Chancellor, asking for reassurance about the future:

'Those of us who are due to go down next month, as I am, can appreciate the progress achieved within the House during our three years' stay, but we feel deeply disappointed at the thought that we shall leave F.H. not knowing exactly what further progress has been made towards Collegiate Status since the Report that came out some four years ago. The importance of this matter to men of all years needs no emphasizing, nor the strength of feeling that exists among us; but may I mention, Sir, that my generation, coming up in 1955, has lived through three years of uncertainty. We have willingly tolerated our intensely cramped quarters only because we have expected an early announcement about a building scheme. ...

'The appointment of Dr W.W. Grave to the Censorship has naturally led to much speculation, and we see this as a hopeful sign – an indication that things are at last moving forward in a decisive manner. Is it not possible, Sir, for you to confirm this hope and let us know what has in fact been achieved? We, as Fitzwilliam men, feel – and we hope that you would agree with us – that we are giving evidence in every sphere of University life of a true collegiate spirit and of a true sense of collegiate responsibility. Could not these be recognized by an official statement telling us what lies ahead?

'Finally, Sir, my colleagues, in their understandable concern, have pressed me to ask you whether you could provide us with some authoritative statement so that before we go down this time of prolonged uncertainty may be brought to an end and we shall feel re-assured. It would make the General meeting of our Amalgamated Clubs at the end of this month a very great occasion if it could be presented with a statement of this kind.'

Three weeks later, he was summoned to see the Vice-Chancellor. He spent forty minutes with Lord Adrian, explaining the Fitzwilliam feeling that they were as much part of the University as any college, and had a further discussion a few days later.

The UGC funding gave sufficient expectation for continuity that the Council of the Senate decided that the post of Censor should be filled, after a four-year gap. The new Censor, who took office in January 1959, was Dr W.W. Grave, a Fellow of Emmanuel and Principal of the University College of the West Indies – a man with vast university-administrative experience.

The remaining steps towards independence now proceeded briskly, aided by a number of very favourable – and completely unpredicted – external circumstances. If Fitzwilliam was to be endowed and also able to afford the later phases of its buildings, more funds would be needed. The Non-Collegiate Students Board proposed to the Registrary that an appeal should be undertaken. The Council of the Senate assented, and the Board launched the appeal in July 1962, sponsored by Sir Maurice Bridgeman, then Chairman of British Petroleum. The target was £900,000, but only £200,000 had been raised by 1964, not enough for both buildings and endowment, but fortuitously it was not necessary to fund buildings: the University had allocated resources for the comprehensive replacement of science buildings on the New Museums Site, and the scheme had collapsed – but Fitzwilliam Phase 2 could be undertaken immediately to avoid the loss of the funds. So the proceeds of the appeal were not needed for buildings, and could go into the endowment.

More potential misfortune was turned to good advantage. March 1962 brought the publication of the *Report on the Relationship between the University and the Colleges*, from the Syndicate chaired by Lord Bridges. One issue was the number of University Teaching Officers without college Fellowships, so an increase in the number of Fellowships was proposed. This was perceived by the Board as untimely and a threat, since many of the best available Teaching Officers in popular subjects might be taken up before Fitzwilliam was able to make its own appointments. So they proposed to the Council of the Senate that Fitzwilliam House might be allowed to appoint up to 24 non-stipendiary Fellows. This was approved by Grace in December 1962. Another collegiate attribute had been acquired.

One final step was needed. The University Statutes were constructed on the assumption that an institution would hold the intermediate status of Approved Foundation before it became a College. But the authors of a further Report in 1964 considered that collegiate provision across the University could be improved simply

A GALLERY OF FITZWILLIAM HOUSE PHOTOGRAPHS

Anthony Kersting FRPS, the leading architectural photographer of his generation, was commissioned to take a series of photographs of Fitzwilliam House. The interior views were taken in December 1949, and the exterior views in April 1950.

The Library

The Dining Hall

The Common Room

The Chief Clerk's office

The kitchen

The back of
Fitzwilliam House

R.W. Haywood (Mechanical Sciences), Dr C.L. Wayper (History), Dr T.W. Wormall (Physical Sciences), R.N. Walters (Tutor; English), J.E.G. Utting (Economics), Dr R. Kelly (Assistant Tutor; Modern Languages), B.M. Herbertson (Assistant Tutor; Medicine) and Dr J. Street (Assistant Tutor; Modern Languages). G.F. Hickson, Secretary of the Board of Extra-Mural Studies, was also elected.

Less than a fortnight later, they continued, electing A.G. Hunt (Classics) and Dr A. Lazenby (Assistant Tutor; Agriculture). In addition, they broadened the field beyond the *ex-officio* appointments, to: Dr D. Kerridge (Biochemistry), H. Nicholson (Engineering), and Dr G.M. Blackburn (Organic Chemistry). Further elections took place during 1963, with: Dr S.G. Fleet (Mineralogy), Dr P.J. Padley (Physical Chemistry), B. Hall (Theology), P. Haggett (Geography), Dr H.J. Hudson (Botany), Dr J.M. Coles (Archaeology), and finally Dr A.V. Edwards (Physiology). The elections up to October 1963 put in place many who were to play key roles in the House and the College for the next three decades.

An early action of the Fellows of Fitzwilliam House was to prepare the Statutes: collegiate status would be manifest by the issuing of a Royal Charter and the approval of the Statutes by the Privy Council. This was undertaken briskly, but with some controversy – and some decisions were unfortunate. The first draft was based on the statutes of existing colleges, predominantly

Fitzwilliam House, by Norman Pounds. Above: The main staircase. Right: The Senior Combination Room

and quickly, and recommended: 'because it has been for many years collegiate in character, the Council now think that it should be unnecessary for Fitzwilliam House to seek recognition in the first instance as an Approved Foundation, and that it would be more appropriate if it were included among the Colleges listed in Statute K, 3(a), as soon as arrangements can be made'.

Fellows and Statutes

The Non-Collegiate Students Board lost no time in implementing their new-found authority to elect Fellows for Fitzwilliam House. Only a month afterwards, on 17 January 1963, the first group was elected, those entitled to Fellowships *ex officio*. The very first was the Bursar, W.W. Williams, immediately followed by a group of Tutors and Directors of Studies: Dr S. Dickinson (Agriculture),

Dr Grave's Emmanuel. In the debate, the Censor had – and was very conscious that he had, and was exercising – the advantage that he alone had prior experience as a Fellow of a college.

David Kerridge recalled a meeting 'where the Censor and I had a major difference of opinion over one statute, a situation not helped by the fact that we are both fenmen and therefore stubborn. Geoff Hunt, later University Draughtsman, came to our rescue with a form of words satisfying honour on both sides. At the end of the meeting … Grave came up to me and said "Kerridge, have a beer. You know what the trouble is. You've not served on enough committees, and I've served on too many". It was the perfect way of defusing a difficult situation.' And the new Fellows tried to improve the odds, a small group gathering regularly to plan the line to be taken at the next meeting. Often the younger Fellows would meet in Tony Edwards' room after Hall, accompanied by a good malt.

Debate started with the very first clause of the first statute. It was only to be expected that an attempt would be made to resurrect the name of Fitzwilliam Hall; there was a large majority of 15 to 6 in favour of Fitzwilliam College – expressing unambiguously the long-awaited status.

Nomenclature was to surface one last time, during a Discussion in the Senate House on 23 November 1965 – a session that should have been purely formal, and which in that spirit had already provided Grave with the opportunity to give generous thanks to the Non-Collegiate Students Board and to the central officers of the University for their support over many years. Haywood – expressing personal opinions rather than the common purpose inherent in Governing-Body membership – declared that it would 'have been a source of pleasure for me to see us revert to our earlier title of Fitzwilliam Hall, while retaining the title of Censor. When this was discussed by the body of Fellows, however, I had no success in bringing them round to my view and, in the belief that a rose by *almost* any other name would smell as sweet, I bowed gracefully, though perhaps a little sadly, to their greater collective wisdom.'

Consideration by the Fellows of the next clause of the Statutes, which restricted College membership to men, gave rise to a much closer debate and in retrospect clearly to the wrong outcome. The possibility of mixed colleges was becoming a live issue, and not just amongst eccentrics and rebels – in 1964 the Council of the Senate had mooted the possibility of institutions open both to men and to women. The opportunity for Fitzwilliam to achieve a unique position as the first mixed college with undergraduate members (more than a year before King's College eliminated its gender-restrictive statute) was closely defeated, by 15 votes to 12. The defeated proposal was to add a final phrase 'except by a two-thirds majority of the Governing Body' to the draft 'No woman shall be eligible to be Master, Fellow or Scholar, or shall be a Member of the College', enabling the College to become mixed without needing to change the Statutes. So the College was condemned to statute revision more than a decade later – and to become an also-ran amongst the mixed colleges rather than having the advantages of being the pioneer.

It took eight long meetings closely packed into four weeks early in 1965 to go through the Statutes. Every clause in each of the 61 statutes was looked at in detail. Care was taken to define the arrangements for the Master, and note was taken of changing social mores: College Servants became Assistant Staff, for instance.

Menu for the first Fellows' Dinner

Kerridge, D.

Fellows' Dinner

Wednesday 27 March 1963
FITZWILLIAM HOUSE
CAMBRIDGE

R. I. Severs Ltd, Cambridge

DR W.W. GRAVE

The choice of Walter Wyatt Grave as Censor of Fitzwilliam House, responsible for taking it to collegiate status with new buildings on a new site, was singularly appropriate. He was a highly professional administrator with an excellent academic background; an Entrance Scholar of Emmanuel, he graduated in 1924 with a Double First in Modern Languages. Before he had completed his PhD, his College elected him to a Research Fellowship; he was to be a Fellow of Emmanuel over a remarkable 73-year span.

Whilst previous Censors had been enthusiasts for Fitzwilliam but – at best – amateurs in administration and University politics, Grave was the consummate political operator. He started to gain experience, in addition to College and Faculty administration, as Senior Proctor in 1938–39. After an interlude with the Ministry of Labour and National Service, he became Registrary in 1943 (joining the triumvirate of top administrators who ran the University) – and in this capacity was first exposed to Non-Collegiate issues. His time as Registrary covered the critical period of post-war University expansion, with major developments such as the Arts and Humanities complex on Sidgwick Avenue, and his work was recognized with an honorary LLD. Then another interlude, when in 1952 he went out to organize the recently-founded University College of the West Indies – recognized with a CMG.

Not daunted by the prospect of yet another institution in transition, he became Censor in 1959 and, as the Royal Charter stated: 'The first Master of the College shall be Our trusty and well beloved Doctor Walter Wyatt Grave, Companion of Our Most Distinguished Order of Saint Michael and Saint George, Censor of Fitzwilliam House'.

Grave ran a tight ship, not just in the Governing Body but more generally. He expected as much commitment from others as from himself, and was determined to build up the College to accord with his own experience. So, he expected his Fellows – the possessive pronoun is chosen deliberately – to dine formally on High Table twice a week, and would enquire pointedly about their health if they were absent. And to dine seated in order of seniority, as was still customary in several colleges; this ceased immediately on Grave's retirement. At the end of dinner, David Kerridge recalled, they 'waited until the Master was ready to say a post-prandial grace before leading us back to the SCR. This could be a long wait and Junior Fellows, who were seated at the foot of High Table, were known to take bets on just how long it was going to be. Or if they were really desperate would scrape their chairs back over the Hall floor; it usually worked.'

Dr W.W. Grave, Censor 1959–66 and Master 1966–71, by David Morris

Stephen Fleet wrote: 'He had an enormous capacity for taking pains, would always seek to be thoroughly briefed (questioning relentlessly as necessary, to acquire information beforehand). He had clear objectives and pressed hard and invariably successfully to achieve them, striving to build an academic community of high quality. At the same time, with the support of his wife, he entertained widely at all levels within the College, having an extensive store of humorous anecdotes. His whereabouts in a crowd was readily identified by the sound of his laughter. He had the capacity fully to engage colleagues, however junior, in College business, transmitting enthusiasm and leading by example.'

Given his work for Fitzwilliam, it is impressive that he was able to undertake an extensive review of the organization of the University: the Grave Report in 1968 made radical recommendations including ending the biennial cycle of Vice-Chancellors and enhancing the roles for the Council, the General Board, and the academic Councils of the Schools. Too radical for many – several proposals needed to be reiterated by the Wass Syndicate in 1989 before his recommendations could be implemented in full.

Walter Grave had a long and healthy retirement; he died in 1999 at the age of 97.

Also needed was the Charter. With this, the objectives of the College were defined. Some were inherent:

(a) To advance education, religion, learning and research in the University;

(b) To provide for men who shall be members of the University a College wherein they may work for Degrees in the University or may carry out postgraduate or other special studies at Cambridge provided that no member of the College or any candidate for membership thereof shall be subject to any test of a religious, political or social character;

but others derived from the special circumstances of Fitzwilliam:

(c) To acquire and take over such property and liabilities of the University as the University may transfer to it;

(d) To acquire and take over the properties and liabilities now

ELIZABETH THE SECOND

by the Grace of God of the United Kingdom of Great Britain and Northern Ireland and of Our other Realms and Territories Queen, Head of the Commonwealth, Defender of the Faith:

TO ALL TO WHOM THESE PRESENTS SHALL COME, GREETING!

WHEREAS a Petition has been presented unto Us by the Chancellor, Masters and Scholars of Our University of Cambridge (hereinafter referred to as "the University") praying that We would be graciously pleased to grant a Charter of Incorporation for the purpose of constituting the present community of Non-Collegiate Students in the University known as Fitzwilliam House (hereinafter referred to as "Fitzwilliam House") a Body Corporate to be called "Fitzwilliam College in the University of Cambridge" with the object among others of acquiring and taking over the site and buildings presently occupied by Fitzwilliam House together with the moneys promised or subscribed to assist the University in the establishment of Fitzwilliam College and otherwise of furthering its purposes under such regulations and with such powers as to Us might appear meet and expedient:

AND WHEREAS We have taken the said Petition into Our Royal Consideration and are minded to accede thereto:

NOW THEREFORE KNOW YE that We by virtue of Our Prerogative Royal and of all other powers enabling Us so to do of Our especial grace, certain knowledge and mere motion have granted and declared and by these Presents do for Us, Our Heirs and Successors grant and declare as follows:

1. The first Master and first Fellows of the College and all such persons as may hereafter become members of the Body Corporate hereby constituted shall for ever after be one Body Politic and Corporate by the name and style of "The Master,

Fellows and Scholars of Fitzwilliam College in the University of Cambridge" (hereinafter referred to as "the College") and by the same name shall have perpetual succession and a Common Seal with power to break, alter and make anew the said Seal from time to time at their will and pleasure and by the same name shall and may sue and be sued in all Courts and before all Justices of Us, Our Heirs and Successors.

2. The College shall have full power and capacity to accept, acquire and hold any personal property whatsoever and shall also without any further authority by virtue of this Our Charter have full power and capacity to accept, acquire and hold any lands and hereditaments situate in Our United Kingdom of Great Britain and Northern Ireland and to dispose of either by way of sale or lease and to exchange, mortgage, charge, improve, manage, develop, turn to account or otherwise deal with all or any part of such property real or personal belonging to the College upon such terms and in such manner as it shall see fit and also to do all other matters incidental or appertaining to a Body Corporate provided always that nothing in this Article shall be deemed to empower the College to dispose of or deal with its property in the manner above mentioned without first obtaining such consent as would otherwise be required by law.

3. The College is incorporated and shall be conducted with the following objects:

(a) To advance education, religion, learning and research in the University.

vested in the limited company known as the Fitzwilliam Hall Trust.

So what assets were to be inherited? The Censor wrote to the University Treasurer to establish the fate of the Trumpington Street building, and requested the transfer of the balances on all relevant funds. The response was prompt and positive, declaring: 'the University's intention ... to transfer to Fitzwilliam College the site and buildings of Fitzwilliam House, together with the proceeds of an appeal issued in 1962 ... . The Council intends to transfer to the new College the various balances at present held in the Non-Collegiate Students Board accounts, and to make an allocation from the Chest to meet the payments to Dr Grave, during his tenure of the Mastership of Fitzwilliam College, of the stipend appropriate to a Professorship, which he has been receiving as Censor of Fitzwilliam House.' The accumulated cash balances were of the order of £50,000.

With the last few adjustments to the Statutes approved by the Privy Council on 2 June 1966, Her Majesty in Council approved on 28 July the grant of a Charter of Incorporation to Fitzwilliam House, under the name and style of The Master, Fellows and Scholars of Fitzwilliam College in the University of Cambridge. The Charter received the Great Seal on 9 September, and the next day the Statutes came into effect.

The long-awaited dream of full collegiate status had become a reality and the Non-Collegiate Students Board went into honourable retirement, its endeavours over 97 years having provided a route into Cambridge for so many men who otherwise would not have had the opportunity, and having done for them the best that limited resources could provide. Its passing was noted in the *Cambridge University Reporter* of 5 October 1966:

Statutes approved
Statute H
Chapter II
NON-COLLEGIATE STUDENTS
(Amended) by repealing the whole chapter

WINDING UP THE FITZWILLIAM HALL TRUST

The Fitzwilliam Hall Trust had been set up in 1921 by Reddaway, to hold properties in Fitzwilliam Street and to manage assets such as funds in support of student awards. Showing great foresight – or his customary optimism – he had included in its Memorandum of Association a clause that, if the Non-Collegiate Students function was to be transferred to a corporation with a Royal Charter, the assets would go to that corporation. So, with a complementary clause in the Charter, the Trust would terminate and the assets would pass to the College.

The first step was to rationalize the property portfolio, to provide accommodation near to the new buildings. So 120 Oxford Road was purchased in 1960, and in successive years 90 Canterbury Street and 92 Huntingdon Road. The location of the Fitzwilliam Street properties was not the only good reason for disposing of them: in 1961, the basement of 22 Fitzwilliam Street had been declared unfit for human habitation by the Medical Officer of Health! In 1963 the five houses in Fitzwilliam Street were auctioned, and purchased by Peterhouse.

The Members of the Fitzwilliam Hall Trust were trustees for assets held for the Trust itself, for assets held on behalf of the Amalgamated Clubs, and for cash held for the Fitzwilliam Society; in 1964, they returned about £2,000 to the Society. For the Clubs, they were responsible for the Oxford Road sports ground, for Red Cottage and the adjacent Groundsman's House, and for the boathouse (which had been purchased in 1958). The categories of responsibilities were separated in February 1970 when, by a Deed of Appointment, the Master, Fellows and Scholars of Fitzwilliam College became the trustees for the assets related to the Junior Members' Association (successor to the Clubs).

The other assets were transferred separately. The investment portfolio was sold and the proceeds, together with the student houses near to the College, were transferred to the College. The Trust went into voluntary liquidation. However, its beneficial role lives on, as the Trust funds for student awards preserve a distinct existence in the Accounts of the College. The Trustees of the Fitzwilliam Hall Trust met for the last time in June 1971 – 50 years to the day after the original incorporation of the Trust – and afterwards celebrated with a good dinner in College.

The trappings of collegiate status

To go with a Charter, a college needs a Coat of Arms. The Amalgamated Clubs and the House had used a combination of the University Arms and the Fitzwilliam Arms since 1887, without the blessing of the College of Heralds. The Heralds had noticed this omission in 1947; their challenge had been deflected by the University Registrary, who informed Chester Herald that Fitzwilliam House was not a corporation but 'an unincorporated fluctuating body of persons' – an expression that infuriated Thatcher!

Nineteen years later, that Registrary had become the first Master; Fitzwilliam College was corporate, and the matter could be put off no longer. At its very first meeting, the Governing Body agreed that authority should be sought to use the existing Coat of Arms. The Kings of Arms responded that they would find difficulty in assigning the Arms to the College unless a link could be formed with the Earl Fitzwilliam. This could be by appointing him Patron of the College. All Fellows except for one radical member agreed that the Master should approach the Earl; he was delighted to accept, but pointed out: 'The connection between my family and the Fitzwilliam from whom the College takes its name is one which I have failed to unravel. The Viscount Fitzwilliam who founded the museum of that name of course comes from the Fitzwilliams of Merrion and does not in fact appear to have any connection with us, but as the device of our Coats of Arms is the same there must, undoubtedly, be a connection somewhere.' The Earl Fitzwilliam was appointed Patron in 1972, with little time to spare: he died in 1979 without issue (the last Viscount had died in 1833).

The College of Heralds completed the design with a crest which differed from that of the Fitzwilliam family, and the Grant of Arms was made by Letters Patent on 31 December 1973. The 250-guinea cost was underwritten by the Fitzwilliam Society, as part of their £500 gift to the College to mark the 1969 centenary.

The Amalgamation Club must have taken the Arms from the Viscount, as they took his motto *Deo adjuvante non timendum*. The Fitzwilliam Society favoured its retention, but a competition was launched; the Governing Body and the junior members favoured a submission from R.W. Sharples, Research Fellow in Classics, and A.G. Hunt: *Ex antiquis et novissimis optima*.

So an expensive piece of parchment was created, and passed to the Master in May 1974 by Norray and Ulster King of Arms. The College was heraldically legitimate.

The Grant of Arms

SILVER DONATIONS TO MARK COLLEGIATE STATUS

Collegiate status was marked in a traditional manner, by gifts of silver from members, from friends, and from other institutions. The College collection was greatly enhanced, as several pieces were commissioned from Gerald Benney, probably the most distinguished twentieth-century British goldsmith and silversmith. Benney was born in 1930, studied at the Royal College of Art, and produced both exquisite individually-commissioned pieces and highly innovative designs for mass production. A characteristic feature of his work is the hammered 'bark' texture: a very durable work-hardened surface, reducing fingerprinting and tarnishing, and contrasting with plain, highly-polished regions (p. 48).

The first piece was donated in 1963 by the Master and Fellows of Emmanuel College; it is a deep, rectangular salver, and the least characteristically Benney piece in the collection. The Master and Fellows of

Trinity Hall donated a rose-water bowl in 1965; this one of a coordinated group of pieces commissioned by several donors. The Founding Fellows of the College donated the coffee and milk jugs – beautiful, but exceedingly heavy when full; after dinner, it is the custom that the most junior Fellow serves the other Fellows, and serving a large gathering provides a very adequate substitute for a visit to the gym. A cream jug, a sugar bowl and spoon, and a tray, were presented by members of the House resident in Malaysia (p. 66). A matching water jug was donated by Mrs Armstrong (p. 85).

To complement these pieces, a pair of candelabra by Benney was donated in 1970 by an alumnus, J.N.G. Findlay (1937); they are very dramatic, with tall, slender spikes.

At around the same time, the Master and Fellows of Selwyn College presented a Loving Cup, and St Edmund's House presented a salver.

III

BUILDING THE COLLEGE

7

A NEW START
IN A NEW LOCATION

University purchase and subdivision of The Grove estate

The University began to plan for the post-war era in 1943, anticipating exceptional entry numbers. The Non-Collegiate Students Board sought additional space, and in March 1944 stated explicitly that a new and larger building was needed. They favoured developing Trumpington Street, but recognized that it might be necessary to move elsewhere.

The pace slowed and in 1947 the Board enquired of the Council of the Senate whether they could start planning a new building. No action, but in Easter 1948 the Council appointed a committee to consider the needs of the House. They concluded that 'a new and much larger building was required for Fitzwilliam House, and that it should provide rooms for the Censor and Tutors, a Reading Room, a Writing Room, Supervision rooms, and a Common Room, and a Dining Hall. The Committee considered that in no circumstances could the accommodation available at Fitzwilliam House be made to provide satisfactorily for a student population of 300.' They considered a move to the outskirts of Cambridge, but felt that the site should be within easy reach of the town centre, for the sake of corporate life.

The first notion was to build on the Sidgwick Site, but the Board took the firm view that the House should be residential – if that was not possible there, then they would prefer to remain adjacent to the Fitzwilliam Street houses. They 'urgently begged of the Council that provision should be made for another suitable site e.g. the Huntingdon Road / Oxford Road site near the playing fields of Fitzwilliam House which can give the full accommodation deemed necessary by the Board'.

This mention of the Huntingdon Road did not refer to The Grove, or presage a rapid approach to it. There began a trawl around potential sites, including Clarkson Road and Herschel Road (later used by Girton and by

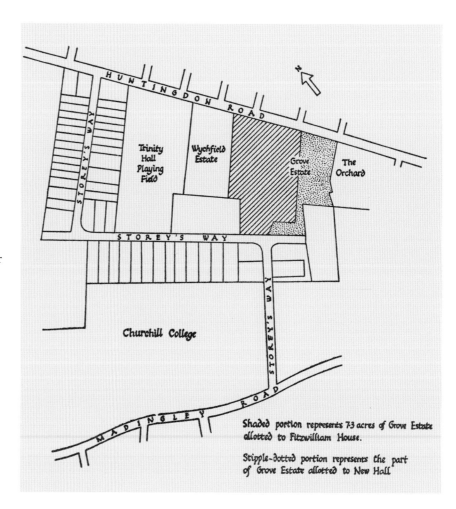

Robinson). Bredon House on Barton Road (now part of Wolfson) was recommended by the Council of the Senate in its *Report on the Future of Fitzwilliam House* in the summer of 1951, but 'It is clear, however, that no steps can be taken toward their implementation until the financial position of the University permits.' It did not permit, and an emasculated Report was published in May 1952, vaguely recommending that 'the general approval of the University be given to the policy of encouraging the

Allocation of The Grove estate to Fitzwilliam and New Hall

The Grove estate in 1830, from the map by R.G. Baker

corporate life of Fitzwilliam House by the provision of new administrative headquarters and residential accommodation'.

The question of the site went into abeyance whilst the matter of the survival of Fitzwilliam House was considered, to be revived after the Memorial was submitted. The Grove, on Huntingdon Road, was drawn to the attention of the Bursar and was first viewed in July 1954. There was a snag: New Hall owned an adjacent plot, but it was insufficient and they wanted The Grove as well; they showed flexibility, so in July 1958 the University Treasurer was able to announce to the Board that 'negotiations for a site for Fitzwilliam House and for the funds required to build a new administrative block were now almost completed. It seemed certain that an agreement would be reached between the University and Mrs W.J. Armstrong for the purchase of 10.8 acres of land on the Huntingdon Road, known as The Grove.' Part of the site was allocated to New Hall, and Mrs Armstrong would retain the house and part of the grounds during her lifetime.

With the site arranged and UGC funding in place, it was possible to select an architect. On the advice of the Professor of Architecture, Leslie Martin, and the University's Director of Estate Management, four architectural practices were invited to make presentations to the Building Committee. Rather than have a full competition, the Committee recommended the appointment of Denys Lasdun.

The report of the Council of the Senate on *New Buildings for Fitzwilliam House* was published in the *Reporter* for 25 July 1960. This referred back to their reports from 1952 and 1954 in which they indicated 'their general policy for the promotion of the well-being of Fitzwilliam House' and announced that the Financial Board had allocated just under 7½ acres of The Grove estate to Fitzwilliam House, together with a further half acre of adjoining land which was being acquired. They also indicated the outline plan (p. 88), assuming a development sequence for a college with 400 under-graduates, of whom half would be accommodated on site.

So they recommended that 'the plans prepared by Mr Denys Lasdun, FRIBA, and now displayed in the Old Schools ... for Stage I of the new buildings for Fitzwilliam House ... be approved and that the Financial Board be authorized to accept a tender'. It was approved on 29 October 1960. Lasdun and his team could go ahead with the attempt to reconcile Fitzwilliam's needs with the very limited available funds.

The Grove estate

At the beginning of the nineteenth century, the site of Fitzwilliam College was part of the West Fields outside Cambridge, unenclosed land forming an agricultural landscape that had not changed significantly for more than five centuries. Then the open fields in the parish of St Giles were enclosed; parcels of land were allocated to existing users and to those with rights to the revenues of the land. Allocation was undertaken by three Commissioners, of whom one was William Custance, a builder, land developer and surveyor who had drawn up a map of Cambridge in 1798. The Commissioners allocated 33 acres, including a 15-acre plot alongside the Huntingdon Road, to a Jacob Smith, who became the second-largest private landowner in the parish; by 1811, Smith had sold

The Grove from the south

the 15-acre plot to Custance – a pair of transactions that, in retrospect, look altogether too convenient.

Custance's plot was accessed from the Huntingdon Road. Baker's 1830 map of Cambridge shows it, together with an L-shaped plot enclosing it to the south and the west which had been allocated to the Storey's Charity (which supported alms-houses). Storey's Way was laid out in 1910; the houses on it were built over the next twenty years, five of them designed by the notable Arts and Crafts architect Hugh Baillie Scott.

William Custance built The Grove on the 15-acre plot; the original house was rectangular, symmetrically disposed about the main entrance. The year 1813 is carved into the cellar brickwork, whilst rainwater heads bear his initials and 1814. The entrance-hall, stair-hall and the rooms on the north-west side – including those now known as the Stapleton Room and the Senior Combination Room – are original. In the mid-nineteenth century the house was extended to the south-east, increasing the area by about half, and was partially re-modelled to provide the three-sided bay which looks down the lime-tree avenue towards Storey's Way.

Custance died in 1841. The property remained in his family until it was sold at auction in 1878 for £8,500. Four years later, it was purchased for Emma Darwin, the widow of Charles Darwin, by two of her elder sons. Emma Darwin wished to be able to live near her younger sons, Frank and Horace. Her grand-daughter, Gwen Raverat, takes up the account: 'After my grandfather's death, Grandmamma spent the winters in Cambridge, at The

Grove, a large house on the Huntingdon Road. It was surrounded by great park-like meadows, and here both Uncle Frank and Uncle Horace built themselves houses: Wychfield and The Orchard. It was a lovely place, where the children and Grandmamma's cows and carriage-horses, and Frances's donkeys all wandered about under the trees.'

Horace Darwin was the co-founder of the Cambridge Scientific Instrument Company, and was looked down on by the family for engaging in trade. As Gwen Raverat wrote: 'A fact about Uncle Horace, which set him in a most amiable light, was that he had the greatest difficulty in learning to spell well enough to pass the Little Go. ... It was understood by us children that Uncle Horace and Mr Dew Smith had started a sort of concern called *The Shop*, where they made clocks and machines and things; and where we hoped that poor spelling would not matter much.' In its heyday, the company played a key role in the development of scientific and industrial instruments, including the first commercial scanning electron microscope in serial production.

Horace's daughters, Lady Nora Barlow and Mrs Ruth Rees Thomas, were leaders in the campaign for women's university education, and in 1953 gave The Orchard and four acres of land to provide a site for New Hall; the house was demolished.

The Grove was sold on the death of Emma Darwin in 1896, 'and then the children felt very much injured at having to be content with their own large gardens instead of roving about over the whole domain; and they were particularly insulted by having to go out onto the common, vulgar road to get from one house to the other. They sat in a row on the fence and solemnly cursed the new owners.' The man they cursed was Charles Armstrong, who owned the Star Brewery in Newmarket Road.

In 1934, Armstrong married his second wife, the widowed Mrs Winifred Reynolds, but lived only five more years. Winifred Armstrong retained a life interest in The Grove when the site was purchased by the University – on her death in 1988, the house and its grounds were re-integrated with the grounds of the College. Mrs Armstrong was a good friend to the College and to its members, particularly to the junior members whom she allowed to hold summer garden parties in the grounds, and she marked Fitzwilliam's attainment of collegiate status by the donation of a splendid silver jug (p. 79).

Mrs Armstrong also owned Atholl Lodge, 74 Storey's Way, on the corner opposite Fitzwilliam. She sold it to the College in 1973, having sold a strip of land as 74A in 1969. Atholl Lodge was used initially for the Chaplain and graduate students, but has been the Master's Lodge since 1988.

Denys Lasdun and his Plan

By the summer of 1960, an outline plan for the development of Fitzwilliam had been prepared by Denys Lasdun, and had been approved.

Lasdun was a modernist, inspired by Le Corbusier, who had worked with Berthold Lubetkin in the Tecton partnership. He undertook adventurous housing projects – from Bethnal Green to Green Park – as well as the headquarters of the Royal College of Physicians, generally regarded as his best work. Accounts emphasize his University of East Anglia buildings in Norwich and his College building at Christ's, but often neglect his work at Fitzwilliam; he seems not to have been especially proud of it, writing that it was '<u>NOT</u> one of my favourites'. Lasdun is most famous – or notorious – for the National Theatre on the South Bank, one of the best examples of *béton brut* architecture in England.

Lasdun's great accomplishment was to meet the major challenges of the low budget and the partial availability of the site. Buildings would be constructed in stages; the

The Grove in the 1930s: Head Gardener, William Bowler, with the house cow; Huntingdon Road in the background

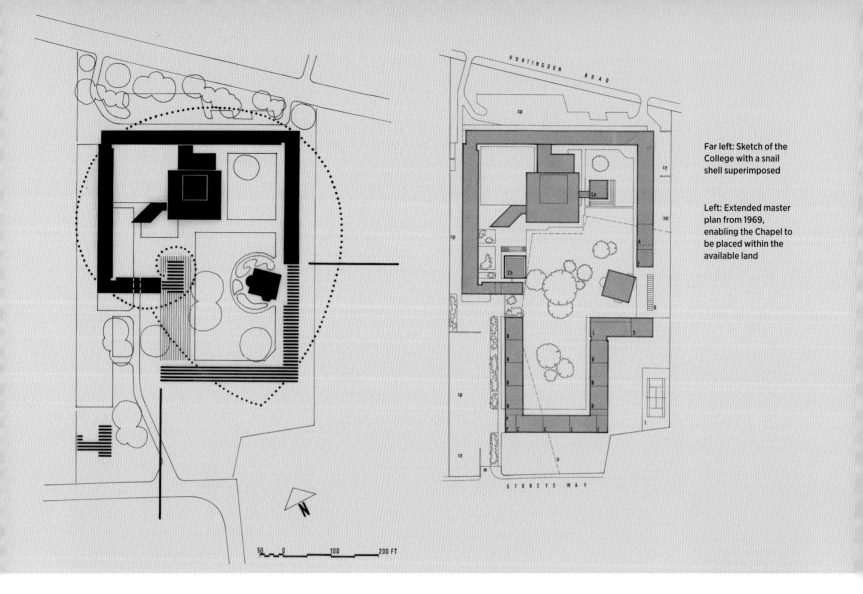

Far left: Sketch of the College with a snail shell superimposed

Left: Extended master plan from 1969, enabling the Chapel to be placed within the available land

College had to be viable from the start, and acceptable visually both initially and as it grew. The notion of growth led to the analogy of a snail shell, focused on the chapel: as it grew, the squared-off spiral of residential blocks would remain consistent in form, with student rooms at similar distances from the Hall.

It is very fortunate that the original Lasdun plan was not implemented in its entirety. The treatment of The Grove – without surrounding space to do justice to it and its gardens – would have been regrettable. Very serious constraints had been built in. It was designed for construction in stages, but after the last stage there was nowhere further for the snail-shell spiral to extend, leaving a substantial proportion of the students off the College site. And space and amenities were seriously inadequate.

Lasdun addressed these limitations in a further master-plan in 1969, driven by the desire to build a chapel without delay (p. 95). He departed from the snail-shell concept, with an additional U-shaped court with about fourteen staircases on the Storey's Way side, and this time

allowed sufficient space for The Grove. But the Chapel fell awkwardly within the available land, and adding accommodation was contingent on acquiring the gardens of The Grove; nothing was done.

The first and second stages of construction

Stage I construction provided the central block with the Hall, Combination Rooms, Library, and Reddaway Room, together with the north-western part of the Huntingdon Road range (Staircases G–J, as currently designated; the letter sequence was reversed after New Court was built), with Fellows' rooms, offices, and the first 20 under-graduate rooms. The University Grants Committee had agreed to fund the buildings and furnishings, costing about £300,000.

The Non-Collegiate Students Board took over the site in August 1960, and Sindall and Co., a local firm, completed preparatory works in June 1961. The main contractor was Johnson and Bailey, also local. Their tender was £20,000 in excess of the grant, but the UGC provided £12,500 more; £7,500 was found by economies.

The bell of HMS *Ocean*, a light fleet aircraft carrier laid down in 1945 and scrapped in 1962 – presented to Fitzwilliam by Admiral of the Fleet Sir Caspar John, who was First Sea Lord in 1963

During the construction of the Lasdun buildings, Ray Kelly built up an extensive collection of photographs.

STAGE I

Left: Dr Grave amidst a demolished house on Storey's Way

Right: Start of work on the Hall Block; The Grove is beyond the boundary fence

Far right: Library windows

Left: Precast concrete segments for the Hall roof

Right and below: The Hall under construction

Stage I complete, from Huntingdon Road

STAGE II Starting work on the Trinity Hall side

Work proceeded almost to schedule, so the buildings were essentially complete in time for the 1963 Michaelmas term. However, the Hall block was used earlier for the May Week Revue, and for General Admission lunch in Hall.

The Stage II plans, submitted to the UGC in August 1962, were well received. More accommodation was to be built than had been envisaged, because the *Report of the Committee on Higher Education* (chaired by Lord Robbins) had proposed a substantial increase in the number of students at universities. Cambridge was to play its part, and the Board agreed a permanent increase of 60 men, provided that the proportion living in College was

maintained at one half. So Stage II provided 195 bed-sitting rooms for undergraduates, as well as more rooms for Fellows, a room for meetings of the Governing Body of the College, and an additional recreation room. The UGC support was slightly insufficient, and the University made up the shortfall.

Not everyone was enthusiastic. When the *Second Report of the Council of the Senate on New Buildings for Fitzwilliam* came up in a Discussion, classical archaeologist Dr Hugh Plomer commented: 'no one seems to have a good word for Fitzwilliam House. Everyone seems weary of its stunted, seemingly gutted elevations and its sad-coloured brickwork. ... Our modern buildings in Cambridge are dull, Fitzwilliam perhaps the dullest of all.' Despite Plomer, the Grace was approved and Stage II construction went ahead in 1964. It provided the remainder of the Huntingdon Road frontage (staircases D–F) and the two side ranges, on the New Hall side (A–C) and the Trinity Hall side (K–P). The archway between O and P, two floors high, provided a grand entrance to the College from the Storey's Way side.

The total cost to the UGC for Stages I and II was about £750,000. The Fitzwilliam Hall Trust gave a £2,000 supplement for panelling the Board Room, which was called The Trust Room.

The buildings provided some of the most interesting modern architecture in Cambridge, although they were almost unknown to the public. They worked surprisingly well, especially considering that the budget per room was under a third of that at Churchill and about half of that at New Hall. But not perfectly. There were design failures. The flat roofs leaked within five years. More dramatic was the cracking in 1971 of two of the great clerestory windows in the Hall – they remained in place but the Hall had to be closed for several months.

Apart from modifications in inconspicuous locations, the main alteration to the Lasdun buildings has been the first-floor in-filling of the archway between O and P staircases, removing the grand prospect of the Hall block through the original main entrance, but providing additional facilities for junior members and more Fellows' rooms.

After half a century, the time has come for more general refurbishment, so plans are being developed to enhance both the Hall block and the residential ranges, to ensure that an iconic piece of architecture continues to meet the needs of the College and its members.

Proposed development of the Fitzwilliam site. Stage I, solid black: the Hall block, rooms for senior members and staff, and about 20 undergraduates. Stage II, shaded: to accommodate about 180 undergraduates. Stage III, stipple-dotted: possible long-term development.

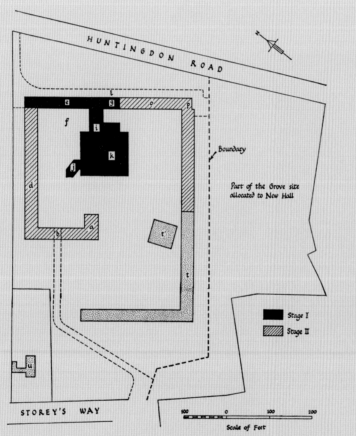

a. Chapel.
b. Main Gate.
d. Undergraduates' sets.
e. Senior Staff and Offices (until Stage II can be built, rooms for approximately 20 undergraduates will be temporarily provided in this section).
f. Garden and cloister.
g. Temporary Porter's Lodge.
i. Kitchen.
j. Parlour.

k. Hall, Library, Lecture Room, Entertaining Rooms, Junior Common Room, Research Students' Room, and Buttery.
l. Service road and service yard.
o. Undergraduates' sets.
p. Porter's Lodge.
t. Possible position of future buildings.
t'. Position of Grove House.
u. Possible position of lodge for Head of House on additional ½ acre which is being acquired.

EXPERIENCES OF THE FIRST RESIDENTS

Views from a student room, 1967: Looking towards Storey's Way (above) and looking inward (left)

Below: A common room with the black vinyl furniture so characteristic of the period

Bottom: The Storey's Way side in 1974

Only a few students were able to live in for 1963–64, but for those who did it was memorable. Chris Bradnock (1961) was one of them. 'Of course, new buildings have teething problems. For the residents, the most significant of these was the failure of the drains, which evidently were too small for purpose! The carefully-laid pipes all had to be replaced, which caused a few problems at the time, but the benefits of the new buildings overall were huge: a great location, the prospect of more and still more new buildings, lovely rooms, tastefully decorated and comfortably furnished, with summer temperatures throughout the year. ... The Dining Hall was particularly magical at night with the patterned ceiling reflecting on and on in the high glass surrounds which reached up to the concrete slabs above.'

Before then, Hugh Sharp (1961) was probably the first student to live in the new buildings. He recalled that 'at the end of the 1963 Summer Term I and two other members of the College were taken on as assistants to the gardener who was preparing the grounds around the new building. ... As I had no obvious place to live, the College very kindly allowed me to stay in one of the Tutors' suites.' There was no catering, and each morning he 'walked along for breakfast at a welcoming transport café at the top of Castle Hill.'

The first impression of Fitzwilliam for Anthony Inglese (1971) was when he came up for interview in 1970. 'The taxi from the station dropped me off outside the College on the Huntington Road. I didn't see a sign for the College and I rapidly concluded that the building in front of me could not possibly be a Cambridge College – I actually thought it was a warehouse.'

Roger Wilkins (1967) was conscious that completion was a long way off. 'With much of the College still to be built, the main entrance ... was still off Huntingdon Road ... . That the architect had decided that the main entrance was to be on the opposite side of the College, and that the back of the College was of no aesthetic significance (even though it was the side seen by the greatest number of people) meant that the view from the main road was ugly in the extreme.'

8

BUILDINGS AND GARDENS

Squash courts

The 1960s had seen immense progress; long-awaited dreams had been transformed into reality, with Fitzwilliam a college in occupation of its own new buildings. So in the 1970s there was some collective exhaustion, and perhaps less desire for endeavour. On his retirement in 1971, the hard-driving Grave had been replaced by the more emollient Miller – and there was little scope for hard driving, as funds were short and physical development constrained.

The master-plan devised by Lasdun for the College held absolute sway, and was contingent on acquiring The Grove; it seemed to provide a perfect excuse for avoiding consideration of development. However, as time passed, new Fellows were elected who were less imbued with the Lasdun concept and who were ambitious to restart the evolution of the College.

The liberation of the College from the Lasdun plan was initiated in 1977 by Dr David Bowyer, a pathologist who had been elected to a Fellowship just two years previously and who held the office of Steward. Lasdun had arranged routes which would be entirely rational once the master-plan had been fully implemented: the College and all the public routes would face Storey's Way; the service routes, particularly for kitchen supplies and waste, would be directed towards Huntingdon Road. Categories of traffic would be segregated. No direct public route was provided between Fellows' Court and Tree Court, even though the most commonly used public entrance to the College was from Huntingdon Road into Tree Court. David managed to persuade the Services Committee that a doorway should be cut to link the courts, going through between the kitchens and the Huntingdon Road range – a convenient, if somewhat squalid, route. This small, symbolic step broke the spell: the Lasdun plan could be challenged.

David now initiated a larger campaign. A keen and able squash player, he was very conscious of the lack of courts at Fitzwilliam, at a time when most colleges

possessed two or three. He was able to carry opinion with him, and in the spring of 1978 the Governing Body agreed that the JMA Executive Trustees should consider building squash courts. Before the end of the academic year it had been established that Barclays would provide a loan, and contact had been made with Sir Denys Lasdun (knighted in 1976). In October 1978 a site was identified on the Storey's Way side of the College, away from the main buildings (approximately where Lasdun had envisaged the Master's Lodge). In retrospect, the location was not ideal, as it constrained the design of New Court.

The project became mired and there was little progress for fifteen months; relations with Lasdun were breaking down and, despite many approaches, he made no response. So another architect was contacted: David Roberts. A block of squash courts was, for him, a small commission, at the end of a very successful professional life. In earlier years, whilst simultaneously lecturing in the School of

The squash courts in 1984

Concept of a New
Court room, by
MacCormac Jamieson
and Prichard

Architecture, he had been responsible for many of the best modern college buildings in Cambridge, including Jesus North Court (1963–66) and Churchill Graduate Flats (1965), as well as much work for Magdalene, where he was a Fellow. Early in 1980, Roberts agreed to act and, by the end of the academic year, plans for a block of three courts were agreed by the Governing Body. An appeal for funds raised only a fraction of the cost.

The courts were completed in time for an informal opening in November 1981, enabling use before the vacation. The official opening, in January, included an exhibition match between Dr Robert Lethbridge, another keen squash player who played for the College team in his younger days, and Liz Makin (1979), the Captain of the Ladies Team. Neither can agree on who won!

New Court

Whilst the building of squash courts initiated the break with Lasdun, it also prompted the College to think in more ambitious terms, to see whether the student-accommodation crisis could be tackled. The Lasdun buildings could house only 215 out of about 450 under-graduates and 100 graduate students of the College. Only club officials and the few Scholars occupied rooms in College for more than one year; most undergraduates had only their first year in College. Elsewhere in Cambridge,

most undergraduates were guaranteed at least two years on site. The lodgings situation was becoming increasingly unsatisfactory, as landladies retired and died. The student intake had to be reduced, additional houses were purchased by the College, and some Fellows' accommodation reallocated and subdivided.

Increasing the accommodation and improving the College environment was seen by the Master, Professor James Holt, as a means for enhancing academic performance as well as bodily comfort. Most students were scattered around the town, and were denied the experience of living in an environment committed to the intellect. Even for those in College, the arrangements were not conducive to good academic performance. Perennially it was full of freshmen, who had only their peers to compare themselves with, and salutary experience and good advice were not passed down – each generation had to make its own mistakes.

The first scheme did not preclude subsequent compliance with the Lasdun master-plan, and was an economical expedient. To provide a further 100 rooms, it was proposed to put a lightweight floor over the existing buildings – this would also keep the rain out. A feasibility study was prepared by David Roberts, for consideration in October 1981. It was recognized to be necessary to consult Sir Denys Lasdun. This, unlike the squash court proposal,

Above: New Court: its relation to the squash courts, and its free end for extension

Below: New Court opening by Edmund Dell, with Professor Holt

produced a response: he was negative in general, and specifically cited structural issues. Another structural report was encouraging, as were discussions with the planning authority, so several architects were invited to a design competition. Lasdun, invited, responded that 'the brief was not capable of producing an acceptable architectural solution'.

Eventually a design was selected. In the Governing Body, the discussion was wide-ranging, but ultimately the meeting was swayed by the opposition of Dr Eric Warner, who made a passionate defence of the architectural integrity of the Lasdun buildings. Eric was an American who taught English Literature and who had strongly warmed to all aspects of his recently-adopted country, including its 1960s architecture; he achieved the preservation of Lasdun's original design, as a prime exemplar of its period.

The proposal for an extra floor was not in vain, however; it ended the perceived stranglehold of the Lasdun plan. The Fellowship had gained confidence and considered substantial and expensive projects; it was imbued with a new spirit of dynamism, ready to make the

This building was erected by Old Members of Fitzwilliam
and by friends and benefactors of the College
in memory of
W. S. THATCHER M.A.
Censor of Fitzwilliam House 1924-54
It was opened on 29th September 1986 by
THE RT. HON. EDMUND DELL

best use of available resources to tackle the critical problem of accommodation. So discussion opened up on constructing a free-standing building, not delaying until the grounds of The Grove became available, but using all the land accessible to the College.

So in October 1983 a decision in principle was taken to build a free-standing block with between 50 and 60 rooms at a cost not in excess of £1.5 million. Five architects were selected for interview, and the recommendation of MacCormac Jamieson and Prichard was endorsed by the Governing Body.

Richard MacCormac has been prolific in both Cambridge and Oxford, and was responsible for the master-plan for the University West Cambridge site (1997). Notable buildings in Cambridge include Launcelot Fleming House for Trinity Hall (Wychfield, 1993) and, for Trinity College, Blue Boar Court (1989) and Burrell's Field (1995).

New Court was designed to be in keeping with the Lasdun buildings whilst having a strong character of its own and providing student accommodation of vastly greater quality and spaciousness – with pitched roofs to keep the rain out. Its stepped façade provides very interesting fenestration, giving bright, airy rooms with a wide variety of shapes and with good views both of the range itself and of the rest of the College.

The new building blocked a few student-room windows in the Lasdun range, but rearrangement provided additional communal space. Tenders were received early in 1985, at about 6% over the nominal cost; the final cost was £1,686,000. This gave 90 spacious rooms, almost all for undergraduates. And good communal facilities on every staircase: rooms where students could cook and sit down together. A great step forward – for everything except the finances of the College kitchens.

New Court was dedicated to the memory of W.S. Thatcher, and was opened by the Rt. Hon. Edmund Dell just in time for the 1986–87 academic year. It received the 1989 David Unwin Award for Best New Building; justifiably, as it was a highly successful project, providing some of the best-regarded rooms in the College and transforming the accommodation. Whereas the Lasdun building was utterly of its period, the MacCormac design has a timeless quality and is as freshly attractive as when it was built.

New Court façade

although never enough space, as room sizes are domestic rather than institutional.

Before The Grove could be used, a very major project was the restoration of the elaborate plastering and gilding on the ground floor; this was made possible by

Left: The Grove: starting the restoration

Below: The Grove staircase

Completion of the site – The Grove refurbished

When Mrs Armstrong died in 1988, The Grove and its gardens could be integrated into the College site, opening up the prospect of completing the College. Further buildings were for the future, but there were immediate issues to resolve. Even though members of the College had ogled The Grove over the six-foot board fence for three decades, there was no plan to implement: it would have been unseemly to investigate the property during Mrs Armstrong's long lifetime.

The house is grade-II listed, imposing constraints on modification. And, as Mrs Armstrong's needs had diminished over the years, so had the proportion of the house in regular use. Much restoration and redecoration was needed to realize its potential. But in what way was it to benefit the College? It had been anticipated that it would become the Master's Lodge, with flats for academic visitors. However, shortly before Mrs Armstrong died, 74 Storey's Way had been converted for the Master.

As 1989 progressed, it was decided to accommodate graduate students on the first floor and in the attic, with access by the back stairs; later to transfer the Senior Combination Room and some administrative functions. So the Master, his secretary, the Senior Tutor, and the lead Graduate Tutor acquired the principal first-floor rooms; the principal ground-floor rooms became the main reception rooms for the College; and the remainder of the ground floor became the Middle Combination Room for the graduate students. Both Fellows and Graduates acquired space of much higher quality than they had enjoyed in the Hall block; space with strong character,

Above: The Grove:
ceiling of the
Stapleton Room

Right: Interior of the
first temporary
Chapel

a substantial benefaction by Nigel Stapleton, and a
principal reception room was designated the Stapleton
Room to recognize his generosity.

Now, as The Grove enters its third century, it stands
amongst its long-established gardens at the heart of
Fitzwilliam, contrasting but also harmonizing with the
generations of modern architecture that surround it.

The Chapel

The chapel in the original Lasdun plan could be built
only when The Grove became available. But a chapel had
been an accustomed feature since 1913, and for many
members was an integral part of communal life.

The immediate need was met by characteristic
improvisation. An ex-RAF prefabricated building of
asphalt-impregnated fibreboard was re-erected as a
temporary chapel. It was inconvenient and insecure,
and the flooring admitted mud; Peter Nott (Chaplain
1964–69) later said of it, 'On bad days it was like the
Western Front in 1916, but those who attended felt
righteous'. It lasted until Stage II of the Lasdun buildings
had been completed. These included a Recreation Room
in the corner above the Huntingdon Road Porters' Lodge
which was used as a chapel from Michaelmas 1966,
serving Fitzwilliam well for more than two decades.

The situation was complicated because a former
officer of Fitzwilliam House wished to fund a chapel. As
an undergraduate, Ian Rawlins had read Physics at Trinity;
he supervised for Fitzwilliam from 1929 and directed
studies in Physical Sciences from 1931 to 1934 (p. 45).
Subsequently, he pioneered scientific techniques at the
National Gallery. In 1964, he donated £10,000; three years
later he gave £10,000 and notified the College that it
would be his residuary legatee, then £40,000 in 1968. He
died in May 1969.

*This Chapel
was built in 1990
through the generosity
of Mr F.I.G. RAWLINS CBE
Director of Studies
in Natural Sciences
at Fitzwilliam House
1931–1934*

Rawlins had wished for brisk action, so Lasdun tried to squeeze a chapel into the available site (p. 86) but it was very close to the existing buildings; in 1970 it was agreed to wait until the full site was available.

Eighteen years later, when The Grove was reunited with the College, the Rawlins Fund had attained about £707,000. The benefaction was an embarrassment in some quarters: funds for primary college functions were short; the College already had an effective chapel; and many Fellows were secular – not militantly as in Churchill, which located its chapel in the most remote part of the grounds – but perceiving it as misguided and certain to

absorb resources in the future. Could funds be diverted? The terms of the bequest were specific, and it had been made recently; the young Law Fellow Andrew Grubb confirmed that it had to be used exclusively for the construction of a chapel.

In consequence of the great success of New Court, an architectural study was commissioned from MacCormac Jamieson and Prichard. Plans were presented in January 1989, and approved by the Governing Body. The first service was conducted in February 1992 by Peter Nott (p. 146; by then, Bishop of Norwich), and the Chapel was dedicated in April in the ecumenical presence of the Bishop of Ely, the Roman Catholic Bishop of East Anglia, and the President of the Methodist Conference.

The circular exterior form of the Chapel provides a well-defined inner end to the Lasdun spiral, and fits beautifully into the gardens of The Grove, with the magnificent plane tree outside its expansive East Window dominating the view over the altar. The effect is heightened since the Chapel is on the first-floor level, with the Crypt on the ground floor. MacCormac employed a similar circular plan for his Ruskin Library at Lancaster University, a few years later.

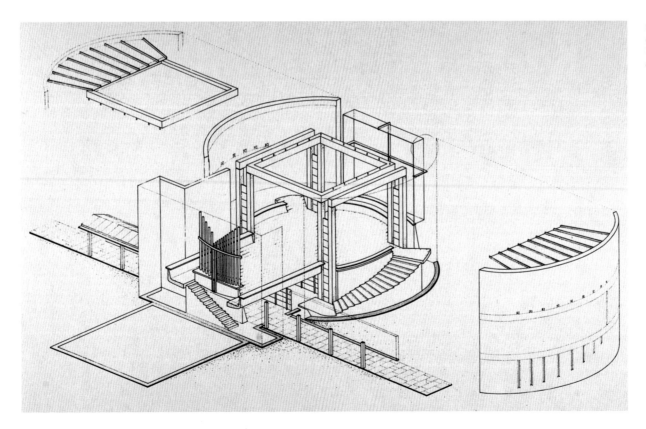

Exploded schematic of the Chapel, by MacCormac, Jamieson and Prichard

**The Chapel and
the plane tree**

Internally, the Chapel is more complex. MacCormac saw it as a ship – an ark – with the wood of the floor and the surrounding parapet forming the hull. The crypt ceiling, underneath, is planked to heighten the analogy. He described the concept: 'In the Christian symbolism of medieval manuscripts, the ship signifies the way of salvation. More literally the scheme draws on the Oslo Viking Ship Museum and the Vasa Ship Museum in Stockholm, where wooden vessels are contained and sheltered by buildings. The building itself is a combination of orthogonal structure and a round enclosure. The plan can be read as a cross, projecting from the residential building, clasped by two arcs. The cruciform is embodied in the raised floor of the Chapel which is supported by four pairs of columns which in turn support the roof.'

The Chapel was widely acclaimed for its design and for its workmanship. It won a Civic Trust Award in 1992, and in 1993 the David Unwin Award for Best New Building and The Carpenters Award, from the Worshipful Company of Carpenters, English Heritage, and other Timber and Wood Federations, 'in recognition of the excellence of design and execution in the joinery work at the Chapel of Fitzwilliam College, Cambridge, judged to be the outstanding example of craftsmanship in a major project'. Richard MacCormac received his knighthood in 2001.

The new chapel and its choir needed an organ, and in 1991 the leading British firm of Peter Collins were given the task of fitting a modestly-sized but versatile instrument into the striking geometric case designed by Dorian Wiszniewski. The inaugural recital was given by Stephen Cleobury, Organist of King's College.

Both visually and musically, the organ fits the building perfectly, and it has proved its worth over 20 years of use by a dozen talented Organ Scholars. As Dr Nicholas Thistlethwaite, the instrument's design consultant, wrote in 1993, 'the College may be proud of its new acquisition which is both an ornament to a remarkable building and a musical work of art for the delight and instruction of many generations of organists.'

Above: Going up to the Chapel

Above right: The East end

Below: The Chapel crypt

Right: The West end and the organ

Above: Wilson Court

Right: Peter Wilson –
bronze by David Wynne

Below right: Aerial view of
the College after
completion of Wilson
Court

Wilson Court

Professor Gordon Cameron, elected Master in 1988, was
in close touch with the professional institution in his
field, the Royal Institution of Chartered Surveyors. Peter
Wilson, a Chartered Surveyor, sold the weekly *Estates
Gazette* in 1990 for nearly £60 million, and Cameron
suggested that Wilson might wish to endow a centre for
the training and further education of surveyors, located
in the College; the College would have the use of the
accommodation in term-time. The arrangements were
made through RICS, which in November 1990 offered a
donation of £2.5 million for the construction of a
building, which was opened in 1995. Wilson was made
an Honorary Fellow in 1997; he died in 2010.

The new buildings, named Wilson Court and including
the Gordon Cameron Lecture Theatre – in memory of
Professor Cameron after his early death – were used by
the Cambridge International Land Institute (CILI). The
original agreement for shared use was to run for 100 years,
with the College having exclusive use thereafter, but CILI
had financial problems and the period of the agreement
was reduced to 25 years in 2002; finally it lapsed, when
CILI went into liquidation in 2011.

Wilson Court was designed by van Heyningen &
Haward, architects whose work in Cambridge includes
Newnham College Rare Books Library in 1982, and
additions to Clare College Memorial Court in 2009. The
buildings provided 48 student rooms (the first in College
with en-suite bathrooms); seminar rooms; offices and a
flat for CILI; and the lecture theatre. Wilson Court won
a RIBA Award in 1996.

Left: The Gatehouse from Storey's Way

Below: The Auditorium and the Gatehouse

Bottom: The Auditorium

Gatehouse Court and the Auditorium

As the end of the century approached and needs for accommodation and facilities had not been assuaged, the College began to consider further building. Some external funding was available, from a Japanese educational foundation, Tsuzuki Gakuen Group, whose students attend Summer Schools in English Language whilst Fitzwilliam graduates go to the Japan University of Economics (p. 178). Donations from Tsuzuki totalled about £1.7 million, much of it linked to building an auditorium.

The ambition was to turn the College to face Storey's Way – the original concept for the site – but design was complicated by the lime-tree avenue leading to The Grove; how could it be integrated into the scheme? The Governing Body gave repeated consideration to a project for a new gatehouse and auditorium, and after several iterations the architects Allies and Morrison were selected. They had designed other college buildings, for Newnham (1995) and Girton (2004), and were undertaking major University buildings. The scheme provided for a Gatehouse Court with residential and office accommodation, together with an auditorium which would, with seating retracted, serve as a multi-purpose hall. The project was not without controversy, as some Fellows considered that building an auditorium implied undue emphasis on conferences – which are disruptive but generate indispensable revenue. They avoided the term Auditorium and referred to it as the Theatre, emphasizing its use for student activities. Gatehouse Court also exposed differences of view. The project presented an opportunity to establish a central office with good direct communications between the Tutorial, the Bursarial, and the

Admissions staff; this was rejected, retaining the traditional pattern of offices scattered around the College.

Gatehouse Court provides the impressive main entrance to Storey's Way that the College had lacked; the clerestory above the entrance hall adds to the impression of spaciousness, and when illuminated is a prominent feature at night. Its two wings provide a mix of office space and 38 student rooms. It follows New Court in its brick

Right: Interior of the Auditorium, showing swing-out acoustic panels

Below right: Auditorium seating retracted for badminton

and mortar colouring, but makes more use of external timber. It was completed just in time for Michaelmas 2003.

The 250-seat Auditorium was designed to integrate spatially with Gatehouse Court, but with a contrasting brick colour and with metal cladding that refers back to Lasdun. It is very versatile, not only because it can be used as a flat hall, but also in its use as an auditorium – acoustically it is bright, with large areas of hard surface, but at the sides there are rows of swing-out acoustic-absorption panels to provide variable damping so that it is excellent for any purpose from an individual speaker or a solo instrument, to a chamber quartet, to a full orchestra.

Gatehouse Court was highly commended in the Small Project of the Year Quality Award, whilst *Building* made awards to Allies and Morrison as Architectural Practice of the Year and to Keir (parent company of Marriott, the contractor) as Major Contractor of the Year.

The new Library

When the first Lasdun buildings came into service in 1963, the Library provided vastly more space than was needed for the few books transferred from Trumpington Street. This changed rapidly: Dr Denis New, reporting as Fellow Librarian to the Governing Body in 1992, emphasized dire shortage of space and sought the old Senior Combination Room (vacated by the move to The Grove) as a Law Library.

Bookshelves were packed into all available spaces so tightly that readers were disrupted when access was needed; shelves were filled solid – new acquisitions were possible only if stock was withdrawn. There were about 33,000 books, about 4,000 bound journal volumes and a similar number unbound; this placed Fitzwilliam relatively low amongst the colleges both for total stock and for the number of volumes per student. However, the

Below: The original Library when new ...

... and solidly packed at the end, right

Far left top: Excavations and basement of the New Library

Far left bottom: Ready to cast the first floor

Left: The Master topping-out the new Library, with encouragement from the Bursar

Below: New Library top-floor bookstacks; the Law section

stock, managed by professional Librarian Marion MacLeod, was well-chosen and current, a useful working library for undergraduates.

Space for readers was completely inadequate, especially at examination time; without carrels, it was poor for extended work with many books and papers. Growth was essential, either elsewhere in the Hall building or by constructing a completely new library.

The situation changed in 2001, when an alumnus proposed to donate funds for a new Library and Information Technology Centre. This substantial and highly generous offer was taken up, and the Fellow Librarian and the Computing Officer (Dr John Cleaver and Dr Richard Ansorge) prepared a proposal to double the Library capacity, and to bring together the scattered IT facilities. There would be simultaneous access to books, journals and IT, and people would be able to work in groups without causing disturbance.

In July 2002, the Governing Body passed the proposal to the New Buildings Committee, envisaging that funds would be available the following summer. The Committee recommended Edward Cullinan Architects. Cullinan had done very impressive work elsewhere in Cambridge, in particular the Centre for Mathematical Sciences and the

Right: Individual working positions in the tower

Far right top: The Norman Pounds Special Collections Room

Far right bottom: The Ray Kelly Reading Room

adjacent Betty and Gordon Moore Library, and the Divinity Faculty building. Ten years previously, he had designed the much-admired Library for St John's College. The Governing Body agreed to appoint Cullinan, but then disaster struck – the donor was unable to liquidate assets at a suitable price.

While the new Library was in limbo, there were two very important developments. The Bursar, Christopher Pratt, increased the liquidity of the College by taking out a very substantial long-term bank loan fixed at the prevailing low rate of interest, and Professor Robert Lethbridge became Master. From his days as Senior Tutor, Lethbridge had been very strongly committed to the intellectual development of the College and recognized the pivotal role that the new Library and IT Centre could play, directly as a resource and indirectly by enhancing the College environment, focusing the aspirations of its members. So the decision was taken to proceed: this highly-important project could be completed from reserves even without support.

The Library and IT Centre provides more than 200 study positions. Many are individual; they provide impressive views across the College grounds, so students can sit and stare in search of inspiration. In this splendid working environment, with several styles of study space, they often have favourite locations. There are three floors of books, and reader positions in a tower extend up to a

ANCIENT FITZWILLIAM

Before a building can be constructed, archaeologists must have an opportunity to investigate the site; clients hope for something interesting – but not so interesting that construction is affected.

When the Auditorium was being built, just a few traces of a ditch were found. But the new Library is closer to the Huntingdon Road, the ancient ridgeway alignment of the Roman highway which led to the north-west gate of the small Roman town, built over the Iron Age hill-fort at the top of Castle Hill.

The investigation revealed that the College site has been occupied since the Bronze Age, with worked antlers, Iron Age pottery fragments, Roman cattle bones, and Medieval pottery. An ideal quantity of archaeological material: enough to enable the Bursar to claim, in the *Fitzwilliam Journal* for 2008, that Fitzwilliam has the oldest occupied College site in Cambridge; not enough to delay the Library.

fourth floor, whilst computer rooms and other study areas are in the basement. The fenestration provides good illumination whilst avoiding glare on computer screens, and the building has been designed to very high environmental standards. The total shelf capacity is two-thirds greater than was available previously.

The new Library completes the site as currently envisaged. Cullinan fitted the Library onto the outer end of the Lasdun spiral, as MacCormac did the Chapel at the inner end; it makes use of the tower to enhance the connection to the original buildings. This is highly appropriate, since with Cullinan the architectural development of the site has come full circle – he worked in Lasdun's office and took part in the design of the original buildings for Fitzwilliam.

And in another way the story has come full circle. The intending donor passed to the College the assets that had been earmarked for the Library and IT Centre, and their liquidation was completed early in 2012, for over £2 million. Consequently, the building has been named The Olisa Library, in honour of the benefactors: Ken Olisa, who came to Fitzwilliam in 1971 and was Junior President – he is an active member of the Fitzwilliam Society and a venture-capital practitioner – and his wife Julia, an alumna of Homerton College.

Left and above: The Gardens of The Grove, c. 1905

The Gardens

In the beginning, shown in Baker's map of 1830 (p. 83), The Grove was set in extensive parkland. Wychfield and The Orchard took much of this land, and the grounds of The Grove were more elaborately and intensively planted, although still with room enough for a cow and the horses; its high point early in the twentieth century was recorded with a set of meticulously hand-coloured photographs.

Once the grounds had been divided and the first stage of the College completed, work started early on the gardens. In January 1964, Dr Hudson reported to the Meeting of Fellows that a plan for the shrubbery and the trees along the Huntingdon Road frontage had been drawn up by the Garden Committee. That was one of the few parts of the site where substantial planting was possible; amongst the Lasdun buildings there was little scope. The formality and austerity of the courts reflected the style of the buildings; plain, grassed in Fellows Court and Tree Court, lightly relieved with roses near the Senior Combination Room and with a variegated bed near to the kitchens. Paths ran immediately adjacent to students' rooms, completely disregarding privacy.

The situation changed radically when The Grove and its gardens became part of the College and a garden consultant, Andrew Peters, was engaged to develop the site and to unify the region between the house and Tree Court: not just a superficial re-design, but a unique opportunity to bring in heavy machinery and replace the original poor soil in the Court, before access was lost. A half-metre depth of high-quality top-soil was provided, and the profile of the sloping site was adjusted. Realigning paths permitted large beds in front of the staircases; the extensive work was facilitated by an unusually dry summer.

In front of The Grove, a new circular area paved with setts was linked by paths and steps to the rest of the College, emphasizing the two magnificent mature beech trees between the house and the Hall block. On the other side, a new lawn linked the house to the lime-tree avenue;

Contrast in gardens: the wooded grounds of The Grove, and the original austere courts of the College

Topiary snail

The Grove in winter

beyond the Middle Combination Room paving on the New Hall side a small formal garden was laid out, with herbs in formal beds demarcated by dwarf box hedging and brick paths.

The general form devised at that stage remains, and has been developed and adjusted to suit the needs of the subsequent buildings. In particular, the building of Gatehouse Court has given greater prominence to the lime-tree avenue, and the Auditorium is complemented by a sunken garden. When the new Library was built, the circular paved area in front of The Grove was lost, but the region between the fronts of the buildings has been extensively planted. The more private space at the East side of the Library is united with the box-hedged beds, whilst adjacent to the Murray-Edwards boundary a wild-flower meadow has been established.

Formal garden with box hedges, beside The Grove

Above: Tree Court two decades after remodelling, looking towards the new Library

Below: The new Library, from Tree Court

Bottom: The peaceful environment of the new Library

Above: The Grove, from Tree Court

Below: In front of the Old Senior Combination Room

Tree Court in autumn

Right and far right top: Graduate Hostel at 139 Huntingdon Road

Far right bottom: Graduate Hostel at Halifax Road

Building developments off site

The Fitzwilliam Hall Trust and the College often acquired houses opportunistically to meet urgent needs for accommodation. Over time, the external properties have been rationalized, with a concentration of undergraduate houses on Huntingdon Road directly opposite the College, and an adjacent purpose-built hostel on Westfield Road.

The purchase in 2010 of the former Cambridge Lodge Hotel on the corner of Huntingdon Road and Storey's Way has provided excellent rooms for graduate students, and has become the nucleus for a graduate colony. Directly opposite is Neale House (a fine Arts and Crafts house dating from 1911) and purpose-built units at its rear, now used for graduates.

Altogether, the College now has 613 units of accommodation. Undergraduates have 368 rooms in College and 63 in houses and hostels, whilst graduate students have 42 in College and 140 externally (of which 14 are for couples or families).

IV

FITZWILLIAM COLLEGE – THE FIRST FORTY YEARS

9

SENIOR MEMBERS

A gallery of Masters

Edward Miller was Master from 1971 to 1981. Born in 1915, he was a Johnian, taking his BA in History in 1937 and holding a Fellowship from 1939 to 1965, when he became Professor of Medieval History at the University of Sheffield. His time at St John's was interrupted by wartime service, with the Durham Light Infantry, the Royal Armoured Corps and the Control Commission for Germany. He died in 2000.

Sir James Holt was Master from 1981 to 1988. Born in 1922, he went to Bradford Grammar School; his studies were interrupted by wartime service in the Royal Artillery. On demobilization, he went up to The Queen's College, Oxford, and took his DPhil at Merton. After a spell at the University of Nottingham, where he became Professor of Medieval History in 1962, and a Chair at Reading from 1966 to 1978, he came to Cambridge as Professor of Medieval History and Fellow of Emmanuel. He specialized in the era of King John and Magna Carta, leavened with investigations of Robin Hood. A Yorkshire man, he is a keen follower of cricket and was an effective batsman for very many years. He was elected Fellow of the British Academy (FBA) in 1978, and received his knighthood in 1990.

Gordon Cameron was Master from 1988 to 1990. Born in 1937, he took his first degree in Economics at Durham. He was at Glasgow for many years, becoming Professor of Town and Regional Planning in 1974, and moving to Cambridge as Professor of Land Economy in 1980. He undertook a major overhaul of the Department, changing it from its traditional emphasis on rural estates, emphasizing urban issues, and adding law and economics. Cameron consulted widely, for bodies including the EEC, the OECD, and the World Bank. He died in 1990, only 18 months into his Mastership.

Alan Cuthbert was Master from 1991 to 1999. Born in 1932, he studied at Leicester College of Technology, then became an undergraduate at St Andrews, and took a PhD in London (as well as spending three years as a Royal Navy Instructor Lieutenant). He came to the Department of Pharmacology in Cambridge in 1963 as a Demonstrator, and became the Sheild Professor in 1979. He was a Fellow at Jesus from 1968 before coming to Fitzwilliam. He was elected FRS in 1982.

Brian Johnson was Master from 1999 to 2005, as well as being Acting Master after the death of Gordon Cameron. Born in 1938, he took his first degree and his PhD at Nottingham, and held lectureships at Manchester and UCL before coming to Cambridge in 1970. He was a Fellow of Fitzwilliam from 1970 to 1990, when he went to be Professor at Edinburgh. He returned as Cambridge Professor of Inorganic Chemistry in 1995, and resumed his Fellowship. He was elected FRS in 1991. He has been President of the Cambridge University Rugby Union Football Club.

Robert Lethbridge was Master from 2005 to 2013. Born in 1947, he graduated from the University of Kent at Canterbury before taking his PhD at St John's College, Cambridge. He was Fellow of Fitzwilliam from 1973 to 1994, serving as a Tutor for 17 years and as Senior Tutor for the decade 1982 to 1992. He was University Lecturer in French between 1980 and 1994, when he was appointed to the Chair of French Language and Literature at Royal Holloway, University of London. He was Vice-Principal there from 1998 to 2003, and subsequently Director of the University of London's British Institute in Paris, before returning to Cambridge in 2005. He was made *Commandeur dans l'Ordre des Palmes Académiques* by the French government in 2013.

Officers – and problems and tragedies

Fitzwilliam became a college just in time for the 1966 academic year, as a fully-functioning institution with a Master and Fellows, with College officers, and with the second phase of new buildings on Huntingdon Road.

Edward Miller, by Michael Noakes

Sir James Holt, by Michael Noakes

Gordon Cameron, by Bob Tulloch

Alan Cuthbert, by David Oldam Crone

Brian Johnson, by Adam Preston

Robert Lethbridge,
by Beka Smith

DR LESLIE WAYPER

Leslie Wayper was dedicated to education – of undergraduates, extra-mural students, and members of the armed forces.

Leslie was born in 1912 into a skilled working-class family and educated at Newcastle Royal Grammar School. He went up to St Catharine's as an Exhibitioner in History and continued for his PhD; his work on Anglo-Austrian relations exposed him to pre-*Anschluss* Austrian politics. Initial war service was in the Royal Ordnance Corps, but after a serious motor-cycle accident he was transferred to the Army Education Corps. In 1946, Leslie came back to Cambridge as an Adult Education Tutor in the Department of Extra-Mural Studies; from 1977 to 1980, he was Director of Extra-Mural Studies.

His association with Fitzwilliam began in 1947 as Director of Studies in History, a position he was to hold for 30 years. He was a founding Fellow, served as a Tutor, and was President. He became a Life Fellow on retirement in 1980, and was the first Secretary of the Cambridge Society. He died in 2006.

Leslie played a leading role in military education, providing urgently-needed information about the Middle East at the time of the Suez invasion in 1956, and developing strategic seminars at the highest level; he brought together representatives of the three Services to discuss current affairs and their strategic implications. These developed into more frequent and more formal gatherings – bringing a stream of fascinating figures from public life to High Table. Not just as visitors; in 1973 he initiated a Services Fellowship, whose first holder was Sir John Chapple, at that time a lieutenant-colonel and CO of a Gurkha regiment, but eventually Chief of the General Staff and a Field Marshal. In 2004, at the age of 92, he published *Mars and Minerva: A History of Army Education*.

There was a common thread linking his military interests and his College teaching. Looking back to the politics of his youth, David Starkey pointed out that 'Leslie's intellectual appreciation of the case for force and his acceptance of it made him unusual in the Cambridge of the 1960s. It explains why, amidst the Gaddarene rush to pacifism, he continued to delight in his role in military education ... . It also gave his teaching freshness and

Leslie Wayper in 2006, by Beka Smith

astringency: not only was sloppy thinking hunted down, so too was sentimentality, however well intentioned.' And the steel beneath the courtesy surfaced in his teaching: 'He took teaching seriously. In those days, most supervisors simply listened (if that) as essays were read out. Leslie took notes, occasionally with unnerving results. I'd discovered that I could *read* my essays from notes. Leslie let me get away with it a couple of times. Then, complimenting me on my turn of phrase, he asked me to repeat the second sentence of my fifth paragraph! Confusion and shame were followed with gentle but infinitely effective rebuke.'

The priority that Leslie gave to teaching, unfashionable as it is in the modern world of Research Assessment Exercises, was central to Leslie's contribution to the development of his students, of whom several became distinguished professional historians. 'But the young are not always grateful. Even at the time we wondered why Leslie hadn't written more books. There were rumours of manuscripts too unwieldy to print or lost on a train. It never occurred to us or to some of his more dismissive colleagues that he did not write because he had something more important to do – like teach. For what is the point of a college that does not place teaching at the centre of its mission? Students do not directly experience research, however profound or important. They do teaching and they judge and value their undergraduate experience accordingly.'

Dr Stephen Fleet, mineralogist and Founding Fellow. He was Tutorial Bursar, then Junior Bursar, and was the first secretary of the Governing Body. Later he was University Registrary, and Master of Downing

Amongst its officers, changes have, all too often, resulted from illness and death – linked to dedication and sheer hard work. Norman Walters died in 1967 (p. 62). His successor, from January 1969, was Alan Watson – a psychologist who was both Senior Tutor and Undergraduate Admissions Tutor until he had to take sick leave just before the beginning of the Michaelmas term in 1982. An emergency meeting of the Governing Body appointed Robert Lethbridge as Senior Tutor, and David Kerridge took on Admissions. In summer 1984 Watson resigned his University Lectureship, so his Fellowship lapsed. This was particularly sad as he had contributed greatly to the College and had nearly the

20 years' service to qualify him for a Life Fellowship. So he was appointed to a College Lectureship, and elected to a Life Fellowship from October 1984 – a graceful solution. It was not to last: he died in December.

Another ill-fated Fellow was Dick Hardy, a physiologist who was elected in 1970. He was an excellent and energetic teacher and a highly-productive researcher, conspicuous by his rare Gordon-Keeble sports-car RNH1 and by his contributions across the College; Edward

Miller wrote: 'like a good Tutor, he did not suffer fools or knaves gladly, but even fools and knaves got help in time of trouble'. As a teacher, one of his pupils wrote, 'In spite of his many commitments, Dr Hardy always had time for his students, the brilliant and the struggling alike. To those who needed special coaching, he would offer his time freely, carving time out of the vacation. He would shrug off his generosity with: "I would only be sitting looking out of the window!".' In his high-intensity life –

DR RAY KELLY

If one Fellow may be perceived as the embodiment of Fitzwilliam in the second half of the twentieth century, it must be Ray Kelly. Blessed with inexhaustible enthusiasm and an extraordinary memory, he occupied a unique place for so many of those who passed through the House and the College.

Ray was born in Leeds in 1920. His studies in French and Spanish at the University of Leeds were interrupted by wartime service in the Intelligence Corps. He served in North Africa and the Middle East, in Greece, and in Italy and Austria; by the end of the War he could at least mediate in Arabic, German, Italian and Greek. He was Mentioned in Dispatches. Afterwards, he completed his degree in Leeds and went to the Sorbonne for three years. He gained his doctorate from the Université de Lyon in 1957.

Following appointment as University Assistant Lecturer in French, Ray became Director of Studies in Modern Languages for Fitzwilliam House in 1952, an office that he held until 1967. He became Assistant Tutor and Assistant Bursar in 1955 and was a Tutor from 1966 to 1981. He was Domestic Bursar and Steward from 1960 to 1967, when he was appointed Bursar. Ray was amongst the first Fellows, and served as President; he retired in 1981 and became a Life Fellow.

Ray Kelly in 2007, by C.R. Morie

His service to Fitzwilliam was unstinting. He managed the building construction on Huntingdon Road. With collegiate status came investment portfolios, pension funds, auditors, accountants, staff and militant unions. Robert Lethbridge recalled that, in the dire financial circumstances of the time, Ray was 'environmentally Green before its time, late at night before going home personally switching off lights left wastefully on and never, even on the coldest of days, wearing a pullover, as a gentle admonishment to we younger Fellows pathetically pleading for the College heating to be turned on!'.

For the students, Ray was a formative influence. John Adams (1958) recalled that he 'took great interest in whatever we did and gave unstintingly of his time to support and encourage us in all our endeavours, studies and other activities – music, art, drama, sport, whatever. No wonder he knew so much about us all. And he never forgot, and right to the end could bring details readily to mind. He was always there – always on the towpath for Bumps, at Oxford Road for important games and at club dinners.' Other reminiscences of Ray 'underline his warmth and tolerance, neatly

synthesized in evocations of a fug of pipe-smoke aided and abetted in the sharing of his tobacco-pouch, ... a Tutor supportive in bereavement, academic wobbles and japes gone wrong, a source of advice and wisdom for generations of young men.'

Throughout, he was involved with alumni. He served on the Fitzwilliam Society committee for 54 years, and was President twice. He was Treasurer of the Billygoats from the 1950s, and President 1979–82; they donated the eight *Ray Kelly* in 2002.

Ray married Dodie in 1949; they invited his pupils into their home on Sunday evenings in Full Term, every week for most of his 26 years as a Tutor. Dodie predeceased him in 2005; at that time he was seriously ill but recovered and was a familiar figure around the College in his last year, valiantly maintaining a cheerful exterior. He died in 2008.

He is commemorated by the Prize endowed by the linguists of 1964–67 and by the Ray Kelly Room in the new Library, which bears the names of those who made donations in his memory.

DR DAVID KERRIDGE – ENCOURAGING RESEARCH IN FITZWILLIAM

David Kerridge made a unique contribution to Fitzwilliam through his advocacy of the interests of the research students, at a time when the emphasis was on raising the profile of the College by developing the undergraduate side.

David was born in 1930 deep in the fens north of Ely, and became passionate about science at Soham Grammar School. He came up to Gonville and Caius to read Natural Sciences, and received his PhD in 1957 for research into the functioning of bacteria. After two years at the Lister Institute of Preventative Medicine, he returned to Cambridge to the MRC Unit for Chemical Microbiology; he became an Assistant Director of Research in Biochemistry in 1960. Three years later he was appointed to a Lectureship, which he held until his retirement in 1997. Amongst his numerous University positions, it was particularly appropriate that he served on the Board of Graduate Studies from 1978 to 1990.

David was a Founding Fellow. His offices included those of Tutor for Undergraduate Admissions, of President, and of Steward, and he had wide interests in the life and community of the College, and proposed setting up the Foundation Lectures. To every call on his time he responded positively and with good grace. His greatest contributions were his teaching and Direction of Studies in Biological Sciences and his 20 years of service as Tutor for Graduate Students – the College's first such Tutorship, created in response to his ceaseless support for their needs. He made a great impact on innumerable students from this country and from overseas who remained in touch with him for years afterwards. In 1999, the College named its new postgraduate hostel in his honour: David Kerridge House.

But for all his self-deprecating modesty, there was a further side to his character which a former Master of Fitzwilliam identified as the 'Young Turk' in David: in his resistance to the University's rules about Approved Lodgings and landladies; in his disbelief at the way in which women were excluded from collegiate life; in his unfashionable championing of postgraduate

students; and in his insistence that the wider staff should be involved in as many College occasions as possible. He was never more Turkish than in the very early years when the College Statutes were being evolved; he considered that an institution taking on a new embodiment had the duty to question traditional patterns.

After 34 years of service to the College, championing research and progressive causes, he became a Life Fellow in 1997. David died in 2008.

including his passion for playing cricket – he defied his long-term heart trouble, but died in 1982 at the tragically early age of 43.

Administratively, the later 1970s were full of problems. Funds were tight, additional work came from developing properties and building squash courts, and staff relations were stressful (p. 159). Academically, undergraduate performance gave concern. There was a very heavy overload for Officers and committee members; meetings greatly over-ran, and very many additional meetings were called – in the worst period, the Finance Committee met several times a week. This had a very deleterious effect on the health of the Bursar, Ray Kelly, who gave up his duties in November 1980.

Although the administrative load got heavier every year, the College persisted with academic part-time Bursars for a further decade – citing the traditional concern that a full-time Bursar could hold different objectives from those of the wider Fellowship. So officers could continue with research and teaching, part-time posts multiplied and many Fellows played heavy and noble parts. Following Ray Kelly, David Bowyer became First Bursar, Derek Fray continued as Junior Bursar, Richard Smith became Tutorial Bursar, and Geoff Walker was Steward. Changes were rung on this pattern through 1981, but it was unsustainable without further support and before the end of the year a full-time non-academic Domestic Bursar was appointed.

By 1993, such arrangements were clearly unfit for purpose. Not only did administrative interactions with the outside world grow unremittingly, but Departmental pressures grew on Fellows as the University was compelled to engage in Research Assessment Exercises. In July, the College appointed its first full-time professional Bursar: Christopher Pratt, who had demonstrated his administrative and financial capabilities as Company Secretary of a major local company; that it had been a building and civil engineering contractor put him in a remarkably strong position to complete the fabric of the College whilst keeping rigorous control of the costs.

Christopher Pratt

DR TONY EDWARDS – A DEDICATED SCIENTIST, TUTOR AND TEACHER

Tony Edwards played many roles in Fitzwilliam over nearly half a century. He was born in 1936, the son of a missionary – he enjoyed his childhood in the Pacific, but was not enamoured of the Church – and educated at Eltham College. He came up to the House as an undergraduate in 1955, then read for the Veterinary MB and undertook research in Physiology for his PhD. In October 1963, he became a Fellow

and a University Demonstrator in Physiology. He was promoted Lecturer and, in 1989, Reader in Neuroendocrine Physiology. His ScD came in 1983.

His strong interest in finance and investments led him to become Treasurer of the Cambridge Philosophical Society; he restored its finances after the recession of the early 1990s.

Tony was Director of Studies in Medicine and Veterinary Medicine for nearly 20 years. Despite his research, he had a great commitment to teaching; for many years he gave more supervisions than any other Fellow. One former pupil wrote after his death 'I was lucky enough to know someone who I thought of as a brilliant scientist and a true inspiration to me in my medical career. He made me feel, more than any other individual at Cambridge, that I could be successful.'

He was a Tutor for nearly 20 years and was the College's first Dean. He was very committed to his pupils: to their faces he could be highly critical, especially when they failed to achieve their true potential, but he would defend them vigorously against anyone else or any committee. Throughout his time as a member of the Governing Body and the very many committees on which he served, he was uninhibited in his interventions and awkward questions, and his sardonic manner only emphasized his forthright views. He was a very effective member of the Fellowship, not just in his official roles; he was keen to engage with others and would enthusiastically interrogate new Fellows about their work and their interests even when they were remote from his professional specialities.

Tony was the first to achieve 40 years as an official Fellow. In later years his health was not good, but he continued to teach and to pursue his research interests beyond retirement in 2003, when he became a Life Fellow. He died in 2004.

Tea with the Chancellor in 1979

In 1985, with plans for New Court

The Visitor of the College – the Duke of Edinburgh

In Statute II of the College, it is defined that *The Chancellor of the University shall be Visitor of the College*. The Visitor has ultimate authority should the Fellows fail to elect a Master or if other serious constitutional issues arise. In June 1977, the University installed His Royal Highness The Prince Philip, Duke of Edinburgh, as Chancellor. Fortunately, he never had to resolve a constitutional issue, but he has been present at key stages of the College development. He retired in 2011, at the age of 90.

The Visitor took an early opportunity to become acquainted with the College, in 1979 meeting Fellows, students and staff over tea. He demonstrated the characteristic of which all planners of such occasions needed to be aware – satisfying his curiosity by sudden departure from the scheduled route, so all accessible spaces and people had to be prepared for inspection. He came back to the College in 1985. In 1995 the Visitor took part in the celebration of the 125th anniversary of the Non-Collegiate Students Board; he unveiled the statue of *The First Undergraduate*, which had been donated by Professor Norman Pounds, and attended the Anniversary Dinner. Then in 2004, he opened the Auditorium and Gatehouse Court.

The First Undergraduate, by Christopher Marvell

In his penultimate year as Chancellor, he opened the new Library. Detailed planning took several months – complicated by the need to liaise with the Vice-Chancellor's Office in the Old Schools and with police and security personnel. Security requires control of the release of information: those outside the planning group learned only at a late stage that the Library would be opened by HRH the Duke of Edinburgh on the afternoon of Monday 19 April 2010. Alongside the briskly choreographed formalities, the Library maintained near-normal operation, with much real work going on.

LIBRARY OPENING IN 2010

Top left: Approaching the Library

Top centre: Unveiling the plaque

Top right: Meeting graduate students

Above: With undergraduates

Left: With Dr Geoffrey Walker

The later Nobel Laureates

All four of the later Nobel Laureates joined Fitzwilliam House as overseas students or researchers, and all were elected to Honorary Fellowships by the College. Three received the Nobel Prize in Physiology or Medicine.

Albert von Szent-Györgyi was born and studied in Budapest. He came to Cambridge in 1927 as a Rockefeller Fellow, matriculating as a member of Fitzwilliam in 1928 and receiving his PhD in 1929; he then returned to Hungary. Although it was known in the eighteenth century that fresh fruit could protect against scurvy, it was not until Szent-Györgyi's work that the active agent, ascorbic acid (vitamin C) was isolated. He received the 1937 Nobel Prize, and in 1963 an Honorary ScD.

Ernst Chain was born in Berlin, where he remained until 1933, graduating in chemistry and researching for his doctorate. When the Nazi regime came to power, he came to Cambridge, a refugee in very straitened circum-stances. He worked in the Department of Biochemistry and joined Fitzwilliam House in 1934, obtaining his second PhD in 1935. In 1939 he began, in Oxford with Howard Florey, a systematic study of substances produced by micro-organisms; they transformed Alexander Fleming's 1928 observation of the antibacterial action of the penicillium mould into a practical antibiotic drug. The 1945 Nobel Prize was awarded to Fleming, Chain and Florey. Chain became FRS in 1949 and was knighted in 1969. That year, the College established a Centenary Lecture. Chain spoke on antibiotics; the lecture was an outstanding success, and Grave wrote: 'Even the least numerate of us could hardly fail to discern something of the thrill of scientific discovery.'

César Milstein was born into a Jewish-immigrant family in Argentina, and took his first degree and PhD in Buenos Aires on enzyme kinetics. He came to the Cambridge Department of Biochemistry and to Fitzwilliam in 1958, working with Fred Sanger and obtaining a second PhD in 1961. Back in Argentina, the political environment was difficult, and in 1963 he joined Sanger in the Laboratory of Molecular Biology of the Medical Research Council, to work on immunology. The Nobel Prize was in 1984 awarded to Niels Jerne, Georges Köhler and César Milstein for theories of the immune system and the discovery of the principle for producing monoclonal antibodies. He became a Fellow of the Royal Society in 1975, receiving its Royal Medal in 1982.

Joseph Stiglitz was born in Indiana and came to Cambridge in 1965 as a Fulbright Scholar. He was a research student at Fitzwilliam for two terms before Gonville and Caius offered him a Research Fellowship. He became a professor at Yale in 1970 and subsequently Professor of Economics and Finance at Columbia University. He was awarded the 2001 Sveriges Riksbank Prize in Economic Sciences in Memory of Alfred Nobel, with George Akerlof and Michael Spence, for their analyses of markets with asymmetric information. He was Chairman of the Council of Economic Advisors in the Clinton administration, and later went to the World Bank as Senior Vice-President for Development Policy, and Chief Economist.

Left: Albert von Szent-Györgyi (1893–1986)

Centre, above: Ernst Chain (1906–79)

Centre, below: Joseph Stiglitz (1943–), in Cambridge in June 2013 to receive an Honorary ScD, with the Master

Right: César Milstein (1927–2002)

10

PERFORMANCE AND RESOURCES

Statistics and performance

Throughout the twentieth century, Fitzwilliam has been buffeted by external events that have affected student numbers and threatened financial viability. The Second World War brought Fitzwilliam close to extinction, but even after the post-war transients had died away it was not possible to achieve stability. In 1966 came the Robbins Report (p. 88) and the target number was increased by 60. As Grave wrote: 'no one can claim that life in the University is in these times without incident; or, indeed,

MEng (bronze silk hoods) and MSci (pink silk shot with light blue) graduands waiting outside the Senate House; LLM (light cherry silk) nearest entrance

DRIVING UP STANDARDS

In the mid-1970s, a new generation of Fellows was admitted, with no prior connection to Fitzwilliam and ambitious for the College that had elected them. First was Robert Lethbridge, in 1973, a Modern Linguist who was to be a determinedly reforming Senior Tutor between 1982 and 1992. David Bowyer, a Pathologist, came two years later; his contributions were to the finance and fabric of the College as well as to academic reform. And Richard Smith, a Historical Geographer, was a Fellow only for a few years but made his mark driving both academic and financial performance.

Enhancing academic performance required both improvements to the physical environment of the College and a change of culture. It was not just that examination grades were poor; too often, students did not perceive failure as unacceptable. Every July, the Governing Body received a long report on those who had failed examinations; many were straightforward academic failures – 11 in both 1976 and 1977. Those whom the Tutorial Committee wished to send down had a right of appeal to the Governing Body; a very protracted and unpredictable process. Misguided leniency not

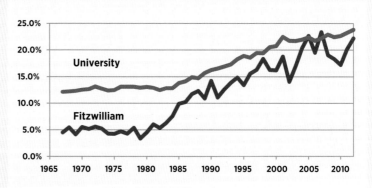

Fitzwilliam and University proportions of Firsts

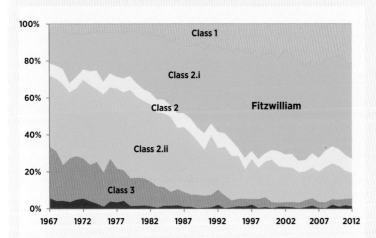

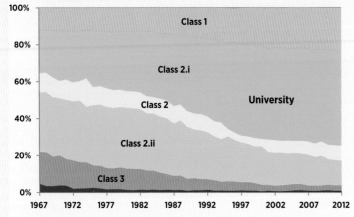

Fitzwilliam and University class distributions since 1967

only sent the wrong signal about expectations; it could be disastrous for individual students who lost the chance of a fresh start elsewhere.

So after the 1977 results the Governing Body resolved to apply the College Regulations strictly. They would still hear appeals, and the limitations of the process continued to cause great displeasure amongst academically-reforming members of the Fellowship. But the protracted effort was worthwhile. In 1981, there were 11 failures and no successful appeal; this clear signal worked, as a year later there were only five failures and not a single appeal to the Governing Body. Another step for modernity had been taken.

What was the effect on overall academic performance? Since the 1960s, there has been a great change in the pattern of the academic results across the University, as well as within Fitzwilliam. Some is grade inflation – a problem prevalent across all tiers of education – but there have been genuine improvements as students have become more serious and more aware of the need to demonstrate their abilities to future employers. The developments in attitude and environment in the 1980s were illustrated dramatically by the results in 1987, when the College had a record number of Firsts for the fourth year in succession. This was reflected in the league-table positions; in the Tompkins Table the College was 11th overall, and top in the Sciences.

Academic reformers have to set their aspirations against moving targets. Even so, great strides have been taken. Up to the beginning of the 1980s, only one Fitzwilliam undergraduate in 20 obtained a First when taking a University examination – only 40% of the rate prevailing across the whole University. The strong drive to improve performance has brought the typical level of Firsts to around 90% of the University rate. For an institution that does not aspire merely to be average, that shortfall means that there is no room for complacency. And with the unrelenting fall in Government support, the College must continue to build up its resources to enable it to provide ever-better teaching into the future.

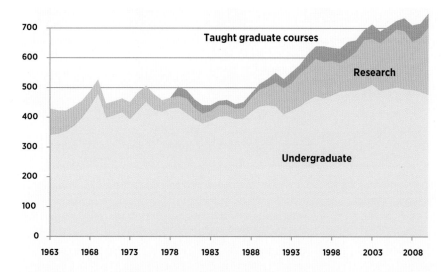

Undergraduate and graduate-student numbers between 1963 and 2010

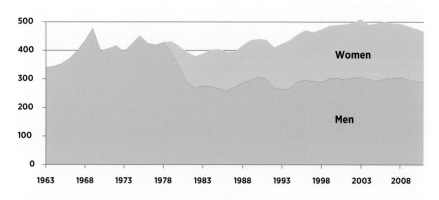

Undergraduate men and women between 1963 and 2010

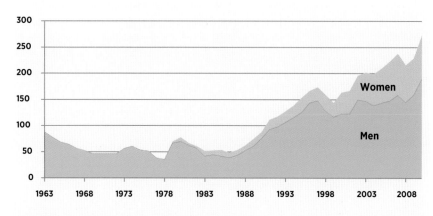

Graduate men and women between 1963 and 2010

that it rides on a particularly even keel'. His comment would have been equally valid in the early 1980s when the University Grants Committee cut funds and compelled the University to reduce the number of Home and European Union students.

In Fitzwilliam, there were conflicting demands on student numbers. Students generated revenue, and finances were perennially under pressure. But there was increasing awareness of the need to reduce admissions to enhance academic performance.

The situation was complicated by changes to course duration. Up to the 1990s, the three-year first degree was almost universal but – led by Engineering from 1992 and Physics one year later – many courses moved to four-year durations as their content increased, final-year research projects gained in importance, and preparedness of incoming undergraduates declined. Four-year courses led to Master of Engineering (MEng) and Master of Natural Sciences (MSci) degrees.

The number of graduate students was building and the composition changing. The Diplomas and other short courses common in earlier eras faded away (many had met colonial-service needs). In the 1990s came a rapid growth of one-year courses, including the Master of Business Administration (MBA) and the Master of Finance (MFin). The principal one-year course is for the Master of Philosophy (MPhil) – partially as a free-standing course, but also as a precursor to PhD studies. This, like the designation of fourth-year courses as MEng and MSci, became necessary as funding bodies required PhD candidates to have had at least four years of university studies and to hold Masters Degrees – financially penalizing students required to take MPhils, since grants were not provided for the extra preparatory year. So that future scholars are not lost at this critical stage, the College seeks continually to build up its provision of studentships for graduate students.

The growth in the number of graduate students, surpassing the traditional Fitzwilliam House position before the erosion of graduate numbers by the twin factors of the undergraduate emphasis of the 1960s and the introduction of the graduate colleges, is shown graphically. There are many ways to count graduate students; the plot is based on University figures for numbers of students in residence and paying fees, and omits graduate students in their fourth and higher years. The growth in the four decades to 2010 is very clear.

Increases in the number of graduate students have put pressure not only on studentships but also on accommodation, and on funds to support research. The number of Tutors for graduate students has grown – until 1992, a single Tutor sufficed. Out of 3,360 graduate students accepted by the University in 1991 and 1992, only 20 applied to Fitzwilliam as their first choice, perhaps because of shortage and price of accommodation, and limited funds for awards. Since then, the importance of the graduate students within the College has been recognized fully, and much more extensive provision made.

Building the endowment

When the College was founded, it had net assets of £299,000. This excluded the value of the College site which, according to the records, would have been around £800,000. Its net assets of approximately £1.1 million in 1967 would have been equivalent to £17 million at 2012 values. At the end of the 2011–12 financial year, net assets were actually £57 million (of which the endowment was £42.3 million); over the 45 years that have passed since the College's foundation, net assets have grown by £40 million over and above inflation.

This growth has come from gifts, from investment returns and from surpluses accumulated from day-to-day operations. Over the period the College has received about £31 million in gifts from alumni and from the colleges of Cambridge. Of the donations, £13 million have been in support of College buildings[1] and £6 million to various Trust funds, with the balance being taken to the unrestricted element of the College endowment. Prudent management has led to an accumulated revenue surplus and the capital value of the College's investment fund has generally kept up with inflation except in the years of extraordinary inflation in the 1970s.

Transfers from the Cambridge Colleges

The Colleges Fund is a mechanism set up under University Statute G.II, to transfer resources from richer to poorer colleges, to reduce the discrepancies in their relative assets. Grants from the Colleges Fund have to be taken to endowment; they cannot be spent on operating expenditure (including repairs or alterations to operational property). As a poorly-endowed college, Fitzwilliam has been a regular recipient of funds. Since the first grant of £8,000 in 1972, the Colleges Fund has contributed almost £10.5 million to the College endowment. In 2012 Fitzwilliam was one of only four undergraduate colleges to receive an award.

The Cambridge Colleges have been generous to Fitzwilliam in other ways. Trinity responded to the College's financial strains by giving £80,000 in 1984, and again in 1986 to endow a College Lecturer post and a Research Fellowship. St John's responded magnificently to the appeal for Gatehouse Court by gifting £400,000 over five years.

Appeals to College members

The 1962 Appeal for the establishment of the College was launched publicly in *The Times* on 12 July 1962. The appeal target was £900,000 'for the completion of buildings already begun and for the provision of endowment income'. Within this figure, the aim was to raise £500,000 for endowment. In the event the Appeal only raised some £200,000, but because of the release of additional funds

---

WHAT IS 'THE ENDOWMENT'?

The endowment can be thought of as the financial base of the College, which enables it to have the assurance that it will continue to be able to meet its charitable objectives in perpetuity. The UK Charity Commission explains it thus: 'In general terms, the term *permanent endowment* covers any land, investment or other asset which trustees cannot spend because of a restriction in the charity's governing document'.

The College uses the income generated by the endowment to subsidise its day-to-day educational and research activities. As the economic and political environment in which it operates changes over the years the income from the endowment represents a cushion to absorb external shocks without damaging the experience of our students. It is the key to the continuing independence of the College.

Endowed funds are handed down from generation to generation; the Fellows, who are the trustees, have to manage the difficult balance between maximizing the benefits for the current members and ensuring that future generations of students are able to enjoy at least equal benefits from the College.

The term *endowment* has a particular meaning in charity accounting which excludes the value of certain *operational property* and the free reserves which the College is able to allocate freely in accordance with priorities. Readers are more likely to be interested in the way the entire financial base of the College has grown over the years; this account refers generally to *net assets* – the difference between total assets and total liabilities as the measure which best represents the growth of the College's capital base.

---

1. Depreciation of College buildings over the 8 years since 2004 will have come to approximately £3.5 million, which should be taken into account as many of the gifts were for buildings.

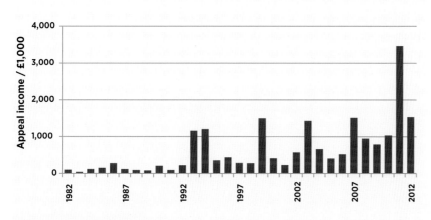

Appeal income, from 1982 to 2012

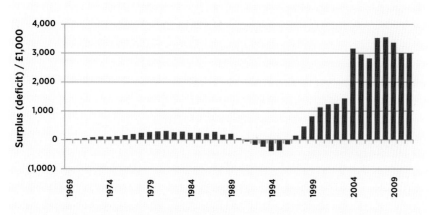

Cumulative revenue balances, from 1969–70 to 2010–11

from the University (p. 72) all of the proceeds went to endowment. The Vice-Chancellor was sanguine, considering that the Board's target of £500,000 for endowment should be obtained if possible, but that the conversion of Fitzwilliam House into a College 'was not contingent on finding the whole, or even the greater part, of that sum; a college with a full array of buildings could very largely support itself from its Internal Revenue account'. This is what happened: the College accounts demonstrate an operating surplus throughout the 1960s and 1970s, which in itself contributed over £200,000 to the endowment.

The proceeds of this Appeal were supplemented in the first year by the gift of £40,000 from Ian Rawlins (p. 95),

earmarked, along with two earlier gifts each of £10,000, for the building of a chapel. By the time this was realized in 1992, 25 years of investment growth and reinvested income had increased its value to £791,000.

In 1971 the remaining assets from the Fitzwilliam Hall Trust, valued at £120,000, also passed to the College.

The next formal approach to old members for support was for new **Squash Courts,** launched in the *Journal* of 1980. The Appeal raised about £36,000 towards total costs of £149,000. The College was disappointed with the result, the Bursar noting that fewer than 10% of old members contributed.

The 1985 Appeal was a great deal more ambitious. By the early 1980s the problem of insufficient student rooms had become acute, and the College determined in 1983 to work on a project to develop new accommodation (p. 93) which was to become New Court. The building was undertaken over the financial years 1985 and 1986, and the Appeal was launched in November 1985 'with the aim of raising £3 million to complete the building of New Court, to provide endowments for new teaching and research fellows and to raise funds for further graduate accommodation'. The College contributed over £800,000 'from its own resources', being the accumulated balance in the College Building Fund and the sale proceeds of 96 Huntingdon Road. The Appeal fell some way short of its ambition; by the time it was closed in 1992 it had raised, net of costs, approximately £500,000 for buildings and further sums in support of the Trust funds.

Despite its disappointing outcome the 1985 Appeal had some lasting impacts. Firstly, it led to the establishment of the College Development Office. Over £8.3 million was raised between the end of the 1985 Appeal and the launch of the 2008 Appeal. The gifts of Peter Wilson, Tsuzuki Gakuen Group and the bequest of Hubert Walker (1935) were the largest contributions, enabling the development of Wilson Court, the Auditorium and Gatehouse Court respectively.

Secondly, it marked the beginning of the active involvement in the College's fundraising of Norman Lamont MP (1961), who was a patron of the Appeal. Lord Lamont, as he now is, has continued to give his time and energy with great generosity to the College's fundraising efforts for 27 years and still plays a prominent role as Chair of the Campaign Council for the 2008 Appeal.

By 2008 the need for continual fundraising had become clear across the entire collegiate University. The University launched its own 800th anniversary appeal and, with the 150th anniversary of the College's foundation on the horizon and the immediate requirement to raise funds to complete the new Library, Fitzwilliam raised its game again by launching its own **150th Anniversary Appeal.** The objective was to raise £20 million to support the College's endowment by 2019.

At the time of writing the Appeal is almost half way towards meeting its target, with funds raised for teaching, for student opportunities, and most importantly for The Olisa Library, whose name reflects the generosity of Ken Olisa (1971) and Julia Olisa which has enabled this iconic building. Great strides have been made in developing the culture of giving which is so well understood in the United States and which is so critical to the success of this College.

Trust funds

Given the early constraints, it is no surprise that so much of the fundraising energies of the last 50 years have been devoted to buildings. However, we should not overlook the growth of the Trust funds, which help to meet the cost of teaching, of student support, scholarships and prizes and other benefits for the student body. By the end of the financial year 2011–12 the total of these funds stood at just over £9 million, of which 33% was supporting teaching and research, 25% was directed towards student support and 16% was for scholarships and prizes. Other funds have been established to support the Chapel, to enable travel, musical activities and subject-specific activities. Notable among individual gifts are the legacies of Sr Josep Batista i Roca, which sustains the College's reputation at the forefront of Catalan studies, and of E.D. Davies for music and student support. Student support was also the objective of a major donation received from Goldman Sachs in 2011, and the generosity of K.L. Wilson (1946) over a number of years has established a Sports Facilities fund.

Endowed funds are the bedrock of provision for the future, but expendable funds also have been essential to the growth and development of the College. Fitzwilliam's relationship with the Leathersellers Company goes back into the nineteenth century. Since the establishment of the College in 1966 the Company has given over £300,000 in funding to support teaching Fellows and studentships.

More recently the establishment of the annual telephone campaign has demonstrated how numerous small and regular donations can create substantial amounts of money to help students, who otherwise would not be able, to take advantage of the many educational opportunities that Cambridge has to offer.

Reserves

The period from 1967 to 1981 proved the prediction of the Vice-Chancellor in 1962 to have been largely correct. With a new set of buildings expenditure was low and regular financial surpluses enabled the build-up of reserves to provide for future maintenance and replacement of the College buildings.

The building programme of the 1980s and early 1990s took a heavy toll on the College's reserves; 1982 marked the beginning of a 13-year run (with only one exception) of operating deficits and by 1991 the revenue reserve was in negative territory. New Court had used up all of the money put aside for renewal of College buildings, and the continuing need for refurbishment of College rooms and the unplanned expenditure on The Grove could be financed only out of current expenditure.

By 1992 the need for urgent action to balance the books had become clear. At the Governing Body in June 1992 the Acting Bursar introduced a budget for 1992–93 which looked to achieve savings of approximately £150,000 over the year. These savings, together with realignment of rents and a drive to build conference business (made possible by the purpose-built Wilson Court rooms), enabled the College to return to surplus in 1995.

This pattern was maintained for another 13 years – again with only one exception. However, in 2008 and 2009 a substantial increase in staff and financing costs caused a return to deficit which took two years to correct.

Conclusion

By any standards the growth of the College over the 45 years from 1967 to 2012 is a remarkable achievement. However, Fitzwilliam remains amongst the least wealthy of the undergraduate colleges – investments of only £29 million in 2012 were more than £40 million below those of the average college (excluding Trinity) and £60 million below the level some consider to be necessary to ensure continued independence of a college. There remains a long way to go!

CLOTHWORKERS AND LEATHERSELLERS

It was very opportune that, in 1874, a generous initiative by the Worshipful Company of Clothworkers coincided with the needs of the Non-Collegiate Students Board. This City of London Livery Company provided Exhibitions for non-collegiate students in Natural Sciences (p. 19); the scheme ran until 1896, and 21 awards were made. All the Exhibitioners took Honours, with seven Firsts. In 1880, the Clothworkers' introduced a further Exhibition at £30 per annum; between 1904 and 1952 it was restricted to students destined for Holy Orders in the Church of England, and attracted few high-quality candidates.

In 1975, the Clothworkers gave the College discretion over the number, value and conditions of awards, up to £240 in any one year, and three years later only Scholarships were awarded. Now typically there are four Clothworkers' Scholars at any one time, with awards made on the results of University examinations. They have supported students almost every year since 1875: a total of about 214 Exhibitioners and about 45 Scholars. A remarkable record – but not the limit of their generosity: in 2003, they gave £50,000 towards Gatehouse Court.

The other Livery Company with long-term association with Fitzwilliam is the Worshipful Company of Leathersellers, which first offered four Exhibitions (with a total value of £100 per annum) in 1894. Up to 1913, there were 41 Exhibitions, awarded to men after at least two terms of residence. This permitted good selection, and all but three took Honours and obtained good results. Then, probably on financial grounds, the Leathersellers discontinued the Exhibitions, and it was to be a further half century before the link between the Company and Fitzwilliam was reinstated.

Restoration came, on a very generous scale, when collegiate status was attained. In May 1966 the Clerk of the Leathersellers' telephoned the Censor to enquire as to whether he would be interested in funding for Fellowships, and subsequently informed him that the 'Court of Assistants of his Company had resolved to provide for the establishment of a tutorial Fellowship by way of a covenant at £3,000 p.a. for 21 years, less tax'. That was sufficient to support one or two teaching Fellows at any one time, and enabled the appointment of a sequence of Fellows – providing initial posts on which were based many distinguished careers.

The first Leathersellers' Fellow, from October 1966, was David Thompson, who was already a Research Fellow. Subsequently he was Moderator of the General Assembly of the United Reformed Church, and is Emeritus Professor of Modern Church History at Cambridge. Dominic Baker-Smith was a Leathersellers' Fellow from 1968 to 1972. He went on to the Chair of English at Cardiff, and is Emeritus Professor of English Literature at the University of

Clothworkers' crest in the Chapel Crypt; stained glass, originally in Fitzwilliam Hall Chapel

Professor David Thompson, the first Leathersellers' Fellow

Amsterdam. Robert Lethbridge, Master of the College, was a Leathersellers' Fellow for five years from 1973.

Other Leathersellers' Fellows have been Roger Smith (Law), John Woolford (English), David Crew (History), and Ruth Morse (English). To help support more than one Fellow at a time, from 1971 the Leathersellers donated an additional £1,000 per annum.

In 1990, the Company substantially increased their donation, to £10,000 per annum, for a Tutorial Fellowship in Mathematics, recognizing the particular difficulty of obtaining such teaching. The first Fellow was Michael Potter (1990–98); he is now Professor of Logic at Cambridge. He was followed by Matthias Gaberdiel, now Professor at ETH Zürich; Olivier Collin, now Professor at the University of Quebec at Montreal; and Rachel Camina, currently in post. Supporting teaching in another way, in 1971 the Leathersellers contributed £500 to purchase books for the Library.

The Leathersellers also reinstated student support, donating two three-year entrance Scholarships each year at £60 per annum. In 1980 a graduate Research Studentship was added, and three years later the undergraduate Scholarships were allocated on University examinations. Finally, in 1987, they decided to terminate their undergraduate scholarships at both Oxford and Cambridge, to concentrate entirely on awards for graduate students. Currently there are four Leathersellers' Graduate Scholarships at any time, each providing £2,000 per annum for three years. These are given for research in Physical or Biological Sciences, in Mathematics, or in Engineering, to home graduates from any British university.

So two ancient Livery Companies have made great contributions to the development of Fitzwilliam by supporting its teaching and its students over very many years – and continue to do so.

THE DEVELOPMENT OFFICE AND SYSTEMATIC BENEFACTION

The New Court appeal gave a salutary demonstration of the limitations of the College's operations. Up to that time, alumni information was maintained both by the Fitzwilliam Society and by the College, but records were incomplete and not always consistent. A major effort, undertaken by volunteers led by Professor Holt's wife Betty, tracked down large numbers of alumni – even some in *Who's Who* had become lost to the College – and from that time the records have been maintained internally. Dedicated full-time Development Office staff were appointed. And, just as it was recognized belatedly in the 1990s that the office of Bursar must be professional and full-time, a decade later it became clear that the continual interaction of active fundraising could not be a part-time task for the Bursar. The College appointed its first full-time Development Director in 2007: Dr Iain Reid (1978), who reached the rank of Captain in the Grenadier Guards before reading History at Fitzwilliam. He retired in 2011, to be succeeded by another Fitzwilliam historian, Dr Helen Bettinson.

A review by Reid showed there had been some success in obtaining major gifts, such as that of Hubert Walker towards Gatehouse Court, but the general participation of alumni was low. Of the alumni, 22% had made a donation, but mostly far in the past. In 2008, only 6% of alumni had given anything in the last two years, and under 3% were making regular gifts – possibly the lowest percentage of any Cambridge undergraduate college. So it was vital to build a bedrock of regular donations from alumni with lasting commitment to the College.

Communication with alumni was frequent, as the *Fitzwilliam Society Journal* had been complemented in 2001 by the introduction of *Optima*. Alumni interest was high, with the largest Alumni Weekend attendance of any College, the London Dinner at capacity, and London Drinks events needing larger venues. So the 150th Anniversary Campaign fell upon well-prepared ground.

The needs of Fitzwilliam were placed before the alumni, putting into College context the changes to the funding of higher education – changes since the days of generous student grants and governmental support of universities in which many of them had been brought up. Looking to the future, it was important that current students were made aware that many benefits resulted from their predecessors' generosity, so in their turn it would be natural for them to support their successors. It was necessary also to convince the Fellowship that this could be achieved without offence to alumni or students.

The 150th Anniversary Campaign seeks to ensure that every student admitted can take their place in Cambridge regardless of their financial means; once there, they must have the best possible resources for study – whether they are undergraduates, or on taught graduate courses, or undertaking research – and receive the best possible academic support. Individual tuition is very expensive, but is at the very heart of what it means to study at Cambridge. Resources are needed to expand the collegiate experience,

Above: David Starkey speaking at the launch of the 2019 Appeal

Right: Lord Lamont, chairman of the Campaign Council for the 2019 Appeal

complementing the academic work of the students and so enriching their quality of life. The Student Opportunities Fund enables the College to support Fitzwilliam students though maintenance bursaries, studentships and hardship grants, and provide help with educational expenses.

The first year of the Campaign was marked by the start of an annual series of telephone campaigns – not the first mounted by the College, as one had been held in the 1990s, but on a large scale and assisted with modern technology. A dozen undergraduates contacted nearly 700 of their predecessors; wherever possible, common ground had been identified, and lively conversations were stimulated. In that year over £115,000 was raised for the Library and IT Centre and for the recently-created Student Opportunities Fund, and information about the careers and achievements of alumni was updated. Subsequent telephone campaigns have been equally successful.

THE RECOGNITION OF BENEFACTORS

When substantial benefactions are made or promised, it is important that donors are recognized. Traditionally this has been by donor boards and by the naming of prizes, scholarships and travel awards; this has been augmented by the formation of benefactor groups and the creation of the title of 1869 Fellow Benefactor for exceptional donors. So far, just two 1869 Fellow Benefactors have been elected: Peter Selman in 2011, and Ken Olisa in 2012. Substantial contributors are members of The Master's Circle, whilst The 1869 Foundation is for those who have undertaken to make bequests to the College; there is a gathering in College in the summer for Foundation members which provides an opportunity for them to learn of the current activities of the College, with presentations by research students and music.

A specific target within the Library Appeal was for the creation of a lasting memorial to Ray Kelly. Over £63,000 was contributed in gifts, large and small, by 350 alumni, Fellows and friends; their names are recorded on a plaque in the splendid Reading Room (p. 103) which commemorates Ray's contribution to the College.

Left: Donor boards in the entrance foyer; at right, the screen gives notification of the annual service of Commemoration of Benefactors

Below left: Ken Olisa, in his 1869 Fellow Benefactor gown, at the 2012 Reunion

Below: Members of The Master's Circle at the 2012 Reunion

Bottom: Members of The 1869 Foundation learn about a graduate student's research

The telephone campaign

11

ADMITTING WOMEN

A protracted matter of Statute

When the first Fellows constructed the first Statutes, the second clause was that the College was to be exclusively for men. This was not handed down from the mists of antiquity – in antiquity, no-one envisaged mixed colleges. It was an innovation following the Royal Commission report of 1922, which contained the notorious and illogical statement that 'we desire strongly that Cambridge should remain mainly and predominantly a *men's University*, though of a mixed type, as it already is'.

The exclusion of women was not quite so absolute as to suit diehard traditionalists. In 1964 Grave wrote 'It might be taken amiss if I were to omit reference to what some will, no doubt, seem a significant or even startling innovation: the decision of the Fellowship to set aside one night in each week in Full Term for the reception of lady guests on High Table'. Only academic guests; spouses and fiancées (even if academic) could dine only on the annual Ladies' Night – a taboo not lifted until 1973.

As the 1970s progressed, it became apparent that the gender-mixed college was a concept whose time had come. The new colleges for graduate students admitted both women and men. Established colleges moved slowly, until King's and Churchill matriculated their first women undergraduates in 1972. Four years later a group of major colleges followed: considerable impetus was building up.

In 1973, the newly-constituted General Purposes Committee discussed co-residence; it was suggested that admitting women might have a civilizing effect, but practical difficulties were recognized. Later in the year the Governing Body started to consider changes to the Statutes, a process requiring special meetings of the entire Fellowship, including Life Fellows. The Minutes of the first Special College Meeting record 'a long discussion about the extent to which the principle of co-residence could be separated from the detailed practicalities of admitting women'. A straw vote decided that practical issues should be considered in detail.

It was not surprising that detailed analysis was sought: weak financially and desperately short of accommodation, the College was not well placed to meet the practical challenges. The greatest was how to support women students: would women Fellows be needed before co-residence (with posts funded by the College, as women University Teaching Officers were rare), or would non-Fellows such as external College Lecturers suffice? In retrospect, that notion seems astonishingly unrealistic. Another practical issue related to College rooms – it was suggested that funds were so tight as to preclude full-length mirrors! Essential modifications for privacy in bathrooms were long overdue; the communal facilities were suited to a barracks. Much more substantial issues were identified, such as the effects on the quality of admissions candidates, and the reaction of potential benefactors with fond recollections of the all-male, sports-oriented House.

The next Special College Meeting, in March 1974, addressed academic issues in more detail. It explored alternatives: to remove the statute which excluded women, or add an enabling clause similar to that rejected in 1963. It was known that the women's colleges were concerned about losing applicants; admissions procedures would have to be developed; and the subject balance could be affected. Dr Ian Nicol (Secretary-General of the Faculties of the University) anticipated extra Arts teaching, at a time when Science teaching facilities were under-utilized. And the meeting returned to practical issues: 'the College had the lowest proportion of residential accommodation of any in Cambridge. It was not particularly attractive to men at present or women in the future.'

It would be wrong to imagine that discussion was conducted entirely at the rational level of cost–academic-

Dr Ian Nicol, Fellow and Secretary-General of the Faculties. Sir Peter Swinnerton-Dyer said at the end of his Vice-Chancellorship: 'It is now about fifteen years since I first joined the General Board and in consequence first met Ian Nicol. Ever since then, I have relied on his good advice, and his knowledge and understanding of the University. How much I owe him, I have known for a long time; how much the University owes to him, I have only fully learnt in the last two years.'

benefit analysis. There was an emotional level, too, especially for those accustomed to the traditional environment of the House. David Kerridge recalled that W.W. Williams, by then a Life Fellow, was so opposed to admitting women that he came down from the Scottish Highlands to vote against the change. Even he was to be somewhat reconciled to the inevitable: 'I was able to convince him of the error of his ways when a few years later I admitted his grand-daughter. He was delighted.' But that was years away: there was no agreement to alter the Statutes.

In response, the Junior Members' Association sent a petition with 300 signatures to the Governing Body in favour of co-residence. A Fellow who attended an open meeting noted that they attached particular importance to having women Fellows in advance of the undergraduates.

Two years passed, with just one unproductive Special College Meeting. College statistics showed that there were fewer Firsts than the University average, and the proportion of graduate students was below average. The College was

stagnating in a changing world. In May 1976, financial implications were considered, together with a new sexist topic: landladies would be reluctant to take women, as they would cause trouble in their kitchens. It was minuted that 'the hope was expressed that a gradual movement over what would probably be the best part of ten years might lessen the impact' of co-residence – a recipe for the most pain and the least gain!

A further meeting rejected a proposal for an enabling statute. However, the topic was opening up, and in January 1977 the fundamentals were addressed: Fitzwilliam was very short of first-choice applicants (even shorter of high-quality ones) and was using the intercollegiate Pool for about a quarter of its admissions, about five times the University average. Mixed colleges were receiving more applicants per place than single-sex colleges, and Fitzwilliam was amongst the worst of the single-sex colleges. The academic arguments were overwhelming, and in March the decision was taken to repeal Statute I.2.

So the formal process could proceed, with a Special College Meeting in April; no vote was cast in opposition, and the opportunity was taken to undertake many necessary but unrelated changes to Statutes. The revised Statutes were approved by Her Majesty in Council, on 7 February 1978. Implementation began for under-graduates from 1979, and graduate and affiliated students from 1978. It was anticipated that the total number of women would build up to about 100. Admission was to be on merit, without quotas, and women would be distributed across all tutorial sides. The election of women Fellows and their appointment as Tutors was a matter of urgency. And, as minuted, 'It was again stressed that Fellows would have to work hard to make the admission of women a success'.

In spring 1979, the first women Fellows were elected: Dr Elisabeth Marseglia (Post-Doctoral Research Associate in Physics), and Dr Sathiamalar Thirunavukkarasu (University Lecturer in Pathology). Another pre-requisite had been achieved. Unfortunately Dr Thiru was able to serve only for a year, but Dr Rivkah Zim was elected to a Fellowship and appointed College Lecturer in English. No Tutorial appointment was made, but a special entertainment allowance was provided for the women Fellows to help them to support the undergraduates.

In 1979, 39 women students were admitted, a little above the anticipated long-term level. Generally all went

A woman student in her room

well, although the domestic staff reported privacy issues with the primitive bathrooms, and they were caught unawares by women wishing to cook in the gyp-rooms – which were suitable only for making cups of instant coffee.

Ten years later, there were still concerns about the proportion of women in Fitzwilliam and about academic performance, and a working party was set up. Its report drew attention to matters that should have been resolved from the start – it was still necessary to require all bathroom doors to be lockable. More substantially, there were still issues affecting security, lighting, sexist 'humour', and ethos more generally; equal respect had not been achieved. The Admissions side was encouraged to take more action to attract good applicants, improving contacts with schools, providing better-targeted information, and making sure that the implicit messages conveyed by the publicity material and at Open Days reinforced the explicit statements about the College being co-residential. To support the Tutorial provision, a woman Tutor, Dr Hazel Mills, was appointed Advisor for Women Students.

Admitted women

So what did life have in store for the 39 young women (of whom two were graduate students) who in October 1979 joined a mixed College, though a College mainly and predominantly of a men's type?

Liz Makin recalled: 'the majority were very strong willed and able to stand up for themselves, so I think that must have been one of the main selection criteria. This was a good thing as we received lots of attention from the men, whether this was being watched, being heckled or being chatted up. We were never short of party invites, or men to fix our punctures either!' Co-residence presented opportunities: a teacher at her comprehensive school suggested 'Why not try applying to Fitzwilliam College as it will be the first year that they admit girls – I shouldn't think many other girls will want to go there if it is all men.'

The flexible approach of the College attracted Cheryl Winter, as it was one of few that took applicants from sixth-form colleges. Melanie Colthorpe found an unexpected opportunity: 'If someone had said to me as I embarked on the sixth form in an all-girls public school that I would find myself … studying at the previously all-male Fitzwilliam College, I would have been incredulous'. She grasped the opportunity: 'once I had made the decision, with single-minded determination I decided that somehow I was going to get in and make the most of every minute spent at the College.'

Personal contacts provided opportunities. Valerie Pearson came to Cambridge with her Spanish teacher 'to meet Geoff Walker with a view to discussing our school's A-level orals, which Geoff normally undertook'; she 'got chatting to Geoff, who sent me away with an application form. Prior to that day, it honestly had never crossed my mind that applying to Cambridge was something people like me did.' Melanie Colthorpe's Spanish teacher also knew Geoff Walker, and she 'was enticed by the … chance

to make my mark as one of the first women there'. Sarah Asplin knew about Fitzwilliam because her brother had been there.

They lived in first-floor or second-floor rooms, on three or four staircases. All knew each other and the men knew them all. Reminiscent of concerns that had been expressed about landladies, Liz Makin recalled: 'The bedders weren't impressed by us, as we tidied up, made our beds and washed up the pots in the kitchen – they much preferred pampering the boys!'

There were very different responses to entering Fitzwilliam. Valerie Pearson had come from a mixed grammar school, and was not particularly conscious of her pioneering role. But Natalie Kaye 'found the environment at Fitzwilliam absolutely overwhelming. I had been educated at an all-girls' school and arrived in a nearly exclusively male college.' She responded very positively: 'trying to change the culture of the College was possibly the reason so many of us were keen to get involved in organizing social events and various clubs and

A garden party in 1979

committees. That first year, for example, we set up a March Ball Committee which eventually I chaired.' Cheryl Winter, too, recalled feeling very excited about the efforts with the March Balls. She found 'Fitzwilliam had a more informal and contemporary atmosphere than other Colleges and this suited me well. It may not have had the prettiest buildings, but I liked the fact that my peer group came from a wide range of backgrounds and schools ... Obviously there was a masculine feel ... but I do not recall feeling particularly intimidated because we were out-numbered. If I felt daunted, it was because I thought that they had made an enormous mistake allowing me into one of the premier universities in the world!' From her room overlooking Tree Court, Cheryl could watch the many comings and goings, 'impressed by the number of smart invitations we received to different functions ... I do not think I fully appreciated the wonderful social life we enjoyed – of course, as one of the few women, I was invited to everything!'

Sport remained central to College life. Judith Oliver's initial impression was of an all-pervading smell of *Deep Heat* embrocation. She recognized that male sports captains 'struggled with a far smaller pool of players from which to pick their rugby and football teams. Lest we should be accused of scuppering Fitzwilliam's sporting reputation, very many of the women rose to the challenge of attempting some sport or other. Looking through the old *Fitzwilliam Journals*, I see I made the College women's squash team in 1981. As I can't play squash, I reckon that was quite a feat.' In her third year, Judith became Vice-President of the Junior Members Association. 'Women who wanted to get involved in clubs, sports and societies certainly found there no barriers to participation. On the contrary, I think some female enthusiasm and organizational skill were welcomed.'

An almost universal recollection was of the slow adaptation of the catering in Hall, as the kitchens were accustomed to satisfying hearty men with substantial portions of fried food. For Natalie Kaye 'The food, as I recall, was terrible and mostly aimed at rowers and rugby players. We had to lobby the College to get salads served.'

Life and work settled to a pattern, and for Melanie Colthorpe 'it was my second year at College that I enjoyed the most, and that I have the most vivid recollections of. ... The second year brought ... a sense of comfort as I pulled open my trunk in my lodgings across the road from the

LISA O'NEILL – INADVERTENT PIONEER

Matriculation 1978: Lisa O'Neill and Kathleen Taylor ...

Lisa O'Neill, from the USA, was admitted in October 1978 as an Affiliated Student. The Senior Tutor wrote 'for your first year you will be one of the very few women students in residence. We have not proposed to make changes in bathroom facilities before 1979; there will, however, be no difficulty in arranging for you to have a room in College during the first year suitable for use by a lady.' This was optimistic: she was in splendid isolation in College (Kathleen Taylor was at Wesley House), and the lack of facilities made it necessary for her to reside in the Sick Bay.

... amidst all the men

LISA TREI – NEW GIRL, BUT OLD CONNECTION

Adelaide attended the 1921 Fitzwilliam Ball

It was appropriate that Lisa came to Fitzwilliam. Her grandfather had been amongst the officers invited to Cambridge in recognition of the service of the American Expeditionary Forces (p. 45). Second Lieutenant McNamee was six months in Cambridge, attending lectures – and learning to punt and going to tea dances; he met Adelaide Coote, whose father was provisioner for the dining hall of Trinity College. They married in 1926. Lisa recalled that her grandfather 'was very proud of our family's connection to Fitzwilliam. He was thrilled when I became a Billy and he often wore his Fitzwilliam tie, tiepin and cufflinks on his daily walks in the Marina district of San Francisco.'

Lisa, too, made the most of her opportunities. 'I thought I had died and gone to heaven. ... The fact that we were outnumbered ten-to-one by male students was far more thrilling than frightening to me. ... Academics took a back seat during my first year. ... After I switched from History to Social and Political Science, I began to enjoy academia. Following a long career as a journalist, I'm still at it – reporting on breakthrough research in the social sciences as a writer for Stanford University News Service.'

College on a sunny and summer-like autumn day – knowing that I had made it as a seasoned student, and ... no longer having the awkwardness of a Fresher.' So 'my years spent at Fitzwilliam ... turned into some of my happiest years of my life so far, with vivid recollections now of my time there, and a proud sense of still belonging to Fitzwilliam as an alumna. ... I wouldn't have missed it for the world.'

Valerie Pearson recalled with fondness Harry Hudson and his fungi stories, and Robert Lethbridge and his pipe, whilst Sohee Park 'loved my physics supervisor, Dr Pooley. He was kind and forgiving even though I was a god-awful student, possibly the worst he had ever taught. Once I forgot to turn up for my supervision and was lazing about in Tree Court doing nothing. He actually came and found me. Nobody would do this at Harvard' (where Professor Park obtained her PhD, in 1991). 'I hated my maths supervisor. He said girls should never have been admitted because we could not do maths. They said things like that then, without any qualms!'

Natalie Kaye felt that the College did not 'appreciate the pressures women in that first year were under. ... But I now look back at my years at Fitzwilliam with affection and some bemusement.' For Natalie, 'things definitely did improve over the three years as more women entered the College. Slowly the hard-drinking, hearty, sports-dominated culture began to change. It was inevitable, I guess, as we acted as a civilizing influence. Being the first intake of women also meant we could make our mark in the ways we wanted – I rowed in the very first women's eight, and tried out coxing too. It was rumoured that we had improved the exam results too, although I think that actually happened much later.'

An account of the consequences of co-residence would be incomplete without the romantic dimension. Much can be left to the imagination and to the memories of those who were there, but it is a matter of record that six of the first-generation women married Fitzwilliam men: three exact contemporaries, and the others from earlier years. Some connections were established very early: Valerie Pearson met her future husband on her first evening in College, and married a year after graduation.

Cheryl Winter wondered whether she was 'looking back with rose-tinted glasses, but I am very happy to remember my association with Fitzwilliam. ... It was a challenge being part of the first intake of women, but not an unpleasant one, and I enjoyed the experience of being a pioneer.' And Liz Makin supposed 'students now probably think it must have been very strange being part of the first year of women at Fitzwilliam, but we didn't know any different. I had a brilliant three years, and being part of the first intake of women just made it more special.'

12

JUNIOR MEMBERS

Lifestyles and politics

The end of the 1960s was marked by changes in student attitudes and lifestyles. The reduction of the age of majority from 21 to 18, in 1970, ended the traditional *in loco parentis* role of the College Tutor; henceforth, the roles of advisor and advisee could not be taken for granted. There was instability in universities across the world, particularly in the United States and France, often exacerbated by heavy-handed over-reaction by authorities.

But in England, and especially in Cambridge, matters were less pressing. There was an imitative component to rebelliousness, which was seen as an inherent student characteristic; with generous student grants and full employment, there were few disincentives. A sit-in at the Senate House, in support of students at the London School of Economics, provided an opportunity to raise issues such as gate-hour reform. And there was a disturbance – a *riot* was journalistic wishful thinking – at the Garden House Hotel, in opposition to the autocratic Greek Colonels. A later Senate House sit-in demanded representation of students on committees and sought nursery provision. Baron Devlin conducted an extensive enquiry both into the sit-in and into student representation; this led to junior members on Faculty Boards and, as observers, on the Council of the Senate.

Fitzwilliam was split between the more conservative, sports-orientated Hearties and more left-wing elements. In 1968 there was controversy about the way in which students should be represented and about the expenditure of the fee component for support of student life. The Amalgamated Clubs committee represented all clubs and societies, weighted heavily towards the sports clubs; uniquely amongst colleges, there was no democratically-elected Junior Common Room Committee. This deficiency was eliminated by direct election for officers; in particular, direct election of the Junior President (rather than nomination by committee members, as in some colleges) made him representative of the student body rather than of factional interests, whether sports clubs or left-wing politically-motivated committee members. The arrangements have stood the test of time and have contributed greatly to the quality of student life and to the effective operation of the College.

The 1973 *University Challenge* team

BASSETT   CURRY   WURTZEL   HALLS

FITZWILLIAM CAMBRIDGE

A POLITICAL GALLERY

Following the General Election in May 2005, Fitzwilliam had an impressively disproportionate presence in the House of Commons, with five out of 646 Members of Parliament – only Clare, with seven, had more. Three were re-elected in 2010, joined by one new entrant.

Norman St John Stevas MP, c. 1968; he was President of the Fitzwilliam Society for 1968–69

Members of Parliament in autumn 2012

Dr Vincent Cable (1962), Liberal Democrat, Twickenham, since 1997.
After his PhD at the University of Glasgow, he worked for the Foreign and Commonwealth Office, then went to Shell, becoming their Chief Economist in 1995. He is Business Secretary in the Coalition Cabinet, and was Shadow Chancellor of the Exchequer before the 2010 election.

Andy Burnham (1988), Labour, Leigh, since 1997.
Before the 2010 election he was Secretary of State at the Department of Health and previously had been at Health, at the Treasury, at the Home Office, and at Culture, Media and Sport.

Mike Gapes (1972), Labour and Co-operative member, Ilford South, since 1992.
Very active in Labour Party politics in his student years, he worked full-time for the Party from 1977. From 2005 until the 2010 election, he was Chairman of the Foreign Affairs Select Committee, on which he still serves.

John Glen (2002), Conservative, Salisbury, since 2010.
His first degree, in Modern History, was from Oxford.

Until the 2010 General Election

Julia Goldsworthy (1997), Liberal Democrat, Falmouth & Cambourne, 2005 to 2010.
She is now at the Treasury, as Special Adviser to Danny Alexander, the Chief Secretary to the Treasury.

David Wilshire (1962), Conservative, Spelthorne, 1987 to 2010.

Members of Parliament in earlier times

David Martin (1964), Conservative, Portsmouth South, 1987 to 1997.

Denys Bullard (1930), Conservative, South West Norfolk, 1951 to 1955, King's Lynn 1959 to 1964. He died in 1994.

Former members of the House of Commons Norman Lamont and Jim Knight are now in the Lords.

Lords Temporal in autumn 2012

Norman Lamont (1961), Baron Lamont of Lerwick, made a Life Peer in 1998.
Formerly Conservative MP for Kingston-upon-Thames, 1972 to 1997; Chancellor of the Exchequer, 1990 to 1993.

James Knight (1984), Baron Knight of Weymouth, made a Life Peer in 2010.
Formerly Labour MP for South Dorset, 2001 to 2010; ministerial roles included Minister of State for Schools.

Leslie Griffiths (1967), Baron Griffiths of Burry Port, made a Life Peer (Labour) in 2004.
The Rev. Dr L. J. Griffiths was at Wesley House and is a Methodist Minister.

Lords Spiritual in autumn 2012

Michael Hill (1985), Lord Bishop of Bristol, in the House of Lords since 2009.
Bishop Hill was an Attached House member, at Ridley Hall.

Michael Langrish (1971), Lord Bishop of Exeter, in the House of Lords since 2005.
Bishop Langrish was an Attached House member, at Ridley Hall.

Members of the House of Lords in earlier times

Norman St John Stevas (1947), Baron St John of Fawsley, made a Life Peer in 1987.
Formerly Conservative MP for Chelmsford, 1964 to 1987; Leader of the House, 1979 to 1981.
He was Master of Emmanuel from 1991 to 1996. An Honorary Fellow of Fitzwilliam, he died in 2012.

Michael Nazir-Ali (1971), formerly Bishop of Rochester, in the House of Lords 1999 to 2009.
Bishop Nazir-Ali was an Attached House member, at Ridley Hall; he is an Honorary Fellow of the College.

Norman Lamont (front row, centre) as Union Society President, Lent Term 1964. Vincent Cable (back row, second from right) was to become President the following year

The *Fitzwilliam Magazine* for 1968 rehearsed the arguments. Nicholas Whines (1966) wrote: 'The JCR Committee must also have a right of veto over decisions of the Amal. Clubs committee, reversible by a majority vote in an open meeting of the JCR. Open meetings must be held at least fortnightly to ensure that the JCR Committee is reflecting the feelings of the undergraduate body and is acting in its best interests.' Fortnightly open meetings – sating the faithful and driving everyone else away – so emblematic of the era!

The Cambridge Students' Union (CSU) sought representation in the University, often ignoring the differences between a collegiate and a unitary university. Problems arose between the JCR and CSU. Ken Olisa (1971), in his manifesto for JCR Committee membership, wrote: 'I believe that an open union is, in principle, a good idea. However, I feel that its role is purely as a social centre, completely divorced from political activity. This year, the College has given £170 to CSU – and has received what? The money could far better have been spent in Fitzwilliam. Next year, the CSU will be asking us to contribute £900, a sum which we would be unable to afford except at the expense of College Clubs and Societies. Would it be worth it?' Ken was elected to the Committee in 1971; he became Junior President the following year.

Participation of Junior Members in the government of the College was taken seriously, and the Governing Body instituted a joint committee of Senior and Junior Members; students on it would attend the Governing Body for its business. The General Purposes Committee first met in Lent 1973; its first representatives to attend a Governing Body meeting were undergraduates George Jarzab (1970), David Powell (1971) and Ken Olisa; John Venning (1967) represented the graduates. Over the following years Junior Members attended Governing Body meetings more extensively; since 2000 they have been present for all business except that relating to individuals. They participate in many of its committees, where their contributions are valued greatly.

At a time when students were receiving a bad press, Fitzwilliam talent was exhibited to the country on *University Challenge*, then in its heyday with the original question-master Bamber Gascoigne. In 1966, the team of John Ritchie (1962), Geoffrey Carreck (1964), David Starkey (1964) and Ronald Clifton (1965) got close to the final – Roger Wilkins (1967) recalled that a bar snooker

NICK DRAKE – TROUBLED TROUBADOUR

Just a couple of years in the short, tragic life of singer-songwriter Nick Drake were spent at Fitzwilliam. Highly formative years; his is an extreme example of the Cambridge environment providing opportunities for diverse talents to flourish.

Nick came up from Marlborough in 1967 – via a crammer, to bring his A-level grades from impossible to dire. Studying English, he passed his examinations, but his thoughts were elsewhere and he withdrew from Cambridge against the advice of his Tutor, Ray Kelly. But the laid-back student was only an insubstantial part of Nick Drake. As a musician, he was highly driven and exacting – not a dreamy plucker of guitar strings, but an expert instrumentalist on the piano, the clarinet and the saxophone as well as the guitar, a refined singer, a sophisticated composer, and conversant with the technicalities of recording.

Much of his undergraduate time was spent in London, developing his music, making recordings, and taking drugs – his absence from Cambridge could be physical, mental, or both. But it was not surprising that he remained an outsider: his solitude, his music and his marijuana separated him from the beer-befuddled Hearties. How to judge between different agents for blurring reality?

His debut album *Five Leaves Left* (alluding to the note in Rizla cigarette papers) was recorded in 1968 on a minimal budget, to be followed by *Bryter Layter*. As time went on, Nick became steadily more isolated, withdrawing to the alien environment of his respectable family home in a Warwickshire village and making only occasional forays into the London music scene. He made his last record, *Pink Moon*, in 1971. He was treated for depression, and died in 1974 from an overdose of his medication.

Nick Drake's reputation has grown steadily; four decades after his death his sad, detached music is readily available, known and highly regarded as it never was in his lifetime.

ALASTAIR HIGNELL

Once an inspirational sportsman, Alastair Hignell remains inspirational – but for his work with multiple-sclerosis charities. Alastair came up in 1974 to read History, three months after his debut in first-class cricket with Gloucestershire; he played for the county for a decade. But cricket, with a Blue, was only part of his sporting life; rugby union became dominant through the 1970s as another Blue – he was the first since 1895 to captain the University at both sports – was followed by 14 England caps. His sporting contributions to Fitzwilliam led to Reddaway Prizes in his first two years; in his final year, a special prize recognized his contribution to the life of the College.

On retirement from playing, he joined BBC Radio, but in 1999 was diagnosed with multiple sclerosis and progressively withdrew from broadcasting. Hignell became Patron of the Multiple Sclerosis Resource Centre in 2002. He won the BBC Sports Personality of the Year Helen Rollason Award in 2008 for his work in spreading awareness of multiple sclerosis, and the following year received a CBE for services to sport and to charity.

table, purchased with the winnings, took pride of place in the Junior Common Room. Seven years later, the team of Philip Bassett (1970), David Curry (1970), Michael Halls (1970) and David Wurtzel (1971) won, and were presented with a set of Hogarth prints, *The Harlot's Progress*. Some of the cash winnings provided a harpsichord kit (which required extensive effort to produce a harpsichord). The winning team came together again three decades later to play in *University Challenge Reunited* in 2002, and won their round against Churchill.

Student societies

The societies in the twentieth century reveal the interests – and the apathy – of members of Fitzwilliam. Most venerable was the Debating Society, active before 1874, but prone to re-invention; it became the Literary and Debating Society, with a very wide remit including music (mostly smoking concerts). In 1908 an 'at home' concert was held, for which

– uniquely – members were allowed to bring female guests. Short-lived ensembles in the Edwardian era included the vocal Fitzwilliam Quartette. In 1908, it debated the serious issues of Socialism and Temperance, but also that 'this house views with grave misgivings the further development of the art of aerial navigation'.

In the early 1920s the Society decided by a fair majority against Prohibition and, presumably, adjourned to The Little Rose. Not all topics were so close to the hearts of audiences, however, and by 1929: 'We can only assume that the Society is still in existence'. A temporary revival had an energetically-debated motion *That England thinks too much of her athletes* being carried but, with prescience, the House did not *welcome a United States of Europe*.

Characteristically for the period, political societies arose. In 1931, an International Society flourished – or at least its first batch of ties sold out. The underlying ideology of the League of Nations Union is clear, with papers on Unemployment Insurance, Reduction of the Hours of Work, and a review of the book *Un plan quinquennal Européen*. Its disappearance from subsequent *Magazines* may correlate with the heavy defeat of a Debating Society motion that *This House would welcome the speedy formation of a Socialist Government*.

The Literary and Debating Society was re-named the Somerset Society in 1950, a revival under President John Sturt (1949) and Secretary Peter Saunders-Harrington (1949) bringing a full programme; in 1954 it became the Ralph Somerset Society. In the 1960s, the 'greatest passions were aroused over political motions. In fact, no matter what the nominal motion, Mr Graham (1958) and Mr Green (1958) managed to have a set-to over Suez.' This revival provided opportunities for 'A.N. May's unbridled ebullience and scholarship – Fitzwilliam's most promising Marxist and epicure', according to the *Fitzwilliam Magazine*; Alfie came up in 1963 to read History, and received his PhD in 1970.

In 1966, the Society had external speakers, including Canon Montefiore (the very popular Vicar of the University Church) who 'convinced a large audience to deny the irrelevance of religion to modern man' and academics such as Peter Laslett, who recently had founded the Cambridge Group for the History of Population and Social Structure. The maintenance of a programme of talks and debates requires sustained leadership and persistence, as demonstrated by Michael Halls (1970, subsequently a Research Fellow) and his successor Simon Olding (1973), who attracted distinguished speakers such as Professor L.C. Knights and Professor Frank Kermode. Decline followed, resisted by Richard Clayton (1981). But as the century drew towards its end, there was a general tendency for societies to become primarily social and less active.

The History Society was the earliest subject-based society, founded in 1900 with Reddaway as its first President – he also gave the first paper. In the 1920s, it was very much an establishment society; Gaskoin was its President, and Reddaway and Thatcher its Vice-Presidents. It flourished: for its 300th meeting Professor G.M. Trevelyan was guest of honour at the dinner. It maintained its tradition of both meeting and dining; Patrick Allsop (1971) wrote in the *Journal* that in 1973 there were two dinners and six meetings, with distinguished speakers such as the Tudor historian Professor Elton and Dr Linehan, whose account of researches in Spain

DENNIS BYRON

Dennis Byron came to Cambridge in 1962 on a Leeward Islands Scholarship to read Law, which he combined with rowing – getting his oar in the Mays in 1964. He was called to the Bar at the Inner Temple in 1965, and practised as a barrister throughout the Leeward Islands until 1982, when he was appointed a High Court Judge for the Eastern Caribbean Supreme Court. He became Acting Chief Justice in 1996 and Chief Justice three years later.

In 2001, Byron went to Zimbabwe for the Human Rights Institute of the International Bar Association investigation into Government Abuses against the Rule of Law. This led to a four-year term as President of the United Nations International Criminal Tribunal for Rwanda. He is now President of the Caribbean Court of Justice, and has been the President of the Commonwealth Judicial Education Institute since 1999.

He was knighted in 2002, and was appointed to the Privy Council two years later. Sir Dennis Byron was elected into an Honorary Fellowship in 2010.

Sir Dennis Byron and Lady Norma Byron, in Fitzwilliam with Professor Hooley and Mrs Padfield

provoked in the Secretary 'the phenomenon known as *tears of laughter*'. Later in the decade, the Society augmented its programme with field excursions, led particularly by Dr Richard Smith (Fellow, 1974–83, now Emeritus Professor of Historical Geography and Demography) into East Anglia.

The Theological Society was long-established, having been founded in 1902, but steadily reduced in significance as the Attached Houses absorbed an increasing proportion of the religious activity of the non-collegiate students. And inevitably the polymath Gaskoin was heavily involved in the Law Society between the wars.

ANDY HARTER RECALLS LIFE IN THE 1980s

After Fitzwilliam, Andy Harter studied at the Computer Laboratory for his PhD and went on to develop VNC (Virtual Network Computing), providing remote-access technology, and founded RealVNC in Cambridge in 2002. He is a Fellow of the Royal Academy of Engineering. He recalls his days in College:

'I remember my admission interviews vividly. I saw Mr Watson, the Senior Tutor, first. We didn't get off to the best of starts when, in a moment of nervous awkwardness, I answered one of his questions "Elementary, my dear Watson". Things went better with Barry Landy and, after standing up to some mathematical probing, we had a lively conversation about computers. I had just finished building one at home from scratch, so we had much to talk about.

'And so, after a gap year at the Royal Greenwich Observatory, I came up to read Mathematics in 1980. Fitzwilliam was a lively, inclusive place without pretensions, and friendships were quickly and easily made. First, there was our small group of half a dozen Part IA Mathematicians, who clung together for support as we grappled with the abrupt change of intellectual gear. I recall a baffling supervision on group theory where we stared at a blank piece of paper for an hour while the supervisor attended to his pipe, finally smiling at us and saying we had made progress. It couldn't happen now, for several obvious reasons!

'Neighbours formed another ready-made social group. My first room was on the ground floor adjacent to the original Porters Lodge on Huntingdon Road and probably the noisiest room in College. I was inescapably party to comings and goings, which was by turns intriguing, humorous and irritating, especially late at night. In those days, there was no evening meal on Sunday and I turned our very basic gyp room into a sort of soup kitchen, in the end feeding not just my staircase but several adjacent ones.

'In many ways those were much simpler times, before mobile phones, computers and the internet. I think we were probably more social then in the sense of actually doing things together, rather than via FaceBook. Many happy hours were spent in the bar with elaborate table football tournaments, darts games and of course pinball. When the first Pac-Man arcade game turned up, I spent more time on it than I should and received the dubious accolade of being the first person to finish the last level.

'Sport was prevalent, and like many I rowed for a while. Hurtling down Victoria Road on a rusty old bike to take a wooden clinker out of the old rickety boat house on a cold, damp autumn morning is a burnt-in memory. I organized College croquet for a while though, for some reason which escapes me, we had to play this on the Oxford Road sports ground rather than in College, which made for an interesting game.

'Looking back, it was a happy, carefree and hugely influential time. It is enormously pleasing to see how Fitzwilliam has matured and developed, and to feel a sense of pride that it is my College.'

Dr Sally Price with women Natural Sciences graduands in 1987

The Science Society was the first major society to be founded after the First World War. It became the largest society, with an ambitious programme of speakers, including Sir Ernest Rutherford. In the late 1980s a society for sciences was re-established under the title of the Clark Kent Society. It flourished under the presidency of Paul Dupree (1984, undergraduate and research student, now Professor of Biochemistry in Cambridge) and the inspiration of Dr Sally Price (Fellow, 1981–90; now Professor of Physical Chemistry at University College London). It attracted a good range of speakers from the Fellowship, including Professor John Coles on 'Peat Bogs, Pete Marsh, and other drowned things', and in 1988 was able to bring in Joseph Needham, the biochemist and great authority on science and civilization in China. But the Society faded when Sally departed for London at the end of the decade.

The Modern Language Society was established in 1956; later, as the century approached its end, there was an increasing establishment of subject societies, such as those for Geography and for Economics.

Drama

By the late 1950s the Fitzwilliam House Amateur Dramatic Society had adopted a much more adventurous repertoire than the drawing-room comedies of earlier times. In 1959, they joined with St Catharine's to give a specially-translated world première of Ionesco's *The Future is in Eggs*, followed by the second English performance of Brecht's *The Exception and the Rule* – to provide, in the words of the *Broadsheet* critic, 'what must be among the most stimulating and entertaining evenings in the history of Cambridge Undergraduate Theatre'. Two years later, they produced Anouilh's *Antigone*; then, Fry's *The Lady's not for Burning* and Frisch's *The Fire Raisers*.

When Fitzwilliam moved to its new buildings, its theatrical members were enthusiastic to exploit the Reddaway Room, in the Hall block. The new location was matched by a new name – *Fitzwilliam Theatre* – and emphasis on modern plays, stage conventions and dialogue. Terence Smith (1962) envisaged a full pro-gramme of performances and weekly play-readings. The first production in the Reddaway Room was Cocteau's *Orpheus*, directed by Tony Harrison (1962) and Peter Ridgewell (1961), with full audiences.

So it continued: Arden's *The Happy Haven*, and Brecht's *The Caucasian Chalk Circle*, with the first appearance of David Starkey (1964) on a Fitzwilliam stage. Two years later, he and Paul Humberstone (1964) produced *The Trojan War Will Not Take Place*, by Jean Giraudoux, again well-suited to a stylized setting with actors close to the audience. The year 1967 saw freshman Nick Clarke (1967) on stage in *A Scent of Flowers* – just a few years after its first performance.

The Theatre catered for many tastes, not exclusively for experimental modernists. In the same year as *Scent*, the revue *Fitz the Bill* was an unqualified success. But, as Nick Whines wrote in 1969: 'The Fitzwilliam Theatre is a strange animal. An innate tendency to hibernate continually gives way periodically to bursts of the most vigorous activity ... but before one has time to grow used to this new pattern of behaviour one discovers it peacefully asleep again.'

In recent years the FitzTheatre productions have been more variegated, and more classical. Shakespearian productions, *Richard III* and *Julius Caesar*, have alternated with eighteenth-century and nineteenth-century pieces: Sheridan's *The Critic*, *London Assurance* by Dion Boucicault, and *The Government Inspector* by Nikolai Gogol. Modernity

has been represented by *The History Boys* by Alan Bennett, whilst the acoustics of the Auditorium have encouraged musicals: *Sweet Charity* by Cy Coleman and *Sweeney Todd* by Sondheim.

Above: *A Scent of Flowers*, in which 'David Starkey gave a suspiciously convincing portrayal of an attempted seduction' according to the *Fitzwilliam Magazine*

Left: Programme, with signatures, from *The Caucasian Chalk Circle*

Music

After the Second World War, a strong musical presence was established, with two or three events each term; opera and operetta were prominent, with Mozart's *Bastien and Bastienne*, Handel's *Acis and Galatea* (in a Coronation Concert in 1953) and Gilbert and Sullivan's *Trial by Jury* and *The Sorcerer*. Students included Humphrey Burton (1951), who would achieve national recognition as a writer and broadcaster on music. The leadership of Norman Pounds (p. 60) and Peter Tranchell (later Director of Music at Caius) proved vital; Tranchell wrote at least two operettas for Fitzwilliam: *Murder at the Towers* and *Daisy Simpkins*.

Each year started with a Freshmen's Concert. The Fitzwilliam Singers gave their first concert in 1947; recitals by leading professionals such as harpsichordist Thurston Dart and violinist Jelly d'Aranyi were hosted. Grave considered the Musical Society to be 'a means of bringing town and gown together, and also of bringing Fitzwilliam House to the favourable notice of a considerable public'. A ground-breaking event was a concert in 1950 of music by Vivaldi, then almost unknown; it was necessary to collect copies of the manuscripts from Turin. In 1963, new works by students Nicholas Marshall (1961) and John Turner (1961) were presented, and the Fitzwilliam Singers performed Charpentier's *Messe de Minuit*.

At Huntingdon Road, the Reddaway Room functioned as the main concert hall, with smaller events in the adjacent Music Room and madrigals from the Hall gallery; the Hall was pressed into service for orchestral concerts. Some student musicians who later made their names professionally took their first steps, including conductor David Atherton (1962), violinist Roger Garland (1964) and recorder player John Turner (1961). The repertoire was varied, with music by Bartók, Smetana's *Sonata* for eight hands at two pianos – even John Cage's infamous 'silent' work *4'33"* was 'heard'. The core repertoire was chamber music, although groups such as the Fitzwilliam Madrigal Group began.

In the mid-1960s, College music gained an enormous boost from the arrival of Fitzwilliam's first Music Fellow, Dr Alan Brown (expert on the music of William Byrd) and Dr Denis New, a fine pianist – often performing duets. The numbers of Music Tripos students averaged two a year; as today, typical for most colleges. While Dr Alan Brown (1965–73), Dr Mervyn Cooke (1988–93) and Dr Peter Tregear (2001–06) were at Fitzwilliam there was an internal Director of Studies, but otherwise the College relied on external Directors over the half century following the post-war creation of the Music Tripos. These included the distinguished musicians Peter Tranchell, Dr Peter le Huray, Dr Hugh Wood and Dr Rohan Stewart-McDonald. Denis New maintained continuity over many decades, and music in the College has benefited from the support of many Fellows, including Dr John Cherry, Dr Christopher Nex, Dr Elisabeth Marseglia, Nicola Padfield and Professor Michael Potter, as well as that of successive Masters.

To mark the 1969 centenary, a celebratory string quartet was commissioned from leading composer Sebastian Forbes; the Fitzwilliam String Quartet performed it in the Reddaway Room in March 1970.

Musical life on 'the hill' was enhanced in 1966, when Fitzwilliam joined New Hall and Churchill to promote joint concerts, particularly larger-scale performances; almost no college can maintain a permanent orchestra on its own. An intercollegiate orchestra was formed in 1987, as well as a College String Orchestra in 1987–88 , and a short-lived Fitzwilliam College Orchestra in 1996. The West Cambridge Symphony Orchestra was founded in 1991, by two Fitzwilliam students with support from the Music Society, but after a decade it transformed into the University of Cambridge Philharmonic Orchestra.

Dr Denis New, 1929–2009

Its successor, the Orchestra on the Hill, began in 2002 and gives three or four concerts a year (shared between Fitzwilliam, Churchill and Murray Edwards); one features music by student composers, giving budding writers a rare chance to hear their own orchestral creations.

In 1973–74 three concerts in conjunction with New Hall included music by Palestrina and Charles Ives, with the repertoire expanding to Stravinsky, Britten, Walton, Malcolm Arnold and David Bedford – focusing on contemporary music, especially by British composers. A few years later a Sunday concert series was started. The musical year still started with a Freshers' Concert; the Music Society proudly announced 10 concerts in 1979–80. The number of events grew each year, including trips to London, such as to the Coliseum to see the ENO's *La Bohème*. Following in the footsteps of jazz pianist Colin Purbrook (1955), nascent music professionals studying in the 1970s and 1980s included violist Martin Outram (1979), opera director John Ramster (1986) and songwriter Nick Drake (p. 136).

The first annual Music Society dinner was held in 1979, and this tradition, with a guest speaker (a distinguished alumnus or a professional performer like Harry Danks or Howard Davies) continues, as part of a larger Music Weekend. By the mid-1980s the Music Society had a constitution and better record-keeping; Andrew Meredith (1983) was the first President. Finances were never easy, given the range and scope of the Society's activities; in 1988 it reported drily that 'the annual drama of obtaining funds from the JMA commensurate with the Society's status was negotiated more successfully than usual ...'. The position was eased by the creation of the E.D. Davies and Milner Walton Funds, and by Norman Pounds' support of the Fitzwilliam String Quartet.

Music flourished in the mid-1980s: the six-concert Lent Term chamber series was well established; the Music Room had acquired a Bösendorfer grand piano; there was a fine new Goble double-manual harpsichord; a vocal ensemble, Cantabile, was founded by Chris Henderson (1972) and Bob Bryan (1975); and performers like oboist Rachel Frost (1983; now with the Chamber Orchestra of Europe) were gaining University instrumental awards. Denis New reported in the 1984 *Journal*, 'I feel mild euphoria for the present and considerable optimism for the future. More students than ever before can sing or play well enough to take part in musical events'. There followed the creation of the May Week music Garden

THE CHAPEL CHOIR

Thanks to the broadcasts of *Nine Lessons and Carols* from King's College Chapel since 1928, around the world Cambridge is indelibly associated with church music. The post-war period has seen a flourishing of chapel music across Cambridge, with Fitzwilliam taking due part. The Chapel Choir provides music for the Sunday services, sings Compline twice each term, undertakes concerts, tours and services in Cambridge and beyond, and provides music for College events such as the Commemoration Dinner. There is an annual joint choral service with our Oxford sister College, St Edmund Hall.

At Trumpington Street, the Chapel could hold only about 25 people, with no organ or piano. There was much more scope in the temporary Chapel in the Lasdun buildings, permitting a formal Chapel Choir, in 1981 directed by student Paul Chambers, who was made Chapel Precentor. The Choir for many years contained a significant number of singers from New Hall amongst its 25 members. In the late 1980s Dr Mervyn Cooke became Director of Chapel Music, with oversight of these activities.

With the MacCormac Chapel came an excellent organ (p. 97), a Steinway grand piano, and the first of the Organ Scholars, Kathryn Magson (2000–03). Choir tours began, to Ghent in 2003, then Hungary, Italy and France. A few years later Fitzwilliam joined the University's Choral Awards scheme, indicating the importance attached to chapel music, with the first Choral Scholars in 2001; there are six each year. The Choir's repertoire ranges over 400 years of music – enhanced with the première of a new commission each term.

The first known musical setting of the College Grace, *Oculi omnium in te sperant* (*The eyes of all wait upon thee*), is by Dr Alan Brown, first performed in May 1969 – a *Centenary Grace for Fitzwilliam*. Twenty years passed before the next was written, by Dr Cooke for the 1989 Commemoration Dinner. This was the progenitor of Organ Scholars' annual settings: the record is held by Will Warns (2009–12) with four, while Ellie Goodfield (2004–07) and Alex West (2005–09) have contributed three each.

Alex West, Organ Scholar

THE FITZWILLIAM STRING QUARTET

The Fitzwilliam String Quartet has preserved its essence despite repeated renewal of its members. Fitzwilliam violinists Nicholas Dowding and John Phillips first came together in 1968 to perform a Handel trio sonata, and went on to form the Quartet at the College in Michaelmas 1968 with Alan George of King's and Ioan Davies of St John's. Of these original members, only Alan is still playing with the Quartet.

The Quartet made its international reputation early with its interpretation of the works of Shostakovich: they played the British premières of his last three quartets. He regarded them as the preferred performers of his quartets, as he told Benjamin Britten. Although most of their performances emphasize modern and unconventional compositions, they developed capability with historical instruments whilst they were Quartet in Residence at the University of York in the 1980s. Since 1999, they have been Quartet in Residence at Fitzwilliam, and return to College regularly to give concerts and to work with student performers and ensembles.

The Fitzwilliam Quartet at their 40th Birthday Concert: Lucy Russell (violin), Jonathan Sparey (violin), Heather Tuach (cello) and Alan George (viola)

Party, the Professional Recital Series, the foundation of a College Wind Band and the 'Out of the Blues' jazz group; Fitzwilliam was hosting about a dozen concerts each year. One special event took place in May 1990: a musical celebration for the knighthood of the recently-retired Master, Professor James Holt.

The year 1990 was very busy, with the College hosting Yehudi Menuhin (Honorary Fellow from 1991) and his Cambridge Symposium for Young String Quartets. The splendid new Chapel came into service. The Music Society Junior President Simon Keefe (1987; now Professor of Music at Sheffield), reported some of the additional ensembles active in College: a string quartet, a wind quintet, a brass group and a vocal ensemble. A much-needed new Steinway grand piano was acquired in 1991. The Society handbook for 1995–96 listed six active ensembles; the Society then, as now, saw its role as supporting the musical interests of all students. Concert programmes could be very ambitious: in 1998, for example, Philip Collin (1995) conducted the College Orchestra and Chapel Choir in Haydn's oratorio *The Seasons*; contemporary students with later professional careers included bass Matthew Waldren (1995).

The first dedicated Director of Music (previous holders had also directed studies), Jonathan Sanders, arrived in 1994, to be succeeded by composer Andrew Lovett, whose music was performed in College on several occasions. It was during his time that the Fitzwilliam String Quartet became the College's ensemble-in-residence. Oversight by resident professional musicians contributes to continuity, the secret of creating lasting musical traditions.

In 2001 Dr Peter Tregear arrived as College Lecturer in Music and Director of Music, and brought new energy to Fitzwilliam. Enhanced facilities included a Bechstein grand piano donated by Denis New (who had retired in 1997), a harpsichord donated by Dr Kenneth Swinburne, and a pair of timpani. The Music Society and FitzTheatre gave a joint production of *Cabaret* in the Reddaway Room. However, Fitzwilliam music had outgrown its old spaces, and the opening in 2005 of the magnificent new Auditorium gave great pleasure. The inaugural concert included the Fitzwilliam String Quartet and recorder player John Turner, and specially-composed music by alumni Nicholas Marshall and Andy Price (2006). It made a very successful concert hall, even for fully-staged operas and musicals (early productions included *Dido and Aeneas* and *Jesus Christ Superstar*). The creation and re-creation of ensembles continued apace: James Crawford founded The Oriana Singers in 2005, and there was a new College flute ensemble.

When Tregear returned to Australia, Dr Michael Downes became Director of Music. A revitalized professional recital series was sponsored by the College's solicitors, Hewitsons. A New Music group called Ensemble CB3 was founded, and also Fitzwilliam Chamber Opera; the only permanent college-based opera

ALKAN PIANO COMPETITIONS

To promote the music of French romantic composer Charles-Valentin Alkan (1813–88), the annual Alkan Piano Prize was founded in 2001 by Dr Ken Smith (Fellow 1966, and Life Fellow since 1988) and concert pianist Ronald Smith (1922–2004). The contest encourages talented pianists; initially only for Fitzwilliam students, since 2007 it has been open to players from nearby colleges. Each year, the competition is followed by a professional evening recital, for which performers have included Ronald Smith himself, Thomas Wakefield, Lloyd Buck and Emanuele Delucchi.

FITZWILLIAM HOUSE

INAUGURAL CONCERT

in the Lecture Hall, Fitzwilliam House
on Sunday, 17th November, 1963, at 8.15 p.m.

1. HYMNS (1962)   *Malcolm Williamson*

New every morning is the love
Awake, my soul, and with the sun
Faith of our fathers, living still
Crown him with many crowns

John Turner and The Billytones

2. FRIENDLY GROTESQUES (1953)   *Peter Tranchell*
Tempo di Turkey-Trot; Rumboid; Valse d'Ivresse; Pas à quatre mains gauche

Peter Tranchell and David Atherton (*piano duet*)

3. SERENADE in D minor, Op. 44 (1878)   *Dvorak*
Moderato quasi Marcia; Minuetto; Andante con moto; Allegro molto

Margaret Gilchrist, Clare Shanks (*oboes*)
Antony Pay, Alan Maries (*clarinets*)
David Klausner, Alastair Gilchrist (*bassoons*)
Keith Maries, John Escott, Nicholas Marshall (*horns*)
Christopher van Kampen ('*cello*), Simon Carrington (*double bass*)
Conductor: David Atherton

INTERVAL
(during which Refreshments will be served)

4. FLUTE TRIO in G minor, Op. 63 (1819)   *Weber*
Allegro moderato; Scherzo (Allegro vivace); Andante espressivo; Allegro

John Turner (*flute*), Andrew Ritchie ('*cello*)
John Hughes (*piano*)

5. TOY SYMPHONY, Op. 62 (1957)   *Malcolm Arnold*
Allegro; Allegretto; Vivace
Conductor: Peter Tranchell

group in Cambridge, since 2007 it has staged an ambitious series of baroque and modern works in the Auditorium and at the ADC Theatre, including Handel's *Xerxes*, Purcell's *The Fairy Queen* and *Dido and Aeneas*, Monteverdi's *Orfeo*, Gilbert and Sullivan's *Iolanthe*, Judith Weir's *The Consolation of Scholarship* and Ivan Moody's *Fables of La Fontaine* – a world première.

The number of music scholarships expanded from organ, voice and piano to include awards for piano accompaniment and saxophone, and another important new activity was an annual College music festival, with concerts, lectures and workshops to mark the anniversary of a significant composer (to date, Vaughan Williams, Henry Purcell, Malcolm Arnold and Louis Couperin). Two years later Downes was succeeded by Francis Knights. College music activity grows apace: Fitzwilliam now has a more substantial concert series than any other college, and better facilities, more music ensembles and a larger library (much of it from a generous donation by music publisher Clifford Bartlett). Helped by Fitzwilliam's best-ever music academic results in 2012, College music is set fair for the future.

IN LIGHTER VEIN –
BARBERSHOP AND SIRENS

There was much diversification in the 1990s. Robin Morgan founded Fitz Swing (now a University ensemble, but it keeps the title and rehearses in College). In 1994 came Fitz Barbershop, founded by Alex Tester (1993) who composed their theme tune, and The Sirens, two a cappella groups that flourish to this day, gaining awards in national competitions, performing at numerous May Balls every year, at garden parties, and much more widely – Barbershop sang at 10 Downing Street, and in its own show at the ADC Theatre. It is recognizable for its close-harmony singing and its trademark waistcoats, The Sirens for their little black dresses.

Barbershop and The Sirens have renewed themselves successfully over many generations of students, but the more usual pattern is that ventures flare for a moment and die. Thus did the 1950s Rock and Roll band Rich Rich and the Moneymakers, flourishing 2002 to 2004, with Richard Benwell (2001), a long-term and exuberant member of Barbershop.

The Sirens at the 2011 Music Society May Week garden party

Barbershop in the Bar after the 2012 Music Society Dinner

The College Chapel and its Chaplains

The story of Fitzwilliam Chapel since 1945 falls into three clearly-defined phases: 1945–56; 1956–93; and 1993 to the present. The defining feature is finance. In the first period there was no money to support a Chaplain, and those who served were members of the House reading for degrees; in the second, money for a full-time Chaplain was secured first from the Council of the Senate and then from the College; most recently, resources were available to support a Chaplain only at partial stipend. The Chaplaincy Endowment Appeal raised sufficient money by 2008 to support the post at 75% stipend, with the hope that eventually it would return to full-time. This explains why the average length of service was over 4½ years in the middle period, but was 2½ years or less in the first and the recent periods.

Walter Harvey had been Chaplain, Assistant Censor and Bursar, as well as Vicar of Horningsea, until he retired in 1944. After the war the House swelled in numbers, but in 1948 the General Secretary of the Amalgamated Clubs wondered how many members knew where the Chapel was. In that year John Sertin was appointed. By 1950 the average Sunday evening congregation had reached 20. Bruce Reed (1950–54) and John Moroney (1954–56) followed, both Australians already ordained and undertaking studies at Ridley Hall. None could give full attention to the task, but costs were low. All were on the evangelical side of the Anglican spectrum. Reed was an

effective preacher, who secured the use of St Michael's Church for Sunday evening services. By 1953 the Sunday evening congregation had doubled, and by 1955 they were increasing further.

The year of greatest change in the life of the Chapel came in 1956 with the appointment of Peter Schneider (1949), a research student; he was full-time from 1958. Schneider was a remarkable man, from a German-Jewish background, whose later career was devoted to the improvement of Christian-Jewish relations. Under Schneider, Free Churchmen were welcomed into the life of the Chapel and a Chapel Committee was reconstituted. The 1950s were a good time for church attendance more generally and Chapel attendances rose similarly. After a successful Carol Service in 1957 in Ridley Hall chapel, evensong was transferred there permanently. In 1960 Schneider was followed by Francis Palmer (1960–64) and Peter Nott (1964–69).

Palmer also was an evangelical, and eventually became Lichfield Diocesan Missioner and Prebendary of Lichfield Cathedral. Nott (1958) was very different: after serving both in the Army and in industry, he read Theology at Westcott House. He was later Bishop of Norwich. Despite different backgrounds and churchmanship, both shared Schneider's commitment to an open vision for the Chapel community where everyone was welcome. The variety of Sunday evening preachers increased; and a Quiet Day was introduced. The first Roman Catholic member of the

Chapel members in the grounds of Ridley Hall, Easter term 1960

Chapel Committee was appointed in 1961, and Mass was permitted in 1966. By 1967 the new Communion liturgy in modern English had been adopted for Sunday mornings. Sunday evening attendances were around 75 by the mid-1960s.

Vacation activities were organized ranging from retreats to parish missions. In 1961 a small group visited the Iona Community, and in the following year thirty students from six denominations joined in a ten-day mission to Stowmarket, organized by the town's churches. Visits were also made to Lee Abbey, Camberwell and a Birmingham parish with a high immigrant population. In 1966 a group spent a week with the Taizé Community in the Rhone valley. Originally a French Reformed religious community, in the spirit of the Second Vatican Council it welcomed Catholic and Orthodox members. When the Fitzwilliam group first visited, the Community had recently opened its new large chapel and the style of life was rather different from today. But its pattern of worship and reflection had a profound effect, and as a result the regular pattern of Morning and Evening Prayer (including Sunday evenings) was modified with a new Daily Office, and the choir led the congregation in learning Joseph Gelineau's setting of the psalms. A second visit was made in 1967. The first New Hall students began to attend Chapel in 1965. Regular visits to the nearby Old People's Home at Primrose Croft began soon afterwards.

The College Statutes of 1966 provided for a Chapel and a Chaplain, who could be a minister of any member church of the World Council of Churches. Martin Baddeley (1969–74) followed Nott's policy for the Chapel, including responsibility for New Hall, thereby adding a new dimension to the Chapel community; several married couples resulted. Baddeley eventually became Principal of the Southwark Ordination Course. John Beer (1974–80), also from Westcott, eventually became Archdeacon of Cambridge. John Mantle (1980–86) came from the Scottish Episcopal Church, and in 2006 was elected as Bishop of his home diocese of Brechin.

By comparison with the initiatives in the early 1960s, the 1970s and 1980s were quieter. The ecumenical atmosphere of the Chapel was maintained; but just as the 1950s boom in church attendance had blown itself out in the 1960s, so the gradual decline from that decade onwards was reflected in undergraduate support for the Chapel. The ecumenical optimism of the 1960s ran into the buffers, with significant dissenting minorities in the Church of England. Reform of Canon Law, and the new Declaration of Assent, requiring the use only of authorized forms of service, restricted liturgical experiments. Fr Richard Incledon, Catholic Chaplain to the University, preached in 1977, although he was not the first Catholic to do so. The funds from the Thatcher Organ Scholarship were used temporarily to fund a Chapel Precentor from 1980; and another visit to Taizé was made in 1985. While Mark Honeyball (1986–90) was Chaplain, students from the Theological Colleges began to come to the Chapel on attachments for a term or a year; this has continued. By 1989 the choir of 26 was half the evening congregation. However, an era came to an end when New Hall terminated the link with the Chapel in 1990.

At this point the College made an inspired choice of Chaplain, older than anyone since Peter Schneider: he was David Isitt (1990–93), previously Chaplain at both King's College and Trinity Hall. David used his previous experience at King's to guide the College, as it built an organ for the new Chapel and appointed its first Organ Scholars. The new building led to a renaissance in Chapel life, and the choir became even more significant, with more Choral Scholars appointed. David chose as the new hymnbook for the Chapel *Rejoice and Sing*, published by the United Reformed Church in 1991, which replaced *The BBC Hymn Book* of 40 years before. Within the year the first Memorial Service had been held in Chapel (for Jack Street), the first baptisms and the first wedding (Richard Dyball, a Fellow). A Staff Carol Service was introduced, reflecting the fact that successive Chaplains now found themselves ministering also to the College staff, as their links with local churches became more tenuous. David generously gave the money for a new altar in 1994.

After Isitt's retirement the College took a further new step by appointing its first non-Anglican, David Horrell, a Methodist (1993–95). He was a New Testament scholar, who completed a PhD during his chaplaincy. This partial reversion to an older pattern was due to the decision to reduce the chaplaincy to a 75% post in view of increasing financial pressures since the end of New Hall's contribution. When David moved to Exeter University (where he is now a Professor), Michael Lloyd, who had just finished as Chaplain of Christ's, was appointed for a year (1995–96), while arrangements for a new appointment were made. The result was a joint post with Wesley House, to which Ben Quash, now Professor at King's College, London, was appointed (1996–99).

LESLIE GRIFFITHS

Leslie Griffiths is one of the most distinguished Fitzwilliam alumni to have belonged to the Attached Houses. He came to Fitzwilliam in 1967 to train for the Methodist ministry at Wesley House. After reading Medieval English at the University of Wales, Cardiff (1960–63), he was an Assistant Lecturer in English in the University of Wales. He played Rugby for the Fitzwilliam Second XV, as well as refereeing on occasions. For Leslie, his membership of Fitzwilliam 'ensured that my study of theology could never be a cloistered affair, but was always exposed to the fresh breezes of a broad swathe of other disciplines and cultural influences'.

After graduating in Theology, he was a minister in Haiti for two periods in the 1970s and wrote a History of Haitian Methodism. Back in England he did a PhD at the School of Oriental and African Studies (1987) and since 1991 he has been a minister in London, currently at Wesley's Chapel in the City. This historic church was built in 1778 by Wesley to replace his original chapel at the Foundery. Leslie was President of the Methodist Conference from 1994 to 1995, and was made an ecumenical Canon of St Paul's Cathedral in 2000. Four years later he was raised to the peerage as Baron Griffiths of Burry Port, and speaks regularly in the House of Lords.

Baron Griffiths of Burry Port

Vanessa Herrick (1999–2002) was the first woman Chaplain, followed by Lorraine Cavanagh (2003) as temporary Chaplain, while she finished her doctorate. In 2002 the Governing Body took the significant decision to launch a new Chaplaincy Endowment Fund, with the aim of making the Chaplaincy self-supporting at 75% level by 2008. Both Chapel and College gained: the Chapel, by removing uncertainty at each vacancy, and the College, by the release of funds for general purposes. The target of £750,000 was reached by 2008. Simon Perry (a Baptist, now Chaplain of Robinson) followed Lorraine (2003–06). In Simon's time the significance of the choir became more apparent, as well as a new range of week-night activities, especially his 'Beyond Belief' meetings on Fridays, when a larger proportion of the College community could be gathered than on Sundays. Jutta Brueck (2006–08) reported that student initiatives such as a three-day 24-hour prayer vigil and the Friday night café had been successful. The Chapel visit to Taizé in 2008 was regarded as a new initiative, though the earlier visits were not in the company of 2,000 other young people! The smooth succession of Dr Tiffany Conlin (2008–11) illustrated the beneficial effect of the success of the Chaplaincy Endowment. She commented astutely that 'while the Chapel is the visible and audible "ship" of faith within the College, there is a significant unseen "submarine" of faithful activity'. By that she meant the student-led Christian groups, individuals who used the Chapel for their prayers, students who gave time and care to others in Cambridge, those of Christian faith, another faith or no faith, who consulted the Chaplain, and those who supported the Chaplaincy through their prayers, practical skills, giving and thoughtfulness. A better description of the range of the Chapel's significance has rarely been offered. When Tiffany returned to Westcott House as Director of Pastoral Studies, she was succeeded by Dr John Munns, who came from a post in the History of Art at Bristol University.

Since 2006 Chapel worship has moved closer to the pre-war high-church pattern, but without losing its ecumenical openness. A College Communion is held every term for all Christians in College, though this also indicates that the weekly Sunday morning eucharist has generally ceased to appeal to those few members of College in the free church tradition. There is usually a sung Compline on a weekday evening. Throughout the period the regular support of some Fellows on Sundays has always been important, though it has never reached the level of some older colleges. Many students remember the Chapel's existence only in a crisis, but there has always been a group of students who have regularly supported its life, on Sundays and on weekdays, always with a sense of fun. In Vanessa Herrick's words, it has been 'a place of quiet refuge'.

Above: Commemorative prow for the 1955 First May Boat

Right: The 1969 performance was commemorated by an impressive piece of silver presented by Sir John Stratton – a silver boat by the notable silversmith Brian Asquith

Post-war sport

After the Second World War it took time to re-establish the Boat Club, but by 1948 five boats were entered for the Fairbairns. Morale was enhanced in the 1950 Lents, when the first eight made an over-bump. The crew was already competing in regattas and going to the Tideway Head of the River. A year later, the first eight made four bumps; then two eights went to the Tideway. The Club was awarded the Michell Cup for the best performance on the river in the course of the year. In the 1955 Mays the first eight won its oars.

Ray Kelly set a challenge at the 1960 Mays Dinner: the First Boat would need to make only three bumps a year to go Head in the centenary year. And in 1969 the Boat duly went Head. Head also in the Lents, and second in the Fairbairns, winning the Head of the Cam, and having several good regattas – despite contributing men to the Blue Boat and to Goldie.

The First Boat remained Head for two further years, but this was not to be repeated. Even so, there could still be very rewarding outcomes. In 1981, the crew benefited greatly from the guidance of Bob Winckless (1966), and they performed well in the Ladies Plate at Henley.

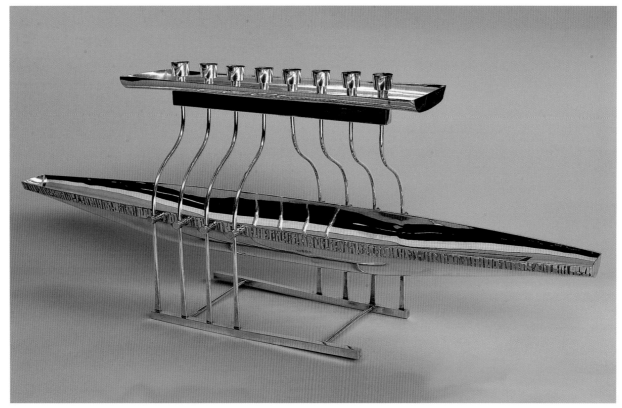

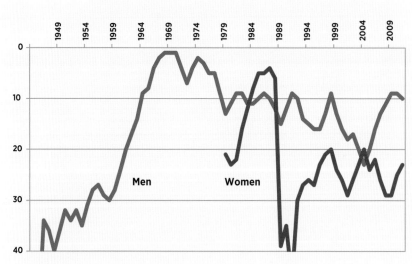

Performance of men's and women's first boats

Left: Carole Burton with the Boat
Race Ladbrooke Trophy

Below: The *Sarah Winckless*

With co-residence came the first women members of
the Boat Club, both in women's crews and as coxes with
male rowers – the earliest in the Club records being Hilary
Farnworth, cox of the 1981 Third Lent boat. The women's
boats initially made rapid progress, reaching fourth
position in the First Division of the Mays in 1988 but
declined thereafter.

There were highly creditable individual performances.
In 1981, Sylvia van Kleef was in the Boat Race Women's
reserve crew. Four years later Carole Burton coxed the
University Women's Lightweights at Henley to a very
clear win over Oxford, and in 1986 she was the first
female Cambridge cox for the Blue Boat, in which Ian
Clarke was at bow – they won. Carole was an exceptional
student, and got a First in Medical Sciences despite
coxing and serious illness.

Sarah Winckless had a very impressive career in
rowing, starting without prior experience when she came
up in 1993 to read Natural Sciences. After competing in
the Women's eights at the 1998 World Championships,
she converted to sculling and won a bronze medal in the
2004 Olympic Games, followed by gold medals in the
2005 and 2006 World Championships.

Above: Andrew Hope (1967) running for Cambridge in the 1968 Varsity Cross-Country Race

Above right: Eddie Butler in action for Wales, 1984

Right: Badminton in the 1950s: Johnny Hock Aun Heah

The policy of Norman Walters in raising the profile of the College through sporting prowess had an enduring legacy at Oxford Road as well as on the river, with successes for the College teams and a very substantial contribution to University sport. In 1971–81, for instance, there were 14 Blues or Half-Blues, ranging from rugby and soccer to real tennis and Eton fives. And the tradition continues: Fitzwilliam won soccer Cuppers in 2013.

Two years after Alastair Hignell (p. 137), Eddie Butler came up – as the *Journal* stated: 'from the wilds of West Wales'. He had Rugby Union Blues in 1976, 1977 and 1978; he went on to be capped for Wales on 16 occasions, six times as Captain. He continues to write on rugby for the *Observer* and the *Guardian*, and to commentate for the BBC.

On the cricket field, Derek Pringle (1978) played for the University, and was called up for England in his final undergraduate year. Altogether, he played in 30 test matches – in his later years as an effective swing bowler. He continues as a cricket correspondent.

MORNIE ONIONS AND OTHERS

The Mornie Onions was a social gathering of Fitzwilliam sportsmen, founded by Grenville Dean, who read Law from 1953 to 1956. Ritual demanded that every member wore its distinctive tie on Fridays; failure to do so, if detected, resulted in a suitably alcoholic forfeit to the detector. So the custom grew up of wearing the tie concealed in ever more unreasonable locations – and false challenges reversed the forfeit. With co-residence came sporting women and they adapted the prevailing customs, forming the Shallots, with their own sartorial embellishment.

Christopher Martin-Jenkins at Lords, c. 1985

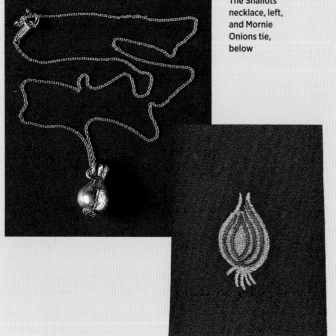

The Shallots necklace, left, and Mornie Onions tie, below

A life-long cricket journalist, Christopher Martin-Jenkins (1964) – CMJ – commentated for four decades. He came up in 1964 to read History; for the University, he had two Half-Blues for Rugby fives, although cricket was his primary sport. As well as commentating, he was cricket correspondent for the *Daily Telegraph* and *The Times*, writing up to his death in January 2013. At his Memorial Service in St Paul's Cathedral in April 2013, the Address was given by The Rt Rev. Peter Nott (p. 146).

Winners of Cricket Cuppers in 1972 ...

... brought together four decades later

13

ALUMNI INVOLVEMENT

Left: The 1965
Reunion Dinner

Below: Relaxing at
a Reunion

The Fitzwilliam Society

During the war, the Society largely went into abeyance; a
diminished *Journal* was published, but social events lapsed.
The first post-war Reunion, in August 1947, coincided
with Reddaway's 75th birthday. Normality returned slowly
for the 638 members of the Society. The first London
Dinner, at the Trocadero in January 1948, saw only 24
attending. However, the broader position was
encouraging, as new members outnumbered losses.

The annual pattern was reinstated, with a London
Dinner and a Cambridge Reunion, attended by a small,
but highly loyal, group of members, many of whom were
active in support of the move towards collegiate status
(p. 69). But typically there were only 36 at the Reunion and
40 at the London Dinner. Each summer, as well as the
Society Reunion there was a Gathering of Old Members to
which the College invited specific year-groups; from 1994,
these were merged to form a single Fitzwilliam Reunion.
Held in September to coincide with the University's
Alumni Weekend, this is now the most successful
Cambridge reunion, and stretches the capacity of the
College for accommodation and dining.

One constant since the Society was founded has been
the *Journal*. The first Editor, Guy Milner Walton, produced
it from 1928 for almost 40 years. He was followed by John
Adams, Roger Coleby, Ernest Saunders, and Norman
Pounds – none in Cambridge. It was only in 1986 that
Fellows of the College started to edit the *Journal*, with
Geoffrey Hunt, followed by the Rev. Canon David Isitt.
Its importance grew after the *Fitzwilliam Magazine* ceased
to provide a record of events. Dr David Thompson was
elected Editor in 1994, and the format that he instituted
has been maintained to the present, with some development by Dr John Cleaver since 2005. The cost is shared
between the Society and the College. Nearly 10,000 copies
are distributed to members and friends of Fitzwilliam
across the world.

The Billygoats, supporting the Boat Club

A major strand of benevolence in Fitzwilliam has come for
many years from the Billygoats. The society was formed
in 1948 under the leadership of John Hunter (1946), to
foster continuity between past and present members of
the Boat Club and to provide moral and financial support;
its first President was John Stratton. As for any good
society, its first action was to set up annual dinners: one in
Hall on Fairbairn Cup night, and the other in London on
Boat Race night (an aspiration – it occurred only once).
There is a dinner in Henley at the time of the Regatta.

THE FITZWILLIAM SOCIETY TRUST

By 1950, the Fitzwilliam Society had built up more than £5,000 from donations and subscriptions; this was eroded in 1958 by the boathouse purchase (p. 157), and in 1963 stood at about £2,000. Funds had been managed by the trustees of the Fitzwilliam Hall Trust but reverted to the Society when the Trust closed (p. 78).

Celebrating its half-century, the Society launched its Jubilee Appeal in 1973; about £4,000 was received and £1,700 covenanted in a year. To manage funds, the Fitzwilliam Society Trust Ltd was set up. Its object was to support the undergraduate and graduate students of the College, in their academic life, in music and drama, and with infrastructure – it contributed to the boathouse in 2007, and paid for the Societies Room in College. In its three-decade life, it attracted more than £50,000 in donations from members of the Society. Funds built up with good-quality management; its charitable status facilitated a good rate of return and freed it from tax liabilities, so the value of the donations was nearly quadrupled by the investment income.

In addition, about £86,000 was bequeathed by Rev. Lester Brewster, a New Zealander who came to Fitzwilliam in 1948. He was a freelance priest who divided his time between the cemeteries of Southwark and the English community of St Moritz; he donated The Vicar's Vase to the Cresta Club.

In 2007 the Trust controlled funds totalling £254,200 (including £38,520 on behalf of the Society); its investment income was £10,140, donations of £1,885 were received, and it made awards totalling £8,533. However, governance costs and administration were disproportionate. All awards (totalling nearly £118,000 during its period of operation) went to College members, so the managers decided to wind up the company and to transfer its assets to the College.

The Society's sum was returned and £203,133 was transferred to the College. Its identity was not lost: within College accounts, a Fitzwilliam Society fund was set up whose income provides grants similar to those made previously by the Trust, and perpetuates its contribution to the life of the College.

In 2011–12, the Fitzwilliam Society Trust Fund made awards totalling £8,195. The largest element was £5,695 for Fitzwilliam Society Research Grants, supporting research travel and attendance at academic conferences for 26 graduate students. There are four Fitzwilliam Society Scholarships, three commemorating Society members: the Coleby Scholarship (Land Economy), the Taylor Scholarship (History) and the Skinner Scholarship (Economics). There is a Stratton Prize, for which some Boat Club connection is required. Books are provided, with grants to the College Library and, as Fitzwilliam Society J.R.W. Alexander Book Awards, to students starting LLM courses. The Fitzwilliam Society Milner Walton Awards support music and drama, and there are prizes for speakers at the annual Brewster Debate.

So the generosity of the Society and its members lives on in the twenty-first century, enriching the work and the experience of successive generations of Fitzwilliam students.

THE CAREER NETWORK

Many alumni are interested in passing on experience to their successors, and for this the Fitzwilliam Career Network has been set up. It is an online network of members of the Fitzwilliam Society who volunteer as Career Contacts, giving students the benefit of their professional experience. The Career Contacts offer advice on careers, on job applications, and on work experience and internships. There are over 250 Career Contacts, from 30 different fields.

The annual Fitzwilliam Society Careers Fair brings Career Contacts back to College to talk directly to current students. In 2012, almost 40 alumni – with experience in employment ranging from five months to five decades – attended the Fair, providing advice with a degree of informality that few other fora could match, to undergraduates at all stages of the process of formulating their life plans.

Careers event in College

Above: The 1958
boathouse

Below: The 2007
boathouse

Initially, support by the Billygoats was limited to
helping crews to attend regattas – primarily Henley. In the
1960s, there were problems with provision of boats. The
1963 Henley crew resorted to purchasing the 1956 CUBC
shell eight themselves – and re-sold it, passing the profit to
the Billygoats. This was not the first occasion for self-help:
a crew in the 1890s had raised half the cost of a new boat.
Something had to be done. Stratton took the initiative
and in 1966 paid for a coxless four, stipulating only that
he wanted the best boat that money could buy.

The Billygoats established charitable status in 1966;
their financial position improved and they were able to
provide substantial support for College rowing. Between
1966 and 2011 they purchased, fully or in part, 19 boats
(including 11 eights).

Amongst the Billygoats' acquisitions was the *John
Adams*, named in 1986 in honour of their Secretary,
even though he had served them for only a quarter of a
century. John was to double that, retiring from office in
2012. This unique role was celebrated by the collection
of a very substantial sum by the Billygoats, to endow
John Adams Prizes for students who have done most to

The Bursar promised to eat his hat if the funds for the Boathouse were raised. They were, and Graham Nutter (1966) and Ken Olisa (1971) presented a monstrous mortar-board with black icing (on left table)!

promote the well-being of the Boat Club, and Bursaries to defray expenses.

In the years to 1958, the House used a very inadequate little boathouse rented from Banhams, two positions downstream from the present location. They gave notice to quit, and the opportunity was taken to purchase (from Banhams) a much more substantial boathouse which had been just been vacated by St Catharine's. This cost £5,250, of which the Fitzwilliam Society donated £1,000. At this early stage, the Billygoats' funds were small, and they made no contribution.

That boathouse served Fitzwilliam for many years – but in increasingly poor condition. With support from the Billygoats, it was replaced over the summer of 2007. After the Lent races, it was emptied and demolished, and its successor was in operation in time for the September Reunion. This brisk progress was possible because its steel frame and industrial roof cladding enabled internal work to begin before the walls were complete – but also because the Bursar (in hard hat, with College crest on the front) chivvied the contractor, who delivered on time.

Altogether, in their 65 years of existence, the Billygoats have contributed the 2010 equivalent of more than a quarter of a million pounds in support of Fitzwilliam.

BEHIND THE SCENES AT FITZWILLIAM

Edward King in front of the
pavilion at Oxford Road

Staff in past times

From the early days, the staff have contributed immensely
to the experience and the quality of life of the students. At
the House, the general factotum was A.J. Holmes, a man
of great character and very powerful physique who had
earned his Distinguished Conduct Medal as a stretcher-
bearer with the Cambridgeshires. Holmes was intensely
loyal to Thatcher and to Fitzwilliam – he had his own
views, but would always respond to a personal appeal.
Anything he took on would be done well. In the very
difficult time after the Second World War he acted as
Head Waiter, and was a tower of strength. Edwin Hawkins
(1946) wrote: 'Much hard work has been put in by the staff,
both in the office and the kitchen. I well remember, in the
first week after the institution of lunches, the sight of Mr
Holmes, perspiration pouring from his forehead, and his
confident declaration *we will manage*. And manage they
most certainly have. I often wonder what *The Billy* would
be like without Mr Holmes, Mr King and Mr Barrett – but
it's fortunate that I have to do no more than wonder.'

What of Mr King and Mr Barrett? Edward King,
groundsman from 1919 to 1957, maintained Oxford
Road to a very high standard. He was a shrewd judge of
young men and of young sportsmen; he had been a soccer
and cricket player for the county before the Great War. His
judgement extended to general character, and he had a
long memory. Thatcher recalled that an American student,
returning to Cambridge after several years, went to the
ground and said 'Hello, King, do you remember me?'; the
answer came at once 'Yes, I do, you owe me 3/6d'.

Harold Barrett was recruited by Thatcher in 1924,
when he was seeking to impose some order in the first few
months of his Censorship. Fitzwilliam was administered
just by Thatcher and the Bursar; Barrett was Accountant,
Chief Clerk, and Tutors' Clerk. Although the accounts
were relatively simple, there was a very severe shortage of
funds – but his cunning built up the reserves which tided

Christmas party for the staff, in the 1950s

the House over the Second World War. He was remembered by a vast number of Fitzwilliam men for his kindliness and helpfulness. He retired in 1960. Barrett's sister became secretary to the Censor in the early 1930s and continued until 1969, working with Grave during the eventful years of transition from Trumpington Street to Huntingdon Road and from House to College. When she retired, she left an environment unchanged in its fundamentals since her brother started.

In the 1970s, radical attitudes were not confined to junior members. Trades-union membership and militancy were developing amongst the staff; unevenly, as the Porters and some other groups did not follow the trends. The College recognized union membership, but the rapid transition from paternalistic staff relations imposed severe stresses. The situation became more complex from 1979 when national officials of trades unions became involved. Professional negotiators were needed, so the College subsumed its own arrangements

into the University procedures and adopted University wage scales.

There were changes in working practice. The College purchased its first word processor, for the Senior Tutor's office. Not a rapid revolution, however, as a 1982 Governing Body Minute continued: 'If it proved useful, a second machine might be purchased for the Bursary in the summer'. And it must have been useful, as another one was purchased 18 months later.

In the early 1980s, Fitzwilliam introduced a novelty to Cambridge – its first lady Butler. Mrs Cann served very effectively for nearly a decade, and had overall responsibility also for the Hall and the Servery; she was supported by Mrs Stosiek (the wife of the Polish chef, p. 65).

Each generation of students recalls the Porters who could make their lives more or less agreeable. Not only the Head Porters – at Huntingdon Road: Sands, Barton, Gray, Norman, Banner, Goodacre, Eisold – but the individual Day and Night Porters. Roger Wilkins (1967)

Right: Marie Hall's boys

Below: Janet Whalley retired in 2009 after 25 years as Master's secretary – with her Masters

IN MEMORY OF MARIE HALL
(1927-2009)
BEDDER (1979-1993) FRIEND ALWAYS
WITH THANKS FROM HER BOYS

recalled that 'in those days, there was still a curfew time of midnight. Some colleges still did lock their gates, but Fitzwilliam Porters were a little more lenient. The gate was left ajar, but you could still get a cautionary word if the gate squeaked as you squeezed in! Some of the Porters were characters and the one that particularly springs to mind was Len Brooker. Len had been a champion boxer in the 1930s and was, in the late 1960s, the coach of the University boxing team. He smoked No 6 cigarettes and had no teeth, but he was full of wonderful tales of the good old days.'

The most personal service to the students is provided by the landladies and bedmakers, who see them at their worst as well as their best. And because of this, down the years, many alumni have maintained lifelong contact with those who looked after them as students. In the summer of 2011, six residents of D staircase in the late 1970s came to College for the inauguration of a memorial bench to commemorate Marie Hall, who had been a bedder for 24 years.

Above left: The Bursar, the Accountant and the Bursary staff

Above right: The Tutorial Office staff

Left: The Library Assistant and the Librarian

Right: The Development Director and her staff

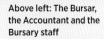

The Domestic Bursar and the Conference Office staff

The IT Department

The Communications Office

Above left: The Head Porter and staff in the Porters' Lodge

Above: The Catering Manager and the Hall Supervisor

Above: Laying up the Hall for the Graduation Dinner

Right: Briefing the waiting staff

'Master, Ladies and Gentlemen – Dinner is served'

Chefs in action

Above: The Maintenance
Department

Left: The Carpenter

Below: In the greenhouse

Above: The Domestic
staff

Right: The Decorator

Below: Gardeners in
autumn

V

THE COLLEGE TODAY

15

AN INTERNATIONAL COMMUNITY

Master and Fellows

Fitzwilliam College is a body of around 900 people: the Master and Fellows, over 300 graduate students, about 450 undergraduates, and about 130 assistant staff. Its operation depends on many further members of the University who help with Direction of Studies and supervision of undergraduates – the Accounts Department makes regular payments to about 600 people – as well as on its symbiotic relationship with the University for Departmental teaching for undergraduates and Masters-degree students, and for the research groups of which its graduate students are members.

A Cambridge college is a highly democratic institution, in which the Master and Fellows form the Governing Body which *shall in all matters whatsoever have the government and control of the College and of its property and income.* Fellows who are members of the Governing Body are in four classes: Class A Fellows hold their Fellowships by virtue of a qualifying office, which may be a teaching commitment or an office such as that of Bursar – there are

about 40 Fellows in Class A; about ten Professorial Fellows, in Class B; about five Research Fellows, in Class C; and about three supernumerary Fellows, in Class D. In addition, there are Life (Class E) Fellows, retired members who have served for a sufficient number of years in other classes; they (about 19) are not members of the Governing Body, but are entitled to take part in special meetings on changes to the College Statutes.

The Governing Body has always favoured democracy over time-saving, and so has not implemented the statute that would enable a College Council to be formed. With Councils, very many issues are never seen by Governing Bodies, dividing the Fellowship into an inner core and an uninformed periphery. With careful management a Governing Body of around 60 can hold effective meetings.

However, there have been improvements to governance, to expedite the handling of business. The Services Committee and the Finance Committee merged in 1981. Then in 1996 that Committee merged with the Elections and Appointments Committee, to form the College Committee.

graduate-student non-voting members. Only business that relates to specific individuals is reserved, and is taken in the second part. By segregating items that require discussion from those which are for information, the conduct of business has been expedited and now only two meetings are needed in the Michaelmas Term and two in Lent, with a total of six or seven in the year.

Bye-Fellows have increased in number and importance in recent years; now there are about 15, of whom most have been appointed to teach undergraduates in specific subject areas. Some are Directors of Studies and serve on committees, and they have High-Table rights, but are not members of the Governing Body. Their positions are renewed annually.

A consequence of democracy is that recommendations and decisions emerge from the sub-committees of the Governing Body, and this enables the College to draw upon the diverse range of expertise and interests of the Fellowship. Amongst the total of about 22 committees, some deal with obvious topics, such as the Education Committee and the Library Committee, but others deal with matters such as the College estates, fine art, and environmental issues. Alumni are co-opted onto the Development Committee and the Investment Advisory Committee, and graduate and undergraduate student members attend nearly half of all the committees – including the venerable General Purposes Committee, set up specifically to give junior members a voice (p. 136), and still fulfilling that role four decades later.

The Education Committee, in the Senior Combination Room, with both senior and junior members

Its powers are those of the original three committees, but transfer of issues between them is eliminated; it has oversight of the management of the College, and makes recommendations to the Governing Body as to policy, elections to Fellowships, appointments to College offices and committees, as well as other academic, financial and staff matters. It meets about eight times each year.

The Governing Body in session in the Trust Room

The Governing Body now divides its meetings into two parts, with the first part open to the undergraduate and

'What does the Master do?' That is the perennial question posed by students, guessing that the response might lie somewhere between figurehead and, in total contradiction, chief executive. What is more certain is that the role of Head of House has changed almost beyond recognition in recent decades. It probably never did resemble the caricatural image rehearsed in period dramas, C.P. Snow's *The Masters* or in the Cambridge episodes of films like *Chariots of Fire*, and still retailed in Inspector Morse's visits to inebriated High Tables in 'The Other Place'. But there was a time, even within living memory, when a Master might *preside* from some distinguished distance. *Chairing* Governing Bodies, Councils and committees, so central to a self-governing and legally autonomous institution, remains a time-consuming if necessary part of a Master's professional life. So too, the social dimension of a collegiate experience requires the Head to welcome guests to his or her House, as well as give endlessly-repeated after-dinner speeches at major College occasions.

Master, Bursar and Senior Tutor

Master and Secretary: the day's schedule

Some of the changes in the role are a function of those in the wider world. In a culture less exercised by hierarchy, the Master is expected to be less *primus inter pares* than a working colleague of the Fellows, in particular the Bursar and Senior Tutor. He has meetings with new members of the Fellowship; he has to *persuade* busy academics to take on important college jobs. With no decision-making authority, he has to take the longer route to building consensus. The Master has to be approachable by junior and senior members alike, explicitly valuing the commitment and efforts of what were once called (we might cringingly remember) 'College servants', and interacting with undergraduates and graduates, inviting them to the Lodge for receptions and supper-parties. Here, in particular, the Master's spouse plays a vital role. Paradoxically, however, the Master knows personally far fewer students than might have been the case in the 1960s or 1970s when an afternoon on the touchline or the towpath made for an agreeable break from administrative tasks. An empty evening could be spent listening to, and thereby enjoyably supporting, a student concert or theatrical performance.

For there has been an exponential increase in demands on the Master's time, registered in a diary now crammed with appointments. At one level, this is the result of developments in higher education, requiring of Cambridge a centralized response to government policy initiatives which can only be achieved through the coordination of the perspectives of 31 – often very different – colleges. The Heads of House have had to elaborate a plethora of

Right: The Master with Mrs Lethbridge, following General Admission

Below: Speech-making – the Master in his capacity as Provost of the Gates Trust with the Vice-Chancellor, Professor Sir Leszek Borysiewicz, the Chancellor, Lord Sainsbury, and Bill Gates Sr.

Below right: A gathering of Singapore alumni

sub-committees and working-groups to this end, and now spend an extraordinary amount of time in meetings with other colleges as well as with senior University officials. Some ritual representation of one's College remains unchanged: in processions; funerals and memorial services; Feasts; reading the Lesson in Chapel. But a Master's involvement in the running of the University as a whole is much increased. The Vice-Chancellor, even though now a full-time appointment, has had to delegate to the Heads the conferment of degrees in the Senate House and the chairmanships of appointments committees, Boards and Syndicates across the departments and institutions. And all these additional formal duties leave aside the changed research context in which Heads who simultaneously occupy academic posts are expected to sustain their work and publication record at the highest international standards.

At least as fundamental, however, is the modern fundraising imperative. This is the direct consequence of progressively reduced tax-payer support for the disproportionate costs of a Cambridge collegiate education which is, in its focus on individuals within communities at odds with economies of scale, what makes it – of course – so unique and valuable. Nearly every Cambridge college is now in 'campaign mode', organized around the pretext of an anniversary or a major project to enhance the student experience, or more explicitly admitting that philanthropy is an essential income-stream to sustain core activities into the future. For the Master, this means a vastly expanded range of events as well

as devoting time to developing relationships with alumni with the means to offer the College significant financial support. Masters travel as never before, in the United Kingdom but also, and above all, overseas, renewing contact with former students who have made their lives and careers far from Cambridge. To put some substance on this, my own travels during my eight-year tenure have taken me and (let us not forget!) my wife to: Japan; Australia and New Zealand (Melbourne, Sydney, Perth and Wellington); Dubai and Abu Dhabi; Singapore, Hong Kong and Bangkok; Canada (Toronto, Montreal and Ottawa); Paris and Geneva; and the USA, on multiple occasions and from East Coast to West. It is not as glamorous as it might sound! And all these visits to airports and foreign venues have to be fitted in to the intensity of a Cambridge term and the quotidian magisterial workload. What has made it worthwhile is the warmth of welcome we have received and the exceptional loyalty towards, and affection for, Fitzwilliam which is being translated into the kind of generosity on which its future depends. The role of Master, as the twenty-first century advances, is unlikely to regress to the sinecure of the popular imagination, in which grandees passed the port late into the night. The role poses all kinds of challenges to one's personal and professional qualities. But the greatest of these is to stamina!

ROBERT LETHBRIDGE
Master

Personal reflections of a Graduate Tutor

Cambridge has entered the twenty-first century with a clear commitment to maintaining its reputation as one of the world's leading research universities. Within this context, the role of the graduate community – a key constituent of the collegiate university – has become ever more prominent and visible. Fitzwilliam, with a long-standing commitment to admitting graduate students from many backgrounds, across a wide range of subjects, has embraced this as an opportunity to create a vibrant 'middle' community of scholars, bridging the space between the undergraduate students and the Fellows.

The graduate community at Fitzwilliam prides itself on being inclusive and friendly, but celebrates its traditions and ethos in a wider context that is unashamedly modern – perhaps best exemplified by the location of the Middle Combination Room within the oldest part of the College, The Grove. It is also a cosmopolitan meeting ground for people from diverse cultural and national backgrounds. The coming together of disciplines, ways of thinking and modes of research and analysis, creates a fertile space for intellectual development which is difficult to match within narrower disciplinary contexts. The College sees one of its key roles being to provide various formal and informal opportunities for graduates to push the boundaries of these scholarly encounters.

BHASKAR VIRA

Dr Bhaskar Vira, University Senior Lecturer in Environment and Development in the Department of Geography, trained as an economist, and has degrees from St Stephen's College, University of Delhi, and St John's College. He is Fellow and Director of Studies in Geography, and Graduate Tutor.

Dr Vira's research interests cross disciplinary boundaries. His work focuses on the changing economic dynamics of development and the political economy of ecosystems and natural resource use. He works on issues of equity and justice arising from development, environmental, and socio-economic change, and how different groups are affected by these processes. Specific work in recent years has included understanding how decisions about forests and wildlife, water, land and food security affect rural livelihoods in India, and the changing dynamics of urban employment in India's new service economy. He also studies public policy and governance issues, especially in the context of development.

GRADUATE-STUDENT STATISTICS

Fitzwilliam is a natural destination for highly able and ambitious graduate students from the entire world. From a total of 308 graduates on the books of the College in Michaelmas 2012, the largest single group is 120 Overseas students, closely followed by 115 from the United Kingdom, and 73 from the rest of Europe.

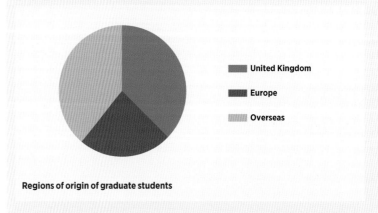

United Kingdom

Europe

Overseas

Regions of origin of graduate students

It is regrettable that the nationality balance is not matched by the gender balance, and perhaps surprising that the category of students with the lowest proportion of women is that of non-UK Europeans.

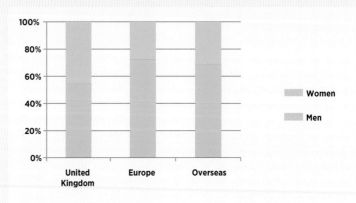

Women

Men

Gender balance, by region of origin

Here, the European category is not restricted to members of the European Union (which is relevant to fee status rather than to culture); the nationality distribution is very wide and includes many from the further regions as well as from the more obvious near-neighbours of the United Kingdom; the North-East Europe category includes students from Russia and former Soviet territories.

Amongst the Overseas students, nearly 60% are from East of Suez, with Chinese students and members of the Chinese diaspora greatly exceeding those from the Indian subcontinent; the balance has changed greatly in the last quarter-century. Students from the United States and Canada are to be

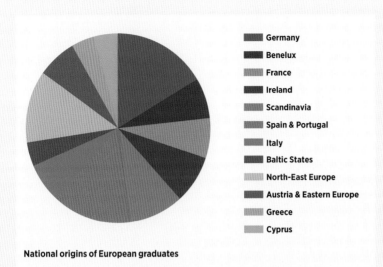

National origins of European graduates

Germany
Benelux
France
Ireland
Scandinavia
Spain & Portugal
Italy
Baltic States
North-East Europe
Austria & Eastern Europe
Greece
Cyprus

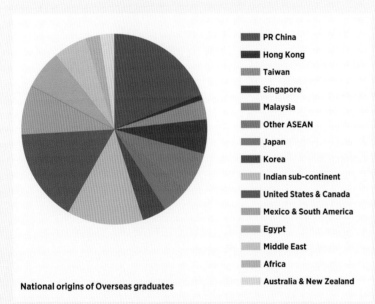

National origins of Overseas graduates

PR China
Hong Kong
Taiwan
Singapore
Malaysia
Other ASEAN
Japan
Korea
Indian sub-continent
United States & Canada
Mexico & South America
Egypt
Middle East
Africa
Australia & New Zealand

The balance is different amongst the students preparing for the degree of Master of Philosophy and similar one-year degrees; the proportion in Arts (including English, Languages, Oriental Studies and Music) is the same, but that in Humanities and Social Sciences (including History, Law and Economics) is doubled. Technology outweighs Physical and Biological Sciences.

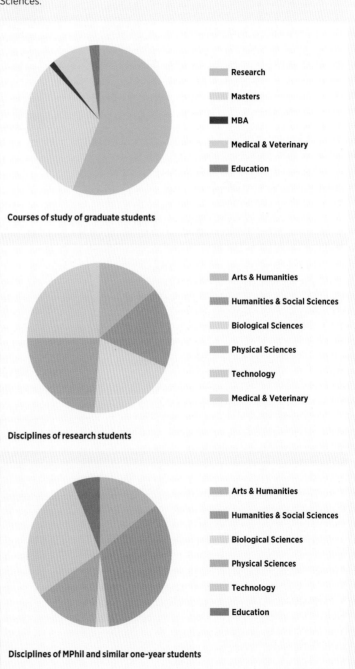

Courses of study of graduate students

Research
Masters
MBA
Medical & Veterinary
Education

Disciplines of research students

Arts & Humanities
Humanities & Social Sciences
Biological Sciences
Physical Sciences
Technology
Medical & Veterinary

Disciplines of MPhil and similar one-year students

Arts & Humanities
Humanities & Social Sciences
Biological Sciences
Physical Sciences
Technology
Education

expected, but it is perhaps surprising that the number of students from Mexico and further south is more than half the number of the northerners. Egypt and the Middle East are well represented.

So what do these graduate students do in Cambridge? More than half of them are engaged in research leading to a doctorate, and a further third in one-year Masters degree studies. With the turnover implicit in the number of one-year students, each year the College now matriculates more graduate students than undergraduates.

Amongst the research students, nearly a third are in Departments within the Schools of Arts and Humanities and of Humanities and Social Sciences, nearly a quarter each in Physical Sciences (which includes Mathematics) and in Technology, and the balance either within the School of Biological Sciences or in Medical or Veterinary research.

Over the last decade, the College has also recognized that, for most graduates, their home in Cambridge will probably be one of their abiding memories of their time at the University and (for many from overseas) in the UK. Investing in accommodation for graduates, through the purchase of a substantial property at 139 Huntingdon Road, the refurbishment of Neale House for graduates, and the construction of new units at Halifax Road are just a few examples of how this commitment has translated into a real transformation of the living space that is available to our students. Keeping our housing modern, well equipped, comfortable, as well as affordable, remains a high priority.

Much remains to be done, as always – but Fitzwilliam is ahead of many other colleges in having thought about its graduates as important constituents of the Collegiate community, and in ensuring that they remain central to its planning for the future.

BHASKAR VIRA
Graduate Tutor

Above: Graduate students entertained by the Fellows in the SCR

Below: Graduate-student conference in the Auditorium

CRIME, PUNISHMENT, AND MASTER OF STUDIES COURSES

Fitzwilliam has a special place in the in-service training of senior officers in the Police and the Prison Service. In the mid-1990s, Professor Sir Antony Bottoms (Fellow, and Director of the Institute of Criminology) was approached by the National Director of Police Training to explore whether Cambridge wished to be involved in training potential Chief Constables. The Institute – and Tony in particular – had long led the field in developing close links between academia and practice, so this was a splendid opportunity. These high-flying professional mature students enrich the student body, so the College has been very pleased to be involved.

First was the Diploma and MSt in Applied Criminology and Management (Police Studies), then a Diploma and MSt in Applied Criminology, Penology and Managements (funded originally by the Prison Service, later taking senior probation staff). Nicola Padfield was the first Director of the prisons programme from 1998 until 2004, when commitments in the Law Faculty limited her administrative role; she and Tony continue to teach the courses. There have been struggles for funding, but now the free-standing fee-paying courses recruit both nationally and internationally. Many Chief Constables and prison governors are now alumni of Fitzwilliam. First-year students come for three-week sessions on criminology, law and practice; second-year research projects contribute to understanding in many fields of criminal justice.

Graduates' barbeque outside the MCR in The Grove

Undergraduates – the perspective of the Senior Tutor

The primary role of the Senior Tutor is to orchestrate the College's educational activities, working through a team of nearly 40 Directors of Studies, and nearly 1,000 under - graduate supervisors (for better or worse, Cambridge supervisors have tended to work in ever narrower fields, to the point that in a typical year the College now deals with twice as many supervisors as undergraduates) to provide the best possible teaching and academic guidance alongside the University's lectures and practicals. Tutors offer pastoral support, to the extent desired by each student: sympathy and counsel in tough times, practical assistance and strategic advice in consideration of academic or career ambitions, encouragement or celebration when things turn out well. With the staff of the Tutorial Office they make arrangements for the increasing number of students who take examinations under special conditions; with the Dean they deal with those few who misbehave; and with members of the Fitzwilliam Society and the University Careers Service they encourage a targeted, timely and ambitious approach to the future. The College offers ancillary provision to undergraduates and graduates alike: a counsellor as well as a nurse, intensive coaching in academic English as well as optional courses in conversational Italian. All these things depend on our generous alumni; but they are only possible, or they only make sense, because we are connected through the University to a vast network of expertise.

That scale promises and delivers real quality and efficiency. Yet the very richness of Cambridge's provision is sometimes regarded as a sure sign of the collegiate university's inefficiency. To be sure, the University's resilience depends on a degree of redundancy which has served it well over the course of centuries. Negotiating within that intercollegiate network is, predictably, time-consuming and occasionally infuriating; yet it leads, on the whole, to well-informed decision making, both collectively and within each college, since that community tends to present ample evidence of the positive and negative consequences of a range of policies and structures. For that reason Fitzwilliam, as a relatively young college (which over the years has benefited from very substantial financial assistance from some of its venerable neighbours), does well to ensure that it retains through its officers an active engagement in intercollegiate committees, that it supports its senior Fellows in taking leadership roles in Departments and Faculties, and that it always welcomes to its table colleagues of goodwill from across the town.

Fitzwilliam remains one of the University's poorer colleges, and Fellows take their role as its stewards seriously.

PAUL CHIRICO

Paul Chirico at John Clare's cottage, with a statue of the poet

Dr Paul Chirico, Senior Tutor of Fitzwilliam College, Fellow Librarian, College Lecturer and Director of Studies in English, previously held lectureships at Jesus College, Cambridge (where he had studied) and at the University of York. He teaches primarily the literature of the eighteenth century and Romantic periods, lecturing on the early development of the novel, on lyric poetry and on late twentieth-century song. His research focuses on the early nineteenth-century poet John Clare and on the dynamics of literary production, circulation and readership in the early to mid-nineteenth century. His book *John Clare and the Imagination of the Reader* was published in 2007 by Palgrave Macmillan. He was founding Chair of the John Clare Trust, which has established an educational, environmental and cultural centre at Clare's birthplace in the village of Helpston, near Peterborough.

UNDERGRADUATE STATISTICS

The composition of the undergraduate body is more biased towards the United Kingdom than that of the graduates, and in 2012 three-quarters of the total of 447 undergraduates were local. Nearly three-quarters of the balance were Overseas, with relatively few from the rest of Europe.

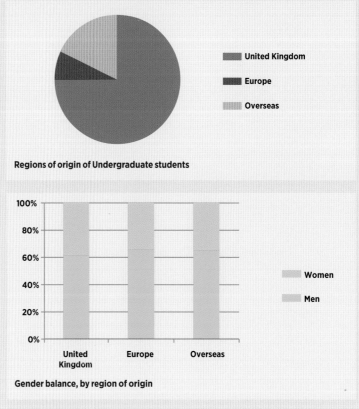

Regions of origin of Undergraduate students

Gender balance, by region of origin

The proportion of women was very similar in all of the regional groups, averaging 38%.

We want value for the money we spend, and we never forget where that money comes from, nor that we spend it for the benefit not only of the present student cohort but of future generations. This is not always straightforward. Many Fellows made clear their sympathy with the students who occupied the University Combination Room in 2010 in protest at the Government's proposals to introduce undergraduate fees of £9,000 per year; yet the College could neither ignore the financial imperatives of the accompanying cuts in direct funding nor, in practice, protect our future students from the effects (felt further in the future) of that settlement. The constructive response is to build up our programme of bursaries to ensure that an education at Fitzwilliam remains in reach for all with the right intellectual drive – a challenge to which the generations who enjoyed heavy subsidies have risen rapidly and honourably.

The other constructive response is to ensure that an education at Fitzwilliam remains the best choice any bright 18 year old could make. In the twenty-first century that choice is informed by more and more comparative data: not just the price of a pint in a college bar, as in the old alternative prospectuses, but everything from room size and room rent to national student satisfaction surveys to the number of supervisions offered in each subject and the average group size. An increasing amount of time is spent

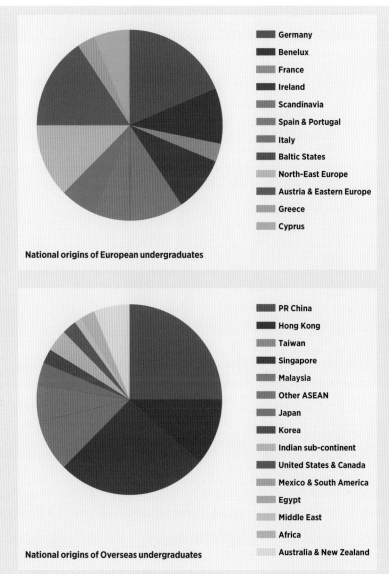

Germany
Benelux
France
Ireland
Scandinavia
Spain & Portugal
Italy
Baltic States
North-East Europe
Austria & Eastern Europe
Greece
Cyprus

National origins of European undergraduates

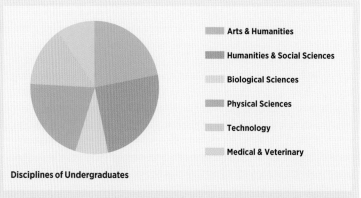

Arts & Humanities
Humanities & Social Sciences
Biological Sciences
Physical Sciences
Technology
Medical & Veterinary

Disciplines of Undergraduates

PR China
Hong Kong
Taiwan
Singapore
Malaysia
Other ASEAN
Japan
Korea
Indian sub-continent
United States & Canada
Mexico & South America
Egypt
Middle East
Africa
Australia & New Zealand

National origins of Overseas undergraduates

The non-UK European undergraduates, like their graduate counterparts, were very diverse in origin; perhaps surprising is that there were five from Austria and Eastern Europe (approximately the lands of the old Austro-Hungarian Empire) and four from the North-East (Russia and Poland), but only one from France.

Amongst the Overseas undergraduates, 70 out of the 80 were from East of Suez, with quite a different balance from the graduates – a much higher representation from Singapore (a quarter of the total, outnumbering even those from the People's Republic of China) and from Hong Kong. The regions with small numbers are striking, and represent a large change from earlier generations: only three students were from the Indian subcontinent, and only one each from the United States and Canada.

The effect of the longer courses in Physical Sciences and Technology is that roughly one-third of students remain in Cambridge for a fourth year.

Inclusion of the fourth-year students would give a misleading view of the subject balance within the College, as perceived by the majority of the undergraduates passing through it, and so the distribution within subjects is plotted for the first three years only. On this basis, slightly less than half (about 47%) were in the Arts, the Humanities, and the Social Sciences. Amongst the others, the Physical Sciences and Mathematics accounted for the highest proportion, with somewhat fewer in Technology, and approximately equal numbers in the Biological Sciences and in their applied counterparts, Medical and Veterinary studies.

responding to Freedom of Information requests on these and many other issues; but once again any frustration is tempered by a realization that it is only through an understanding of the realities represented by such data that we can ensure the College continues to improve.

Fitzwilliam has indeed flourished, with extraordinary speed by Cambridge standards. It has done so through determined policy: during my time at the College the Governing Body has repeatedly been willing to offer enthusiastic support to proposals designed to enhance the facilities offered to junior members: construction of the Olisa Library, establishment of MPhil and PhD studentships and of dozens of new funds for student support, purchase of a former hotel at 139 Huntingdon Road and its conversion within weeks into an outstanding graduate hostel. These examples, among many others, continue a tradition of constant growth and improvement since the move to the present site. But of course these facilities and funds provide merely an enhanced framework; the real flourishing of Fitzwilliam lies in the academic achievements of its junior members, the groundbreaking research of its graduate students and Fellows, and the lives shaped by the opportunities taken within its courts.

PAUL CHIRICO
Senior Tutor

ADMISSIONS AND ACCESS

Cambridge attracts students from across the world, but within the United Kingdom regional, social and educational differences can discourage schoolchildren of potentially high ability from applying. Continuing the non-collegiate tradition of opening up the University, the College has sought to alleviate this problem by removing obstacles and providing information. One of the obstacles to entry was the entrance examination, since many schools were unable or unwilling to make special arrangements for candidates. The Cambridge intercollegiate entrance examination was discontinued, the last cohort being for admission in 1986, and thereafter public examinations were used as the basis for admission. Fitzwilliam recognized that this was an important development, and implemented it a year early. Subsequently, Scholarships and Exhibitions were awarded on the basis of performance in University examinations.

A further step in that era was the introduction of Matriculation Offers, in which a few candidates were given conditional offers of two E-grades at A-level (sometimes known as the Hertford scheme, after the Oxford college which pioneered that approach to broadening access) – not because that was the anticipated result for the candidates, but because Admissions Tutors and Directors of Studies judged them to have very high potential and deserved the opportunity to develop it.

Traditional assumptions about the Fitzwilliam constituency have had to adapt to the changing national-educational environment. For Home students, perhaps the most salient aspect relates to grammar schools, whose pupils now form only about 20% of those admitted (their number belies their significance: they were the highest-performing cohort of Home students in 2011). The distribution of the admitted population between independent, comprehensive and grammar schools, and sixth-form colleges, is not greatly different from the University average. So, in order simultaneously to achieve the highest academic standards and to maintain the honourable tradition of enhancing access to Cambridge, the admissions process cannot be passive; the College seeks the most able applicants of all origins and scholastic backgrounds, including those who would not instinctively apply to Cambridge.

The College holds Open Days, enabling potential applicants to learn about studying in Fitzwilliam and the application process. Contact with potential applicants takes place in schools also; Fellows visit schools, as Governors and to give talks. Since 2006, there has been a Schools Liaison Officer within the Admissions Office – normally a recent graduate, to minimize the age difference with the pupils, she visits schools as well as organizing local events. Such personal contact provides opportunities to raise aspirations and dispel myths. The Colleges and the Intercollegiate Admissions Office divide up the United Kingdom: Fitzwilliam is linked with some London boroughs and two Northern counties, which are visited regularly by the Schools Liaison Officer, often accompanied by a Fellow or an undergraduate. The Schools Liaison Officer was initially a part-time post (with a further part-time commitment to another College), but since 2011 has been full time – made possible by alumni donations. So alumni support outreach towards potential members of the College, as well as providing support for hardship and enhancement of the experience of the students once they are in Cambridge.

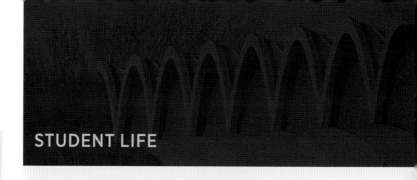

STUDENT LIFE

Left: Arrival in College for the first time

Below: A Porter issues a room key

Left: The café-bar

Below: Setting up the matriculation photograph

Above: College societies recruit

Right: Professor Cardwell with students before the Matriculation Dinner

Below: A Land Economy supervision with Mary Young

Collecting lunch from the servery

Self-catering

Boathouse training

Rugby Cuppers winners in 2011

Ferris wheel at the Winter Ball in 2012

GOING OVERSEAS

Mark Savage Award project: Ronald Ching teaching English to a Cambodian orphan

Student days have always been enhanced by travel but, increasingly, student travel has become purposeful – thereby attracting financial support from the Master's Gift Fund, the Student Opportunities Fund, and several travel awards established by the generosity of benefactors.

A fund commemorates Mark Savage (1999) who died in 2000 whilst an undergraduate at Fitzwilliam. Projects take students across the globe, from legal support of capital-charge prisoners in Texas, to remote developing-world villages – building village schools, teaching, and helping to establish supplies of clean water.

Every summer since 1998, five new graduates of Fitzwilliam have set out for the Japan University of Economics in Kyushu, in the southern coastal city of Fukuoka, to join counterparts from St Anne's, Oxford. They study Japanese language and culture for a year, and teach English conversation. The scheme is funded entirely by Tsuzuki Gakuen Group (p. 100), a trust which supports 70,000 children and young people from kindergarten to university. Participants have many opportunities to experience the country. Liam Price, there in 2009–10, was impressed by their 'friendly and thoughtful disposition and their enthusiasm for life', and interested to find that, by explaining it, he was 'becoming increasingly enlightened to the nuances of British culture', and 'the many idiosyncrasies that we have'. A true instance of travel broadening the mind, so valuable in our inter-dependent world.

Recently, undergraduates have been Teaching Fellows with the Chinese Crimson Cultural Exchange Foundation and the University of Hong Kong, for a six-week school-teaching programme in Hong Kong and in a mainland city. Not only English students have gone; it has also given students from the Chinese diaspora an opportunity to immerse themselves in everyday life in the People's Republic that otherwise they would never experience.

GRADUATION

Left: Before the Graduation Dinner, in The Grove

Below: The Graduation Dinner

Scholar of the Year (2012) – Samuel Strong

Left: Professor David Cardwell and graduands

Above: Sports Personality of the Year 2012 – Matthew Bennison

Right: Demonstrating procedure – Professor Bottoms leads up groups of four graduands

Far right: Demonstrating procedure – Francis Knights stands in for the Vice-Chancellor

Below: Arranging a hood

Setting off for the Senate House, saluted by the Master

The Master, as Vice-Chancellor's Deputy for the conferring of Degrees, in procession

The Head Porter, John Eisold, in his other role as University Constable

Greeting the new graduates

179

Finance in a changing environment

Fitzwilliam has come a long way. The site is fully occupied, and the College can boast a proud architectural heritage. We are now able to house all our undergraduates in College accommodation and some two-thirds of our postgraduates – a far cry from the desperate shortage which characterized the early years. Through the support of alumni and the Cambridge Colleges, and sensible management, the endowment has grown to respectable levels and a 'safety net' of free reserves has been built up, which allows some level of fluctuation in annual financial performance to be tolerated. The College punches at its weight in Cambridge.

Standing still is never an option, however. It is generally considered that a Cambridge college needs an endowment of over £100 million to be sustainable and independent. Despite all the efforts of the last half-century, Fitzwilliam remains among the most under-endowed of all the undergraduate colleges, whilst being heavily dependent upon income from its endowment to subsidize the cost of the top-quality Cambridge education which it provides. In these straightened financial times, it seems unlikely that much respite is going to come from the Government in the form of increased tuition fees or direct support.

The original Lasdun buildings are 50 years old, with roofs and services reaching the end of their useful lives. Accommodation that was suitable for the students of the 1960s no longer meets the aspirations of twenty-first-century students. The original functions of the central building have progressively moved out to newer facilities; its role is being rethought in order to restore it to its rightful position as the social centre of the College in an up-to-date way. Exciting plans have been prepared by Cullinan Studio, the architects of the Library.

All of this will cost a lot more money than the College has available in its free reserves.

These are challenges derived from our heritage. In addition, the world of Higher Education in which we operate is changing rapidly, and emerging trends are placing new demands on College finances.

First is the strong growth in graduate-student numbers, driven by competition for jobs and PhD places, by changes in the secondary education system, and encouragement by University policy. This growth leads to the need for more accommodation. Unlike most undergraduates, our graduate students often live in their

accommodation the year round; it is their home. They need more space and more facilities. Yet they are the most modestly supported group financially; there are many cases of genuine hardship in this community and we urgently need to build up funds to provide support for graduate students.

The new undergraduate tuition fee regime is still in its infancy and it is difficult to know its impact. Students have become more cautious about applying to university and therefore it is important that we are able to offer visible financial support to show those young people from less advantaged backgrounds that it is possible to access the best university education without the inevitable accumulation of frightening levels of debt. To sustain the reputation of Cambridge as one of the leading universities in the world, the College has to be equipped to attract the very best students from all backgrounds irrespective of means.

Then there are teaching trends to consider. With such Government support as exists being directed towards science-based subjects, retaining resources to support the full range of subjects is increasingly challenging. The core of the College's teaching provision is provided by University Teaching Officers, who have full employment contracts with the University and undertake College teaching on a part-time basis. The demands of a University post are increasing, and in some subjects it is difficult to find people to take on College roles. The alternative strategy for the College is to employ lecturers itself. The cost of endowing a lecturer at present rates of return is at least £1.5 million.

Finally, the costs of living and operating in a regulated world cannot be underestimated. Most regulation is well intentioned, but implementing it is a thoroughly bureau-cratic process. More and more time is being invested by administrative staff and Fellows in meeting these require-ments. Colleges are small businesses; although collegiate Cambridge is a giant among universities, we do not have large administrative support available. Every hour and every pound invested in non-relevant activity is diverted away from the core educational mission. However, it is a trend that seems unlikely to reverse.

Fitzwilliam faces these challenges with the confidence derived from 50 years of development and in the sure knowledge of support from its friends within Cambridge and within the wider Fitzwilliam community. Members of the Fellowship take very seriously their obligation as trustees to preserve and enhance the opportunities offered by the College for the benefit of present and future generations of students. However, we live in a very uncertain world, in which decisions and trends operating at national and international levels can have a major effect on the economics of a college. Amongst the big unknowns are rates of inflation, the long-term economic effects of the loan system of financing student fees and living costs, the demand from overseas students, and the pattern of philanthropy.

So what strategies are available to manage successfully through this next period? There are no magic wands. Running a tight ship, maintaining a diverse income stream and continuing to present the College's needs to its friends and benefactors will be essential ingredients. We will need to keep looking into the future and to anticipate when we can, and above all avoid overstretching the College's resources. We will also need to work co-operatively with other colleges; the College model is an essential ingredient of Cambridge's unique offering, but sustaining 31 independent institutions, each with its own infrastructure, is expensive and it will be necessary to be creative to find efficiencies in this area too.

Whatever the future holds, we are determined that Fitzwilliam will emerge ever stronger.

ANDREW POWELL
Bursar

Achievements and aspirations

As the College approaches the 50th anniversary of the Royal Charter granted in 1966, the most self-evident achievement in Fitzwilliam's history is precisely that. For its first 150 years has two narratives: firstly, the long, and sometimes fraught, story leading from Hall to House and, finally, to Fitzwilliam College; and, secondly, that of the last half-century, since Fitzwilliam's move to its present site.

In respect of the latter, every former student, Fellow or member of staff returning to Fitzwilliam, whether from the era of the House or more recent decades, is struck by the most visible achievement of which they have been a part, namely the transformation – which is not too strong a word – of its physical identity and setting. One Master summed up 1983–84 as 'the year of the Building'. He was referring, in that instance, to the planning of New Court, opened in 1986. More accurately, not least for those who have lived through them, very many years since the early 1960s have seen construction in progress, as one architect after another has grappled with challenges posed by Lasdun's original concept and the creative solutions of their predecessors. For all practical purposes, the College's main site is now complete, with its main entrance on Storey's Way and with the Huntingdon Road left – literally – behind. Its buildings, organically related to each other rather than monolithically cloned, are set in wonderful grounds enjoyed alike by residents and visitors.

It is too easy to conclude, however, that it is only now that we can marvel at what has been achieved. For, even during the College's physical development, each milestone was celebrated in its own right. Back in 1974, for example, the *Journal* remarked on its 'magnificent and well-stocked library'. That the necessity of building the College's recent new Library and IT Centre was motivated by the inadequacies of the original is not to devalue what once was good enough, nor to invoke the wisdom of hindsight. It is to be reminded that each stage in the completion of the College site has responded to changing circumstances, and Fitzwilliam has been particularly fortunate to have the space to inflect its requirements accordingly. Some older colleges (exemplified by Trinity Hall, with its new buildings on the Wychfield site next door) have been so physically constrained that they have not been able to insert additional facilities within their historic boundaries. While Fitzwilliam too has post-graduate centres outside its grounds, one key feature of

what it is today is that the College is self-contained, with its community activated by its life and work being in a single location, and given a particular internal dynamic by its criss-crossing paths where people meet.

Nor has the physical development of the College been driven by realizing some master-plan unrelated to academic priorities. It was very specifically in the context of Fitzwilliam losing its competitive edge in the late 1970s, when the College – unlike its rivals – could offer rooms only to one year of undergraduates out of three, at the same time as traditional lodgings were disappearing, that the building of more residential accommodation became a really urgent priority. And it is not by chance that progress on the academic front coincided with New Court, itself symptomatic of Fitzwilliam's new-found confidence and ambitions.

Running through the entire history of Fitzwilliam to date has been a concern about the College's academic achievements. For decades after its 1869 beginnings, the migration of its most able students had been a source of recurrent disappointment. And, even after 1966, 'migration' of another kind meant that intellectually-gifted applicants to Cambridge were too often drawn to the older colleges with established reputations and facilities to match. It seems clear, in this regard, that Fitzwilliam's sporting pre-eminence in the 1960s was integral to a process of getting the College better-known. There were always, as there had been before collegiate status, isolated academic successes. Throughout the 1970s, however, the Master's Letter (in the *Journal*) reported that Tripos results were either 'disappointing', 'no better or worse than usual' or 'very similar to recent years'. In practice, the numbers of Firsts were only in the high teens; even in 1983, there were only 21. But what was described as 'the long haul' then did achieve real momentum, recorded in published inter-college league-tables which – however invidious or problematic – afforded a measure of relative progress, perhaps more significant than the simple statistics of Firsts and Upper Seconds boosted, or not, by grade-inflation (there were 26 Firsts in 1984, 34 in 1985, 37 in 1986, 41 in 1987, 51 in 1990). For, from 1985 until 1990, the College had an unbroken six-year run of successively improved academic results, thinking of itself – and perceived as such – as a college *on the move*. Fitzwilliam had been 22nd out of 24 colleges in the 1982 Tompkins Table; in 1986, the College was 15th; in 1990, it was 8th. Behind the collective

its best results ever, in absolute terms, with a new record number of Firsts reflected in the start of another climb back up the rankings.

Other achievements stand out: winning *University Challenge* in 1973; winning Cuppers time and again across a range of sports; the sheer number of Blues; the number of Fitzwilliam men and women representing their country in the international arena, from cricket to rugby and from squash at the Commonwealth Games to rowing in the World Championships and the Olympics. There have been Fitzwilliam presidents of the Cambridge Union. The College's musical talent has been prominent in CUMS as well as in concerts enhanced by the Fitzwilliam Quartet in the stunning Chapel or the first-class Auditorium. In the more properly public domain, former Fitzwilliam students have had a profile second to none: Nobel Laureates; Fellows of the British Academy and the Royal Society; CEOs of, and partners in, major commercial and professional organizations; leading broadcasters; hospital consultants, professors, bishops, judges and QCs; heads of schools and public bodies; TV executives, composers, prize-winning novelists and authors of well-known screenplays; Members of Parliament of every party; knights and peers of the realm; Cabinet ministers; HM Ambassadors; and Heads of State. And within the University itself (to return to more parochial achievements), Fellows and Masters of Fitzwilliam have taken on major responsibilities: starting with the first time one was appointed a Proctor, described in the 1979 *Journal* as evidence of the College 'coming of age'; in membership of Council and the General Board; as chairs of Bursars or of Heads of House Committees.

All this, both individual and collective, has been achieved at the same time as the College has developed financially. Indeed, not much would have been achieved, it could be argued, without the building of its resources. Even the most vibrant of corporate spirits fails to pay for teaching and overheads. The first 100 years of Fitzwilliam's history are indeed marked by the precariousness of its funding. In a sense, collegiate status (bringing with it independence from the University as 'lender of last resort') only exacerbated its difficulties. The wider national 1970s squeeze on UK universities, allied to Fitzwilliam's new-found liabilities for its own physical infrastructure and educational provision, present a pretty grim picture of intermittent crises and spiralling deficits. The distance travelled since that difficult period is brought into

achievements of the student body, there were more particular triumphs: Fitzwilliam's Lawyers left the rest of the University standing in 1984, with five out of eight of them getting Firsts in Part II; in 1986, it was the turn of Natural Sciences to dominate the class lists; the Modern Linguists were top in 1989, 1990 and 1991. With these kinds of results, the number of University prizes awarded to Fitzwilliam students also exponentially increased. And, as Professor Holt reported in his Master's Letter of 1988, these achievements were a source of pride and satisfaction – not least to alumni who had seen these indications of progress in the national press. And he rightly pointed out that this was a consequence not only of radically revised admissions policies coming to fruition but also of the fact that new residential buildings had provided the students with precisely the improved conditions in which to better fulfil their intellectual potential. The College's academic achievements remain, and perhaps always will do so, a work in progress. In a place as competitive as Cambridge, Fitzwilliam can no more expect to secure a permanent place in the top half of the academic league-tables than as Head of the River, where another historic run came to an end in 1972. The Master's Letter of 1973 started off with that particular 'painful intelligence'. There have been other 'disappointments'. But, in 2011–12, the College had sharper relief by noting that the £1 million endowment of those years has now been expanded to some £42 million. That achievement is the result of good stewardship, but also of extraordinary generosity. Successive requests for support (the 1969 Centenary Appeal, for the Squash Courts in 1982, for New Court in 1986) have not always met their targets. But there is also a longer tradition of donations: Reddaway's from his own pocket; legacies; regular and one-off contributions from the richer colleges; the support given by the Clothworkers and the Leathersellers. The current 150th Anniversary Campaign, with over £10 million raised to date and made up of contributions both great and small, principally from alumni, marks an entirely new phase in Fitzwilliam's efforts to sustain, for future generations, what is so valuable about a collegiate experience and education. In this area, too, however, there is much to be done. Fitzwilliam is one of the largest, but remains one of the poorest, of the Cambridge colleges. £42 million may sound a lot, but not against the £100 million reckoned to be the minimum endowment needed to finance the shortfall between costs and fees as the UK tax-payer relentlessly withdraws the subsidies too long taken for granted.

If these achievements are remarkable, one may nevertheless ask how exactly all this has been achieved. Part of the answer lies in the immensely hard work of generations of Fellows. The College has always had a relatively small and young Fellowship (it currently numbers 54), thereby encouraging the majority of them to get involved and feel they have a real part to play in the College's development. Yet, at the end of the day, it is Fitzwilliam's students who have taken it forward, bringing to it their own energy and aspirations, both while in residence and in the wider world to which they have graduated. Their pride in the story of the first 150 years of their Cambridge college, and their continuing loyalty and commitment to it, are inseparable from one's confidence in the future of Fitzwilliam.

ROBERT LETHBRIDGE
Master

REFERENCES AND FURTHER READING

General references

W.W. Grave, *Fitzwilliam College, Cambridge* (The Fitzwilliam Society, 1983)

J.C.P. Roach, *A History of the County of Cambridge and the Isle of Ely: Volume 3: The City and University of Cambridge.* (Oxford University Press, 1959)

A History of the University of Cambridge: P. Searby, *Volume 3, 1750–1870,* and C.N.L. Brooke, *Volume 4, 1870–1990* (Cambridge University Press, 1997 and 1992)

J.A. Venn, *Alumni Cantabrigiensis Part II 1752–1900, Volumes i–vi.* (Cambridge University Press, 1940-54)

Reports of various Royal Commissions from *House of Commons Parliamentary Papers Online* (ProQuest Information and Learning Company)

Cambridge University Reporter (Cambridge, University Printing House)

Obituary notices of Fellows of the Royal Society and *Biographical Memoirs of Fellows of the Royal Society* (London, Royal Society)

Oxford Dictionary of National Biography (Oxford University Press, 2004)

Fitzwilliam Magazine, 1908–69

The Journal of the Fitzwilliam Society, 1926–2012, with its extensive range of reminiscences, Censors' Letters, obituaries, and reprinted University and Non-Collegiate Students Board reports

Fitzwilliam College Archives

Minutes of meetings of the Governing Body of Fitzwilliam College

Census records, from 1861 to 1911

Specific references

Chapter 2

The Student's Guide to the University of Cambridge (Cambridge, Deighton, Bell and Co. 1874; reprinted Cambridge University Press, 2009)

Chapter 3

S. Bose, *His Majesty's Opponent* (Cambridge, Massachusetts, Harvard University Press, 2011)

S.K. Bose (ed), *Netaji Collected Works, Volume 1* (Calcutta, Netaji Research Bureau, 1980)

K.R. Shirsat, *Kaka Joseph Baptista, Father of Home Rule Movement in India* (Bombay, Popular Prakashan, 1974)

Chapter 4

H.M. Burton (1920), *There was a Young Man* (London, Geoffrey Bles, 1958)

Chapter 5

A.R.H. Baker, *Norman John Greville Pounds 1912–2006, Geographers' Biobibliographical Studies,* 2011

F. Brittain, *It's a Don's Life* (London, Heinemann, 1972)

N. Bitton, *Alfred Sadd of the Gilberts* (London, Livingstone Press, 1944)

Lee Kuan Yew (1947), *The Singapore Story* (Singapore, Prentice Hall, 1998)

Chapter 6

Report of the Council of the Senate on amendments of the statutory provisions for Colleges and other collegiate institutions. Reporter, 18 March 1964

D. Kerridge, *From Common Acre to a Cambridge High Table: a Fenman's progress* (published privately, 2010)

Chapter 7

P. Guillebaud: papers on the development of West Cambridge in *Proceedings of the Cambridge Antiquarian Society,* from 2005 to 2009

G. Raverat, *Period Piece: A Cambridge Childhood* (London, Faber and Faber, 1952)

M.J.G. Cattermole, *Horace Darwin's Shop: a History of the Cambridge Scientific Instrument Company 1878 to 1968* (Bristol, Hilger, 1987)

B. Calder, *Architectural Research Quarterly* 11, 301 (2007) and 12, 65 (2008)

Chapter 9

The sections on Leslie Wayper, Ray Kelly, David Kerridge and Tony Edwards draw extensively on obituaries and Memorial Service addresses reproduced in the *Journal of the Fitzwilliam Society*

Nobel Lectures, Physiology or Medicine 1922–1941 and *1942–1962* (Amsterdam, Elsevier Publishing Company, 1965 and 1964

Chapter 12

Trevor Dann (1971), *Darker than the deepest sea* (London, Piatkus Books, 2006)

SUBSCRIBERS

Cecilia Aas 2005
Dr Richard Abbott 1987
David Ackland 1971
Richard A. Acton 1971
John Adams 1958
Roger Adams 1966
Will Adams 1971
James Robert Addison 2008
Kyo Seong Ahn 2003
John Ainger 1959
Matteo Alchini 2007
Alan Alcock 1988
Professor Richard Aldrich 1955
Amanda Alexander (née Jones) 1981
Michael Douglas Allan 2009
Benjamin James Allen 1962
Roy C. Allison 1957
Myles Allsop and Anna Tee 1993, 1993
Patrick L.F. Allsop 1971
Richard and Ali Allsop 1987, 1987
Natalie Amps
C.J.D. Anderson 1969
Trevor Harvie Andrew 1977
Jannis Jan Angelis 1996
Dr Vivian Anthony 1959
A.L. Antrobus 1956
David Archer 1969
Mark Arends
Rev. Jeremy Arthern 1956
Michael J. Ashburner 1962
Graham Ashton 1968
Neil William Ashton 1967
Sir Bryan Askew 1949
The Honourable Mrs Justice Asplin DBE 1979
District Judge D.J. Asplin 1971
Tristan Aspray 1989
John Atherton 1956
Dr Paul Austin 1985
John Axon 1955
Azizul Azhar 1996
Chris Bagnall 1964
W.G.R. Bain 1971
Caroline Baker (née Mahar) 1988
Louise Baker (née Fletcher) 1985
Dr Mark R Baker 1992
Rod Baker 1981
Professor Dominic Baker-Smith Fellow 1968–76
L.P. Baldwin 1971
Dr David F. Ball 1948
Paul Bancroft 1979
Rick Barfoot 1978
Anthony Barker 1963
Colonel (Retd) Jeffrey Barker 1959
Bob Barltrop 1973
Philip Barnard 1960
Simon A. Barnes 1987
David Barnett 1976
A.M. Barringer 1972

Chris Barrow 1986
Antony Barton 1999
Norman Barton 1965
Nigel Bartram 1972
J. David Bass 1957
David Bates 1968
Peter J. Bates 1959
Peter Battye 1959
David Bayliss 1979
Dr S. Beadle 1975
Dr Frank Beavington 1954
David Bebbington Research Fellow 1973–76
Dr Bettina Becker 1994
The Ven. John Beer
Dr Sasan and Mrs Shirley-Ann Behravesh 2006, 2005
Richard Belger 1979
Robin Bell 1965
Robin Bellis 1957
Dr Elina Vilar Beltrán Catalan Lectora 2003–05, Batista i Roca Fellow 2009–12
Reuven Ben-Dor 1972
Christopher Bennett 1972
David E. Bennett 1953
John Carey Bennett 1964
Robert J. Bennett Fellow 1978–85
Matthew David Bennison 2008
Sally Benthall (née Ranger) 1981
Michael Benton 1960
Neil Beresford 1967
Matthew Bergin 2010
Dr Helen Bettinson 1982
Bhatnagar Siddharth 1994
Dr David Bissell 2000
Paul Blackborow 1977
G. Michael Blackburn
Professor Jonathan Blackburn
Mark T. Blagrove 1979
Andrew Q. Blane 1955
Roger Blaney 1965
Michael J. Blundell 1961
Stephen Blunden 1979
Peter Boardman 1969
Colin R.L. Boden 1956
Philip Keeling Boden 1957
Steve Bodger 1968
Dr Oliver Bohanek 2007
Clare Bolton 1989
Stephen Borrill 1990
Stuart H. Bostock 1971
Dr Gary Bosworth 1998
David Bottomley 1978
Professor Sir Anthony Bottoms Fellow
John Bowen Jones 1952
Dr David E. Bowyer Life Fellow
Roger Mark Lewis Bracey 1955
Emma Bradley 1987
Chris Bradnock 1961

Professor David Bradshaw
Dr John Bradshaw 1968
Michael C. Brain 1968
Bruce Braithwaite 1982
John Braithwaite 1963
Dr Ian M. Bratt 1973
Roger Brawn 1969
Philip Breedyk 1962
Alan M. Bretman 1969
Martin Broadhurst OBE 1972
Bronwyn Broadhurst (now Syiek) 1983
J.B. Brodie 1958
Professor J.H. Brooke 1962
Rev. Anthony F.P. Brown 1953
Charles E. Brown 1972
C.D. Brown 1963
Nick Brown 1987
Nigel David Brown 1972
Tony Brown 1978
William T. Brown 1958
Michael Errol Bruce 1959
Richard Brumby 1966
Edward Bryant (Berdichevsky) 1959
Mike Bucher 1961
Matthias Buck 1987
James E. Buckley 2009
John Joseph Buckley 1975
Dr Ian Bucklow 1948
Ken Bulteel 1966
Nick and Jane Bunch 1997, 1997
Chris Burge 1971
Andy Burrows 1976
Humphrey Burton 1951
Iain Butler 2010
Katie Bycroft 1988
K.A. Bystram 1948
Salvador Cardus
Alejandro Carnicer 2010
Paul Carr 1965
Dr Stephen Carr-Bains 1972
Michael Carrier 1968
Alison Carter
Ian Carter 2003
T.M. Carter 1949
A.A. Cartwright 1946
Jaime Carvajal Urquijo 1960
Paul Cassidy 1981
Dave Castell 1963
Christopher Cathey 1987
Dr C.J.D. Catto 1965
Peter Catton 1963
David Chalk 1977
Dr Hero Chalmers
Nixon Chan 2012
Pradheep Chandavimol 1959
David and Alison Chantrey 1986, 1986
Brian Chapman 1955
Adrian Charles 1978
Chris Charlton 1990

Tom Charlton 1975
Katherine Cheetham (née Read) 1992
Qi Chen 2008
Ruitao Chen 2012
Tongtong Chen 2003
Cheong Kwok Leong Ryan 1990
Stephen Cheshire 1962
MingShun Chiang 2010
Brian Chilver 1954
Dr Paul Chirico Fellow and Senior Tutor 2007–
David Chrisp 1956
Mark Christy 2010
Laurence Churms 1959
Alan Clark
Adrian Clarke 1979
Robert Clarke Catering Manager
Ronald F. Clarke 1954
Steven Ellis Clarke 1995
William Clarke 1953
Ronald Bruce Claxton 1961
C. Claydon
Jane Clayton (née Thorn) 1983
Richard Clayton 1981
Stephen Clayton 1983
Lucy Newman Cleeve 1994
Professor Bill Clegg 1967
Professor R.E. Clements
Simon Clephan 1977
Rev. Alan Clift 1958
Jane Coates (Garrett) 1986
Adrian Coates 1976
Mike Cobb 1970
N.R. Cockburn 1982
Ian Codrington 1956
David Cole 1982
Geoffrey H. Cole 1946
Christopher Coleman 1970
Professor J.M. Coles Fellow
Lauren N. Colley 2006
Derek Collinson 1962
Robert Constable 1951
John Cook 1962
Professor Mervyn Cooke Research Fellow 1987–93
David Coombs 1982
David C. Cooper 1957
J.R. Cooper 1959
John Cooper 1957
Jonathan Cooper 2009
Robert Cope 1971
Andrew Cotton 1983
Bernard Cotton 1967
Dr Alan Cousens 1975
Piers Coutts 1971
M.P. Cowie 1978
Dr Robert H. Cowie 1972
Didier Cowling 1984
Chris Coyne 1977
Ludo Craddock 1968

Nickless Hugh Craft 1968
Dr Mark Crankshaw 1992
James Crawford 2002
John Creasey 1953
Judy Claxton
R. Guy H. Crofts 1961
D.B. Crosby 1967
Professor A.G. Cross Fellow
Simon Cross 1972
Phillip Crowson 1958
Dr Jonathan Cullen Fellow 2009–
Derek Culley 1954
Michael Curry 1974
Alan Cuthbert Master 1990–99
Stephen Cutler 1970
Paul Danes 1990
Andy Daniels 1988
Jane Darbyshire 1982
David da Rosa 2001
Jonty Walter Davies 1989
Dr J. Gregory Davidson 2002
Professor Darryl T. Davies 1974
Professor Graham Davies Fellow
John Davies 1966
John Vivian Davies 1954
Paul A. Davies 1987
Nigel R. Davis 1969
Alan Keith Dawber 1965
Roger Dawe 1959
Melissa de Alejandro Kelly 2011
Michael Dean 1972
Earl Deng 2002
Weishen Deng 2005
Hannah Dent 1998
Pat Walton Denton, Jr 1995
Stephen Derrett 2009
John W.T. Dickerson 1955
Allan Dickie 1963
Ian Dickson 1961
Malcolm Rae Dickson 1999
Geoff Dinkele 1956
Martin Dinkele 1982
Paul R. Dixon 1984
Kelvin and Gemma Donald 2003, 2003
Susan J. Done 1982
Robin Dow 1963
Oliver B. Downs 1994
Dennis Doyle 1947
Graham R. Drake 1965
Ken Drake 1953
Norman Drummond 1970
Terry Duffy 1961
Dr John Stuart Duncan 1948
Emma Dwyer 1991
Maurice Dyson 1970
Philip David Earp 2011
Dr R.G. Edrich
Georgina Bowles Edwards 1996
Graham Edwards 1984
Julian Edwards 1985

Name	Year
Olufemi Elias	1988
Susan Ellicott	1981
Stephen Elvidge	1968
Prebendary Dr Peter Elvy	1962
Dr Clyde Emery	1957
Richard English	1980
John Etherton	1974
Allan and Abby Evans	1988, 1989
M. Havryn Evans DL	1956
Dr Ray Evans	1975
Alastair Everitt	1956
Richard Ewers	2009
Tony Extance	1956
Peter Facer	1958
C. Paul Fairweather	1970
Alex Farnsworth	2007
Steve Farrall	1990
Steven J. Faull	1974
Alastair Ferguson	1979
Graeme Ferguson	1961
Selwyn C.A. Fernandes	1982
Anthony Fielding	1977
Dr Colin J. Fish	1972
J.H. Fisher	1949
Mike Fisher	1975
Fitzwilliam String Quartet	
Dr Don Fleet	1969
Kristina Esther Fleischmann	2007
Matthew Fogg	2012
Gabriel M.K. Fong	1989
Kim Fong	
Michael Forrest	1974
Michael Foster	1965
E.D. Foulds	1960
Emeritus Professor Michael W. Fowler	1966
Barrie J. Frampton	1952
John Sims Francis	1952
Martin L. Francis	1964
Gordon Thomas Frey	1976
Bridget Frost	1986
Roger Frost	1959
Francisco Fuentes-Ostos	1991
Andrew P. Furmanski MSci	2007
Ben Gales	1988
Richard Saward Galliano	1953
John F. Gamlin	1958
John Garbutt	1985
Andrew Garden	1981
Mark Gardiner	
Matthew Gardiner	1996
Roger Kimberley Garland	1964
Colin Garley	1960
Dr Andrew Garmory	2000
Colin A.V. Garraty MA LLM	1958
Nicholas Gartside	1996
Simon Gathercole	
Dan George	1979
Bernard D. Georges	1974
Adrian Vincent Gibbs	2010
Joanna Giddins	1983
Paul V. Gilchrist	1964
Professor Robin Giles	1961
Dr Chris Gill	1965
Geoffrey Glover	1969
Andrew Glynn	1994
Melanie Glynn	1998
Roger Goddard	1971
Philippa Goff	2011
Robert A. Goldspink	1968
Geoff Gollop	1973
Henry S. Goold	1952
David Gosling	1959
Eric S. Goss	1964
Gabriel Gottlieb	1996
D.W. Gower	1964
Vincent Gowler	1991
Roger Graham OBE	1958
Andrew Graham-Stewart	1970
Andrew Granger	1978
Ian Grant	1968
Roddy Grant	1975
T.R. Graves-Smith	1958
Dr A. Ross Gray	1952
Tony Grayling	1982
R.M. Greatrick	1977
John Green	
John Christopher Green	1959
Professor Richard Green Fellow 1989–99	
James Paul Gregory	1995
Chris Griggs	2009
Dave Grimshaw	1977
H.M.P. Gronow	1989
Charles Gurnham	2012
Frieder Haenisch	2011
Russell J. Haggar	
Professor Peter Haggett Hon Fellow	
Dr David Haigh	1978
Peter Haigh	1967
Phil Haigh	1992
The Rev. John Frederick Hale	1951
Peter Hale	1976
Michael Haliassos	1978
Ian N. Hall	1979
Nigel Hall	1974
Chris C. Halliwell	1971
Peter Hamer-Hodges	1973
Rhian-Anwen Hamill	1986
Alistair Hamilton	2010
Duncan Hamilton	1958
Robert Hamilton	1962
Michael Hamlyn	1999
J.R.J. Hammond	1956
Tracey Hancock (née Johnston)	1980
Kevin Hanley	1986
Jonathan Hann	1965
Hannes Harbrecht	2010
Matthew Harman	1973
Brian Harrap	1950
D.J. Harrington-Lynn	1991
Professor Ray Harris	1970
Geoffrey Harrison	1955
Rev. Canon John Harrison	1968
Mike Harrison	1953
Clive Hart	1957
Martin Hart	1984
Dr Andy Harter	1980
Dr Stephen Hartley	1972
Hasli Hasan	2004
A.F. Hassan	1954
Mike Hasty	1971
A.I.C. Haythornthwaite	1957
Haitao He	2012
L. Brian Heath	1953
Chris Heaton	1968
Paul Heffer	1968
Chris Helliwell	1988
Martin Hemming	1968
Robert Henderson	1969
Heng Chee How	1980
Ayako Henson	2011
Nick Heptinstall	1985
The Rev. Vanessa Herrick Chaplain and Fellow 1999–2002	
Andrew M. Hetherington	1988
Peter Hewlett	1968
Shaun H. Hexter	1978
Nicholas J. Hicks	1980
John (Dave) Hidle	1965
David R.F. Hill	1951
Ralph B. Hill	1953
Victoria Hills (née Banks)	1998
Jennifer Hipkiss	2009
Peter H.E. Ho	1973
Ho Meng Hee	1982
Andrew Hobbs	1975
Rev. Michael B. Hobbs	1955
Mark William Hogan	2008
Professor Joseph Holden	1994
Malcolm Hollifield	1977
Andrew Holmes	1983
John A. Holmes	1975
Peter Holmes	1972
Professor Sir James Holt Master 1981–88	
Quentin Holt	1982
D.W.L. Holton	
Keith Horner	1965
Dr Jane Howard and Professor Graham Lord	1985, 1985
Peter Howard	1970
Dr Robin S. Howard	1974
Sally Howes OBE	1979
David Howells	1965
Jess Hrivnak	1999
Bernadette Huang	1985
John (Paul) Hudson	1974
Chris Hughes	1967
Colin Hughes	1962
R.J. Hughes	1970
Ian Hurlstone	1969
George Hutchinson	2003
Selwyn Image	1959
Victoria Imrie	
Anthony Inglese	1971
Dr Riyad Insanally	1977
Dr George Inverarity	1954
Akira Irie	2012
Ted Irving	1948
Dr David M. Isherwood	1964
Roger Jackson	1970
Simon Jackson	1975
Dr Sue Rayner Jacobs	1984
David J. James	1983
Keith W. James	1955
Rev. Paul James	1952
David Jamison	1970
Paul Jarman	1981
Channa Jayasena	1995
Ceri Jefferson (née McInally)	1991
Richard Jefferson	1991
Michael Jeffery	1965
Christopher J. Jenkins	1971
Dr Geraint Jenkins	1985
Sue Jenkins	1982
Keith Jenkinson	1959
Nigel Jepps	1973
Dr Thomas Jestaedt	1990
Rajan Vipin Jethwa	1996
C.L. Johnson	1965
David F.C. Johnson	1974
Dick Johnson	1960
Hannah L. Cromar Johnson	1993
Graham Jones	1963
K.B. Jones	1964
Nigel Jones	1977
Peter Jones	1996
Raymond M. Jones	1967
Samantha Joanne Jones	2008
Tim Jones	1983
Lucy Jordan (née Kilborn)	1993
The Joshi Family	
Marcus Judd	1959
Dr Alex D. Kanarek	1950
Prabhu Kashap	1980
Chris Katkowski QC	1975
Annalise C. Katz-Summercorn	2002
Dr Peter D. Kay	1961
Dr Jonathan Kell	1984
Matthew Kellett	2012
Godfrey Kelly	1948
Dr Roy Kelly	1962
Julie Kerr and Donna Frost	
Michael Tevriz Kezirian PhD	1988
J.S. Khaira	1988
Norman Killey	1960
Professor Sebastian Kim	1997
Catherine M. King (née Gifford)	1981
David William King	2007
Rev. Peter King	1970
Dr Sarah King	1980
Stephen Kingsley	1972
The Rev. Stephen Kingsnorth	1971
John Francis Kingston	1962
Eamonn Kinsella	1962
Dr Charles Kirke	1971
Peter A. Kirkman	1991
Tony Kirkman	1963
Elena Klien	1995
David Knight	2003
John Knight	1952
Francis Knights Fellow 2009–	
Peter Knowles	1964
Professor Huxley H.M. Knox-Macaulay	1955
Kian Hong Kock	2010
Constantinos Kounnis	2001
Carol Lamb	
Nicholas Lancaster	1968
Barry Landy Fellow 1973–2004, Life Fellow 2004	
John Lansley	1961
Robert Last	1979
K. Sarwar Lateef	1962
John Latham	1975
Anna E. Lawrence	2012
Joanne E. Lawrence	1991
Tony Lawson	1969
Alec Lazenby	
The Rev. William Norman Leak	1948
A.R. Leal	1964
David Leaman	1973
Mark Leaning	1973
Dr D.R.M. Ledingham	2008
Dr Alfred H.Y. Lee	1952
Professor Emeritus Clive H. Lee	1960
J.B. Lee	1951
Kenneth Wei Wen Lee	2011
Dr Suan Yew Lee	1954
Dr Harry G. Leitch	2003
Peter J. Leonard	1998
Rev. Dr Elmore Leske	1971
Ivan A.D. Lessard	1991
Professor Robert Lethbridge	
C.F. Leung	1952
Richard Alwyne Lewin	1993
C. RobertsLewis	
John Lewis	1954
Anthony Ley	1956
Peter Lidwell	1991
Richard Lidwell	1965
Henrik Lieng	2011
David Lilley	1965
Eugene Oon Teik Lim	1983
David M.L. Lindsay	2007
Alex Lloyd	1990
Julian A. Lloyd	1980
M.J. Lloyd	1959
Victor Yik-kee Lo	1998
Richard John Edward Lodge	1991
Roger A. Lodge	1953
James Lohoar	1958
Jon Howard Lomax	1989
P.H. Lonergan	1987
Dr Richard Lonsdale	1976
Michael Loveridge	1980
Raymond Ludwin	1965
Daisy Helen Luff	2010
Michael Lumley	1962
Flynn Lund	2003
Raphael Kong Wah Lung	1981
Sidharth Luthra	1990
Bob Lyddon	1976
Richard Lyon	1967
Richard J. Lyon OBE	1962
Dr Iain Macbriar	1968
David MacLean	1968
D.A. (Douglas) Macmurtrie	1954
HH Ken MacRae	1963
G.A. Magee	1946
Clive J. Makin	1981
Liz Makin	1979
Dave Mandle	1968
Professor David J. Manners	1946
David Mansell	1977
Stuart Mansfield	2001
David Manttan	1991
Ian Marcus	1977
Professor Richard Marks Bye-Fellow	
Elisabeth Marseglia Life Fellow	
John Marsh	1971
Simon Marsh	1979
D.B.K. Marshall	1955
Patrick Marshall	1965
Freddy Martell	1954
Andrew Martin	2000
Chris Martin	1976
Graeme Martin	1995
Paul Martin MCR 1965–66	
Francisco Martin Bourgon	1962
Tim Martin-Jenkins	1966
Dr Philip A. Mason	1968
Annika Inga Mathews	2012
David Matthiae	1960
Geoffrey May	1967
Simon Maybury	1975
Harvey Maycock	1989
Ben Mayes	1986
Peter A.McD. Mayes	1951
Barry O'N. McAlinden	1988
James McAulay	2011
Jeremy McBride	1973
C.H. McCarthy	1948
Desmond McCarthy	1958
Professor William L. McClelland PhD	1966–67; 1973–74
Rev. Dr Robert McDonald	2004
Calum McFarlane	1997
Andrew M.J. McGahey	1978
Fergus E. McGuire	2000
Royston McHugh	1957
Michael McIntosh Reid	1962
John McKelvey and Catherine Marston	1994, 1994
David J. McKenzie	1967
Eric H.C. McKenzie	1971
Alasdair McKerrell	1974
Dr Brian McKinney	1981
James McQuhae	1954
David J.P. Meachin	1965
Richard Meads	1963
Tony Meggs	1970
Dr Reginald Melton	1955
Timothy Mercer	1973

John Merrett	1957	Stephen J. Paddison		Stephen Reid	1969	Peter Somerfield	1966	Dr Geoffrey J. Walker	1955

John Merrett 1957
W. Anthony Merrett 1955
Keith Michel 1967
David Miles 1972
Professor Martin Millett Fellow
Alison Mills 1995
Ray Mills MBE 1967
Krzysztof Miszewski 1946
Stewart Mitchell 1954
Jo and Joe Moffatt 1992, 1992
Keith Mok 2002
Shelly-Ann Desree Mol
(née McDermott) 1997
Dr Francisco A.T.B.N. Monteiro
2005
Valter D.R. Monteiro
Rahul Moodgal 1993
R.H. Moore 1966
Sarah Moores 1990
Tim Morgan 1990
Amber Morley 2011
Professor Colin Morley 1962
Julian Morley 1983
Geoff Morris 1962
Alan Morten 1953
Ian Mortimer 1948
John F. Mueller 2009
Matt Muir 2009
Jamie Muirhead 2011
The Rev. Dr John Munns Fellow
Robert H.M. Munro 1960
Phil Murphy 1972
Dr Shettima Mustafa 1973
Mark D. Myers 1984
Hugh Naismith 1956
David Nally Fellow 2006–
Jayant Vishnu Narlikar 1957
Chris and Rowena Neighbour
1997, 1999
Professor Andrew Neil 1967
James M. Nelson 1951
Peter Nelson 1997
Russell Newton 1983
Dr Chris Nex Fellow 1991–99
Wan-Fai Ng 1989
Chris Nicholls 1968
Derek Nicholls
Fiona Nickerson (née Pearce) 1983
Josephine Nicol 1988
Hermann Niederste-Hollenberg
Dr Peter Nightingale 1970
Roger Noble 1955
Professor Glen Norcliffe 1962
T.D. Norman 1959
Julie M. Norris 1986
Rt Rev. Peter Nott 1958
Graham Nutter 1966
HH Judge Patrick O'Brien
Tim O'Dell 1978
Andrew Oakes 1969
Robert Oakes 1971
Susannah Odell 2011
Kathryn Ogilvy 1981
Ken Olisa 1971
David Oliver 2012
James Oliver 1978
Nicholas Olney 1978
Chin Hwee Ong 1992
Richard Frimpong Oppong 2003
Arturo Ortiz-Tapia 1994
Ewald Osicki 1974
Sir Duncan Ouseley 1968
Martin Outram 1979
David Owen 1983
Dr Sara Owen
Dr Ian Paczek 1983

Stephen J. Paddison
Christopher Padfield 1968
Dr Peter J. Padley Fellow 1963-66
A.F.G. Page 1954
Michael Page High Table Waiter
A.C. Palmer 1949
Sohee Park 1979
James Parke 1962
C.M. Parker 2008
Roland Parrott 1994
Andrew Paterson 1976
David Payling 1993
John Payling 1960
Jonathan Pearce 1977
His Honour Judge David Pearl
Life Fellow
John M. Pearman 1958
Peh Eng Kiat 1991
David Penn 1963
Nigel Penny 1966
Charlotte, Thea and Sophie Perry
David Perry 1967
Jane Perry (née Brown) 1995
William Perry 1997
Simon Pettit 1966
J.A. Phillips 1968
J.E.F. Phillips 1976
John Phillips 1968
Matt and Cathleen Phillips
1997, 1997
Peter Phillips 1966
Dr G.D. Piearce 1966
John Noel Pilling 1954
Malcolm Pinhorn 1953
A. Pires da Silva 2012
Elizabeth Plane (née Galloway) 2002
Stephen Plummer 1966
F. Thomas Poole 1959
Andrew R. Pottage 2008
Michael Potter 1946
Andrew Powell
Becca Powell 2009
Geoff Powell 1958
John Powley 1957
Alasdair Pratt 1958
Robin Precey 1968
J.M. Prescott 1967
C.W. Pressnell 1951
Dr Donald K. Price 1949
H.E. Price 2010
Jonathan Price 1967
Professor Sarah (Sally) Price
Fellow 1981–89
Barry Prince 1982
G.M.A. Proffitt 1966
Hugh Prudden 1949
P.B. Pugh 1968
Dr Noel D. Purdy 1991
Sarah Quarterman
(née Robinson) 1984
Philippa Räder (née Jones) 1984
Paul Ramage 1960
Rev. Canon John Rankin 1971
Rachel J. Rayner 2005
C.A. Read 1990
Christopher Read 1996
Group Captain D.J. Read 1952
J.S. Read 1953
Jane Reck and Andrew Lees
1981, 1980
J.L. Reece 1973
Basil Reed 1951
Mathew Rees 1986
Colin E. Reese QC 1969
Richard Reger 1985
Dr Iain Reid 1978 and Fellow

Stephen Reid 1969
Nicholas J. Reidy 2008
J.D. Rew 1964
Barrie Reynolds 1951
Gary Richards 1974
Michael J. Richards 1965
Paul Richards 1973
Dr Geoffrey Richardson 1955
Anthony G. Ritzmann 1972
Dr N.R.C. Roberton Fellow 1979
Clare J. Roberts 1988
J.D.E. Roberts 2011
Michael Roberts 1991
Stephen Andrew Roberts 1965
Justin M. Roe 1990
John Roebuck 1966
Anthony C. Rogers 1964
John Rogers 1959
Cristian Gabriel Romocea 2008
Christopher Roshier 1963
Professor Michael W. Ross 2003
John Rush 1964
Struan Rutherford 2012
A. Rutterford 2010
H. Colin Ryder 1958
Pawel J. Rzemieniecki 2010
Kourosh Saeb-Parsy 1993
Gursimran Sahota 2003
Chris Salt 1999
Dr Patrick J. Salt 1965
S. Samra 1991
Dr Richard Sanders 1966
P.E. Sanderson 1958
J. Sargeant 2010
Simon Schofield 2011
Irving C. Scott 1959
S.D. Scott-Fawcett MA FRICS
FRGS 1978
Camiel Selker 1999
Michael Sellers 1973
Dr C.S.G. Selmes 1948
Dr Robert Rasiah Selvendran 1964
Peter Semmler 1969
Malcolm A. Seymour 1952
Neehal Shah 1991
Professor A.G. Shakespeare 1945
Zoe Shaw 1979
Allan L.M. Shepherd 1953
Dr Asghar Shiri pour Charlou 1991
Richard V. Short 1977
Barry Shorthouse 1971
Gerald Siddall 1948
Dr David Sigee 1961
Group Captain Alan Silvester 1949
Virginia Simmons 1990
David J. Simons 1986
Ed Simpson 2000
M.A. Simpson MA MLit FRHists
1958
R.T. Simpson 1965
The Rev. N.C. Sissons 1989
Lyndon K. Skinner 1983
Professor Nigel K.H. Slater
James Sleigh 1970
Philip J. Sloper 1970
Brian P. Smith 1971
Professor Ian Smith 1968
Jeffrey Smith 1964
Martin Smith 1971
Mike Smith 1965
Nick Smith 1982
Roger Smith 1967
Roger J. Smith
1967, Fellow 1971–74
Tom Smith 1973
Stephen Smyth 1995

Peter Somerfield 1966
Stephen Sorfleet 1970
Graham Sparrow 1990
Elizabeth Spence 2012
Leonard John Blackie Spencer 1967
Dean Spielmann 1989
Malcolm J. Stacey 1960
David Stanley 1973
John Stanley 1956
Jeremy Stattersfield 1975
Theo Stavri 1997
Ian Stead 1955
Mark S. Steed 1984
David J. Stephens 1956
J.J. Stevens 1970
John Dowler Stevenson 1955
Peter Stevenson 1997
David Stewart-Hunter 1966
David and Mary Stewart 1967
Mark A. Stewart 1972
Samuel Strong 2009
Nigel Sunman 1980
Tony (W.A.) Suttill 1957
Stephen D. Sutton 1982
Dr Layinka Swinburne
The Rev. P.F. Swingler 1968
Emma Swinnerton 1996
Alethea Tang 1997
Maria L. Tang 1986
Jeremy Tasker 1981
Shi Huan Tay 2012
Barry Thomas Taylor 1999
Rev. C.L. Taylor 1964
David P. Taylor 1983
John A Taylor 1979
Simon P. Taylor FCMI 2000
Ian Tennent 1956
Alex Tester 1993
The Rev. David G. Thomas 1972
His Honour Judge Paul Thomas
QC 1975
Ian Thomason 1970
Christopher J.B. Thompson 1961
Professor David Thompson
Oliver Thomson 2009
N. Thorne 1976
R. Thorne 1974
Augustine Kamugisha
Tibazarwa 1985
Barry Tipping 1980
N.R. Tittle 1976
Christopher Tod 1966
Adrian Tollett 1972
Paul Tomkins 1967
Rachel Tomlinson 2001
John Toppin 1980
Roger Trafford 1961
Lisa Trei 1979
Richard Trethewey 1987
Rev. Raymond Trudgian 1957
Gerald Tucker 1975
Simon Tuite 1971
Ron Tulley 1964
Dr E.R. Turner 1947
Hannah Alix Martha Turner 2012
John Turner 1961
Martin Robert Turner 1989
Oliver Turvey 2005
Dick Tyler 1978
John V. Tyson 1956
Olivia Ufland 2012
Patrick van Berlo 2011
John S. Vandore 1970
John Venning 1967
Andrew J. Verrill 1984
Antony Wakeling 1962

Dr Geoffrey J. Walker 1955
Kenneth Walker 1950
Steve Walker 1973
John Wallace 2011
P.A. Wallace 1982
Dr Nicola Wallbank 1986
Rowan Waller 1987
Tom Walls 1958
Peter Walton 1956
David Wang 1992
Jeremy Ward 1962
Alan Warren 1953
Tom Warren 1971
Julian Washington 1987
J.G. Weaver 1967
Rachel and Doug Webb 1979, 1979
G.R.E. Welby 1946
David J. Weller 1992
A.J. Wells 2001
Geoffrey E. Wells 1961
Dr Paul Westcar 1978
Richard Whale 1998
Janet Whalley Staff
Neil Wharmby 1976
Richard Whatmore 1986
Michael Wheatley 2003
Richard Wheeler 2004
Dr Martin St.G. Wheeley 1966
David Whitaker 1975
Nicholas White 1986
Tamsin Whitfield 2012
Professor G. Whittington
Life Fellow
Ralph Wickenden 1990
Chris (C.G.S.) Widdows 1964
Mark Wild 1978
Roger Wilkins 1967
Dr Clive Wilkinson 1959
Susan Beris Williams-Jones 1987
Andrew Williams 1973
David M. Williams 1977
Jonathan Williams 1998
Dr Martin R. Williams 1966
N.E. Williams 1948
Nigel Williams 1984
Dr Paul Williams 1965
Rev. Stephen J. Williams 1974
D.M. Williamson 1949
Clive Willis 1957
Stan Willis 1958
Barrington T. Wilson 1970
Christopher Wilson 2010
Richard John Wilson 1994
M.B. Wingate Fellow 2007–
K.L. Wong (Croc) 1989
Chris Wood 1977
Major General Roy Wood 1960
Tobias Wood 2002
Craig Woodgate 1987
Roger Michael Woods 1972
Lindsey Woolley 1989
Andrew Wordsworth 1990
James C.A. Wright 2011
Canon Kenyon Wright CBE 1953
David Wurtzel 1971
M. Xia 2010
Jun Xing 2008
Pui Shing Yang 1992
Chris Yates 1992
Daniel Yee 2012
Dr R.E. Yorke 1959
Nick Youell 1968
Robert M. Young 1998
Yu Tai Hoi 1974
Kevin Yuen 1992
Ken Zhang 2005

INDEX

Senior Members and Officers, including Honorary Fellows and Fellow Benefactors (SM)

Junior Members (JM)

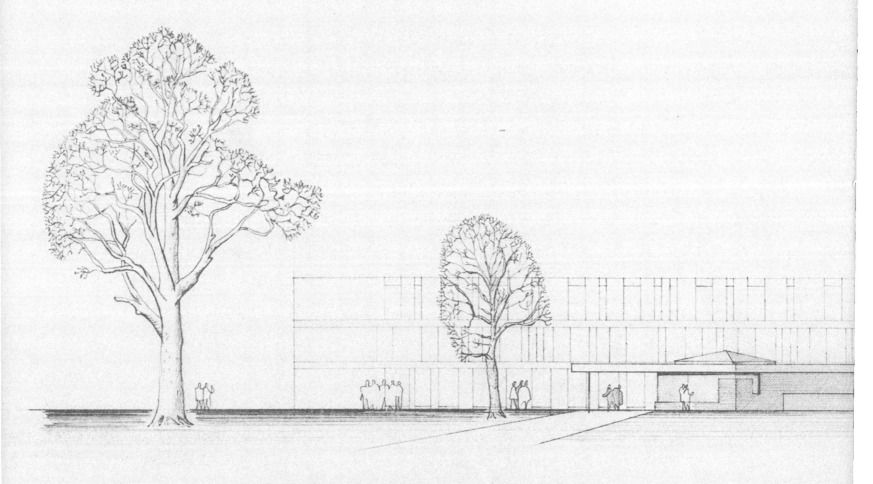

south elevation

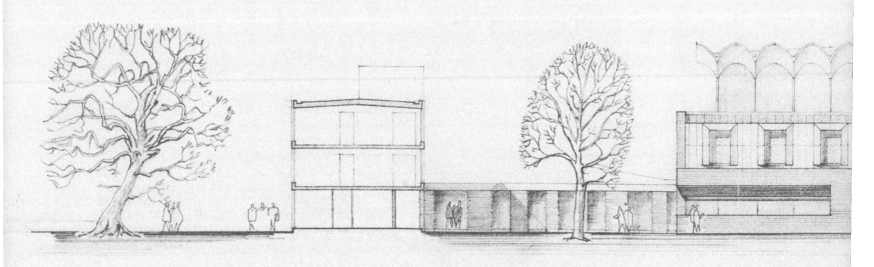

west elevation

PROPOSED COLLEGE FOR FITZWILLIAM · CAMBRIDGE